DON'T BRING LULU

DON'T BRING LULU

Her Family's Tale of Trial and Triumph

Ron, Doris and Sarah Onions

Book Guild Publishing
Sussex, England

First published in Great Britain in 2012 by
The Book Guild Ltd
Pavilion View
19 New Road
Brighton, BN1 1UF

Typeset in Garamond by Ellipsis Digital, Glasgow

Printed in Great Britain by
CPI Group (UK) Ltd, Croydon CR0 4YY

A catalogue record for this book is available from The British Library.

ISBN 978 1 84624 709 5

Introduction

It all began with a teenage romance in a grocery shop. After school, Ron rode the delivery bike and Doris served behind the counter. When they married, along came Sarah and then Lulu. There were serious difficulties after each birth, especially in Lulu's case. However, when the opportunity came, they all went to America where Ron worked for BBC television news as a producer and reporter.

Don't Bring Lulu tells how the family coped during one of the most violent periods in American history and then how they managed to overcome the major problems that confronted them when, after five years in New York, they returned to England.

Ron

There was just the occasional breeze drifting in from the south-west but it was enough for us to catch the intermittent smell of the Fawley oil refinery. It was the day of the annual village fete at Locks Heath on the main road between Southampton and Portsmouth. We had been living there for about a year.

The family comprised my wife, Doris; our eldest daughter, Sarah, who was coming up to four years old; our new baby, Louise, nicknamed Lulu; a cat called Georgie who came to us in mysterious circumstances in Tottenham (we'll explain later); and myself, a London lad whose modest newspaper career had taken me from Sports Editor of the *Tottenham Weekly Herald* to the sub-editors' desk of Brighton's evening newspaper, the *Argus*, where I also sat in as Sports Editor from time to time. The football on the coast wasn't in quite the same class as where I'd come from, but the views in every direction beat London by a mile.

However, in 1960, television beckoned, in the shape of Southampton-based Southern TV, one of the new regional ITV services recently given the go-ahead by the government. A year later, I was lured away to the nearby BBC regional programme, 'South At Six'. Which brought us, via a couple of house moves, to Locks Heath and the fete just down the road. This event was to be the works – all the usual stalls, an egg-and-spoon race and brass band, plus a fortune-teller and tombola or two, and – perfect from our point of view – a children's fancy-dress competition for Sarah, together with a beautiful baby contest for – guess who?

So off we trundled, with Lulu in her best bonnet and Sarah dressed up as a dolly-in-a-box. There were more than a dozen beautiful baby entrants, and each was weighed on an imposing set of scales before meticulous inspection by the judge, who happened to be a local doctor. She seemed to spend rather more time looking at Lulu than she had devoted to the other beautiful babes, convincing us therefore that she had found the winner. Instead, however, she turned to us and said, quietly: 'Has this baby been weighed recently?' She had been studying the competition entry form. This informed her that Lulu's weight at birth was close on ten pounds. Yet the competition scales showed nothing like the increase in weight that would be appropriate for a healthy baby of four months. Then she asked: 'Has she been seen by your doctor lately?' It was a chastening moment.

The following Monday we drove down to see Doctor Scott at Bassett on the northern outskirts of Southampton. He had looked after the family for some while and Louise had been delivered in the maternity unit attached to his surgery, which he ran with the help of his wife, a qualified nurse.

During the course of a careful examination he concluded that there might be a thyroid deficiency; if this turned out to be the case, it could be the reason for Lulu's very slow rate of development since her birth. Dr Scott immediately arranged for Louise to see a specialist at Southampton General Hospital.

By curious coincidence, as we were leaving the surgery we bumped into a BBC colleague, Tony Crabb, and his wife, Brenda, who were on their way in to see Doctor Scott. When we relayed the worrying news about Lulu, they revealed that they had a cousin who was, as they put it, 'backward', and had shown symptoms similar to Lulu's soon after birth.

Two days later we took Lulu to see the specialist. He was tall, silver-haired, Scottish, and a little austere, and he wore an imposing long white coat. Long white coats were an essential part of medical regalia in those days and some said they were responsible for the condition known jokingly as White Coat Syndrome. The theory was that the mere sight of a white coat had an adverse and immediate effect on certain vital organs – the heart and pulse beat faster and breathing went into overdrive. At that time Louise was too young to have that kind of reaction, but she certainly developed an aversion to doctors later as a result of years of medical procedures, and this continued into her middle age.

Anyway, as he examined Louise that day, Doctor 'Whitecoat' suspected that there might be a problem with her thyroid gland, confirming Doctor Scott's diagnosis. This gland, he explained to us, is located at the front and sides of the neck in front of the windpipe, and if it does not function properly, this might result in mental and physical sluggishness.

Then came what seemed to us the startling revelation that it was possible to check how well the thyroid was working by swallowing a solution containing radioactive iodine. *Radioactive!* The word had a mesmerising effect on us. We had been teenagers at the time of the atomic bombing of the Japanese cities of Hiroshima and Nagasaki that caused the deaths of thousands of people from radioactive fallout, and also recalled later incidents in other countries where there had been accidental exposure to radioactivity.

Doctor Whitecoat tried to reassure us. 'We are talking about a very small quantity of radioactive iodine,' he explained. He went on to say that once the dose is swallowed, the radioactivity shows up in the thyroid gland, so it is possible to check the amount by passing a Geiger counter – *Geiger counter!* – across the area of the neck where the gland is located. This procedure triggers a vigorous clicking noise in patients whose thyroid gland is functioning normally.

So the test proceeded, and we relaxed a little when the doctor administered the dose with a humble teaspoon. Somehow this made it seem much more homely. The Geiger counter moved back and forth across Lulu's neck. There was no reaction. Nothing.

It wasn't that she had a sluggish thyroid. What the Geiger counter revealed was that there was nothing there to be sluggish. As another doctor explained later, 'Her thyroid is just not functioning. There's nothing but the husk.'

Subsequent consultations, however, gave us somewhat better news. Lulu's condition could be controlled with a medication called thyroxine. This, we learned, was a substance derived from the thyroid gland of a sheep. It is taken daily in tablet form, the dosage depending on how much or how little the patient's thyroid gland is functioning.

In Lulu's case, we were told that she would have to take thyroxine tablets for the rest of her life.

Further hope that we also clung on to was that the relatively early diagnosis meant that Lulu should be able to lead a normal life. She might not become a genius, but then, how many people do?

So – diagnosis: hypothyroidism; treatment: thyroxine tablets; prognosis: good. Keep taking the tablets, Lulu!

In time, however, we were to discover that it was nowhere as simple as that . . .

Doris

Louise Elizabeth Onions was born sometime after midday on Sunday, 25 March 1962. It had been a long and difficult labour after a pregnancy that seemed to go on forever. When I took Lulu into my arms for the very first time, all ten pounds of her, I looked closely to see who she most resembled, noting especially her reddish hair and intensely blue eyes. Then the thought came out of nowhere: 'This one's going to need a lot of looking after.'

Throughout the pregnancy I had been apprehensive about what might happen in the months ahead. This was because there had been serious problems after the birth of my first daughter, Sarah, three and a half years earlier in November 1958, after seven years of marriage. I was then 30 years old and we had both delayed having kids deliberately so we could both get on with our professional lives.

I had graduated from the Royal Academy of Music with a teaching diploma in Speech and Drama and had taken a job at a teachers' training college in North London. Ron was sports editor at the *Tottenham Herald* and we lived near the newspaper office in rambling accommodation that stretched alongside the local Friends' Meeting House. The rent was all of £1 a week – but for this we were required to act as caretakers and light the stove in the hall where the Quakers' Sunday morning meeting took place.

We had to pass through the meeting hall to reach the front door of the building, and this was also the route to the bedrooms, which were up a short flight of stairs. Truth to tell, the whole place creaked a bit and, to add to that, our kitchen window looked out on a long disused Quaker burial ground. The tombstones had been moved back to the boundary wall of the house, providing space for a vegetable garden which gave us crops of excellent quality and a prolific strawberry patch.

The spooky old place was not exactly for the faint-hearted. We overcame any late-night jitters by conducting the journey to bed in a bizarre free-style dance combining jive and ballet all the way from our sitting room and through the Sunday meeting room till we reached the bedroom stairs.

If anyone rang the front door bell while the meeting hall was in use, we had to respond by going the long way round, out through the kitchen door and skirting the vegetables at the rear side of the building. There were frequent callers seeking help and/or money. It seemed especially a first port of call for prisoners just out of jail and seeking a loan that they insisted was 'just to tide me over. To be repaid of course, missus.' Mmm . . . Sometimes I gave them an old shirt or two and some loose change, but this expansive gesture had to be abandoned when Ron became aware of a rapidly depleting wardrobe.

The square windows, the Georgian-style front door and the overall pioneering look of the building made me think of America, probably because we had just seen a film called *Friendly Persuasion*, starring Gary Cooper, about the problems of a Quaker family living in the backwoods during the American Civil War. Not that there were many backwoods in downtown Tottenham.

At the end of summer my mother and father came down from Blackpool, where they ran a boarding house, to spend a couple of weeks with us. Mother, however, was not very well and spent much of her time in that second bedroom. She had suffered from stomach upsets of one kind or another since I was small, and I can recall too many occasions when I ran off to the chemist to collect one of those old-fashioned bottles of medicine to give her some kind of relief. I asked our Tottenham doctor to come and have a look at her before she went back north. He seemed reluctant to become too involved, but he prescribed something that seemed to do the trick for the time being, and as a result we were all able to enjoy the remainder of their stay with us.

In the late autumn of that year, Ron began to feel that he had spent a little too long on weekly newspapers. He spotted an advertisement for the post of sub-editor on the *Evening Argus* in Brighton. He went down to the coast for an interview and was offered the job. The trouble was that it was just for the few months of summer, covering staff holidays, and it paid about £14 a week – roughly what he earned on the Tottenham job.

I was not convinced that it was a wise move, but he felt that a summer on the coast would lead us onward and upward, as he said rather too often. We would have to find somewhere to live, but we were lucky enough to be on friendly terms with the Ferry brothers, whose mother lived in Rottingdean, just outside Brighton, and she kindly put us up over a couple of weekends. We had met Irwin and Philip through our connection with a north London group of weekly newspapers. Irwin worked on the Wood Green edition, and Philip was a musician and composer who had followed in the footsteps of his distinguished father, Hugh Charles, who, with his partner Ross Parker, was responsible for a string of hits, including those they wrote for 'Forces Favourite', Vera Lynn, during World War II – notably, 'We'll Meet Again' and 'There'll be Bluebirds over the White Cliffs of Dover'.

The Ferry brothers' energy and enthusiasm press-ganged a reluctant company of hacks and others, including Ron and myself, into appearing in a musical revue, 'Stop Press', written by a collective driven by the Ferry duo and with music composed by Philip and performed by him, a one-man band, at the piano. We were able to get the motley cast together for just one show, but it was a sell-out and raised quite a lot of money for press charities.

On our two weekends at their mother's home in Rottingdean we failed to find suitable accommodation for ourselves in the neighbourhood, but we left our details with various agents in the hope that one of them would come up with something suitable before too long.

Meanwhile, life at the Meeting House continued with its highs and lows. The lows included our failure on two occasions in the winter to light the stove in that capacious room where the Sunday morning meeting took place because we had overslept after a late night out. The Friends, through chattering teeth, were much too gracious about our lapse. Ron said they should have doubled the rent.

The relative highs sprang from the fact that a larger hall, adjoining the Sunday meeting room, was hired out for various activities, including dancing and drama classes in which we took part. Then there were the bring-and-buy sales. Just before Christmas was peak time for these, and we used to help out behind the stalls, recruiting to assist us one of my aunts and her daughter who, like us, saw the opportunity to solve all their gift problems without leaving the building. Well, almost . . .

Everything changed in the new year. At the end of February, I realised I was pregnant. There were major decisions facing us. Ron was due to start the new job in Brighton on Easter Monday. We had to find a new home quickly. We faced the prospect of living on only one salary. We decided to go ahead with the move.

Before studying at the Royal Academy of Music, I had worked as a secretary in a clinic for mothers-to-be at Edmonton Town Hall, so I had an understanding, albeit limited, of some of the problems that might arise in pregnancy. I was certainly not prepared, though, for the first question put to me at the local maternity clinic: 'How many miscarriages have you had?' This upset me. The answer was none. What prompted the question was the lifestyle of the fifties, totally different from today, when very few women put their careers first. Back then most first-time mothers were much younger than me. In a few months time, I would be 30. Almost in my dotage.

There were few problems in those early months of pregnancy, apart from the usual early-morning sickness. On a subsequent visit to the clinic, the nurse noted that the baby was being carried prominently to the front and then asked another of those straight-ball questions: 'Is the father a big man?' The answer was no: Ron was five feet nine and slim, though he put on a bit of weight in later years.

With Easter fast approaching, we got over the pressing problem of accommodation in Brighton thanks again to the kindness of the Ferry family in Rottingdean. It was agreed that Ron would stay with them during the week and return to Tottenham at the weekend. He worked a shift pattern that gave him Tuesdays off and therefore time to go house-hunting.

I was not too happy to be on my own in the Meeting House but there were friends and relatives nearby and they made sure that I was well looked-after. The Ferrys were once again generous enough to invite me down for a couple of weekends so we could conduct the search for our own home on the coast. In the event, it took very little time. We found a two-bedroom detached bungalow under construction at Saltdean, a clifftop community distinguished by its Art Deco swimming pool and just a short walk along the clifftops from Rottingdean. The cost? All of £2,650, and ready for occupation in two or three months. Somehow we managed to line up a £2,000 mortgage and the rest was scraped together from our own meagre savings and a generous contribution from the bank of Mum and Dad.

On Good Friday, Ron went down to Brighton to settle in temporarily at the Ferrys' Rottingdean home and start the new job on Easter Monday. The shift pattern on the sub-editors' desk at the *Argus* gave him Tuesdays off, but he had to work a long Saturday shift on the sports edition of the paper, and that meant I did not see him until late Saturday evening. Twenty-four hours after his visit home, he was back on the train to Brighton.

This period of our lives echoed an earlier time before we married, when, during his National Service days in the Royal Air Force, he used to escape from Abingdon at noon, with a fleeting 36-hour pass and hitchhike home to me. On Sunday nights, as he set off back to Abingdon, he sang a World War I ditty beginning, 'Goodbye, Dolly, I must leave you, though it grieves my heart to go . . .' I hated it.

Anyway, in Tottenham I acquired a live-in companion – a cat, who appeared one morning on the kitchen windowsill overlooking the Quaker burial ground. We called him Georgie. In high summer, Georgie was part of the moving-day ensemble that rolled off to Saltdean. I don't think it would happen today, but the removal men happily packed us all in, with Mr and Mrs sitting up front alongside them on the long bench seat and Georgie in a basket somewhere in the back of the pantechnicon. The journey passed without incident, apart from the pitiful miaowing coming from behind us, but on our arrival at the bungalow and opening up the pantechnicon, Georgie shot out of the back as though he'd been fired from a cannon, and disappeared.

Feeling that this might be a bad omen, and five months' pregnant, I dissuaded Ron from the mad idea that he would carry me over the threshold of Chez Nous. As for Georgie, it took him twenty-four hours to emerge from the raggle-taggle of overgrown grass and weeds that were alleged on the bungalow site plan to be the garden.

Late in the afternoon, neighbours appeared with a tray of tea plus helpful local advice, and we celebrated our safe arrival by firing up the solid fuel cooker that had been installed in the kitchen. We couldn't afford an Aga, so we had purchased a Scottish substitute, which was certainly a darn sight cheaper, running on coke and providing plenty of hot water.

I have very mixed memories of the rest of that summer. On the plus side, there was the English Channel, which we could see from the front room of our new home, and two hundred yards up the hill behind us, behind the last line of bricks and mortar, the South Downs stretched towards Lewes and Eastbourne on the right, and over to Brighton racecourse and the hills of West Sussex on the left. There were larks up there, fluttering above the cornfields and singing their hearts out, and badgers that came scampering down to our place at night looking for food.

On the other hand, I soon felt lonely in what was principally a retirement community. Then there was the wind. It was blowing a bit when we first met the builder on the bungalow site. I asked him, 'Does the wind always blow like this?' and he said, 'What wind?' Many years later the conservatory roof was to disappear in a 70-miles-per-hour gale.

The news from Blackpool didn't help. My mother was going through a bad spell and I agonised over whether I should take the long journey north to spend some time with her. In the event I felt that I was not up to it, either physically or emotionally. Ron gave me every support in coming to this decision, but it was not easy. Meanwhile, there was so much to do – seeking advice from my local doctor, hospital consultations and all the aspects of starting a new life on the coast.

I tried to reassure myself that my mother would recover. All my life she had suffered from stomach trouble of one kind or another – diverticulitis was often mentioned – and I recalled too many occasions in my childhood when she had sent me on an urgent errand to get some kind of medicine from the chemist at the top of the road. Now she was a long way away, dependent on others, and the fact that we were still waiting to have the telephone installed increased my sense of isolation. On top of that, the ancient television set had died at some point on the journey from Tottenham to Saltdean. Now it squatted in a corner of our sitting room refusing to speak to me. The trouble was, we couldn't afford a new one.

Communication with Blackpool and elsewhere was by post or by popping round the corner to a public phone box. One afternoon there was loud knocking at the front door. It was a police constable and he said that my husband should call my uncle George – my mother's younger brother – in Blackpool. Ron was still at work, so I went round to the phone box myself. Uncle George answered. He said mother was in a bad way but he wanted to talk to Ron about it.

The fact was, he could not bring himself to tell me that my mother had died of diverticulitis. She was 52. On medical advice, and after consultation with the family, we decided not to go the funeral in Blackpool.

Who can say to what extent my mother's passing at this time shaped subsequent events? Certainly it increased my sense of loneliness. I felt an increasing need to reach out to somebody who might provide support and understanding. I wrote a letter to a woman called Sheila Kitzinger. She was a journalist and author and I had caught sight of an article she wrote about childbirth. In particular it outlined a series of relaxation exercises to be carried out during labour and designed to alleviate discomfort and pain. I told her that I was practising the routine and wondered whether she might visit me if her work brought her down to Sussex at any time. This, I suppose, was a bit of a cry in the dark, and she wrote a sympathetic reply but regretted that she would not be able to do the journey in the near future.

I guess I was asking too much, but to this day I still regret that I was unable to talk to her during that lonely period of my life.

At the beginning of November, my father came down from Blackpool to be with us for the arrival of the new baby. I went into labour on the fourth of the month. Ron said if the baby was born the following day, perhaps we should call him Guy. I wasn't in the mood for jokes as we set off for Brighton Maternity Hospital, and neither did I take kindly to Matron when she insisted that the bottle of black ink I had brought with me must be taken away.

I had anticipated that there would be plenty of time to write to all my friends and had come fully equipped – fountain pen, reams of notepaper and all. No way! Matron was constructed in the sergeant-major mode that prevailed in those days. Nowadays I sometimes think there are very good reasons for bringing that type of matron back.

Guy Fawkes Day came and went. My nearest and dearest sat in

the pub near the Regency Pavilion, popping out occasionally to a phone box to see whether 'Guy' had arrived. No such luck. The labour was proving to be long and difficult. Earlier that year, I had been on a course of relaxation exercises designed to assist delivery, but when it came to it I found it more and more difficult to apply them. Closing time sounded in the King and Queen, and husband and father went back to Saltdean.

Sarah Margaret finally arrived at half-past five the following morning. She weighed eight pounds six ounces and she was everything that I had yearned for. I had had several stitches after delivery and there was also some concern about possible thrombosis, so I stayed in hospital for a week before being declared fully fit. The two main men in my life came in several times and tiptoed into the large room where the new-born babes spent much of the time sleeping, their tiny cots arranged in a semi-circle around a huge coal fire. I doubt that it would get past Health and Safety today, but it was a heart-warming sight and the memory of it is still there for both mother and father.

Five days later, I was back, with my daughter, in the bungalow where, in my absence, my father had built a small greenhouse adjoining the back of our new home, sheltering the kitchen from the occasional fierce winds coming off the Downs from the north-east. It was a happy homecoming – not least because among our meagre possessions was a family heirloom in the shape of an Edwardian swing cot in which Ron spent his early days and which had now been set up in a warm alcove in the kitchen.

My father fussed over the new baby, occasionally holding a hand mirror over her face to ensure that she was still breathing. I think that all this may have sprung from an incident years before when my mother was in hospital and about to deliver their first child. Apparently she got out of bed to visit the bathroom and there, without much indication that he was on the way, the baby arrived. He was still-born. Obviously this was a shattering experience for my parents, and we believe that my dad's routine with the hand mirror, along with other examples of the almost obsessive care and concern he showed towards Sarah, marked a determination that what had happened in that hospital – the death of his first child – must not happen again now that his first grandchild had arrived. I am reluctant to admit it, but Sarah's neurotic parents picked up the hand-mirror habit in those early over-protective days.

Eventually my dad went back to Blackpool and we gradually settled into the new routine. Sarah was fine. She slept well and there was no problem with breast-feeding. I was soon able to cut out the dreaded 2 a.m. feed. Ron had to get up early to do the 7 a.m. shift at the *Argus* and he would bring Sarah to me at about six each morning, announcing that 'Tuppenny Bobert' was ready for breakfast. It was one of those nonsensical nicknames that stuck until a friend began referring to her as 'Suzy Bun'. That one has never really gone away.

On Christmas Eve, just seven weeks after Sarah's birth, we learned from Ron's sister in Hertfordshire that she, too, was now a mother. I think the news must have come by telegram, a Post Office service that brought urgent messages to your front door within a few hours. The postie with a telegram was not necessarily a welcome sight in those days, but this one pronounced that baby Jill had arrived just in time for Christmas and was doing fine. The news brought an extra sparkle to Christmas Day. We had been invited to spend it with the Ferry family, and I recall a great deal of music among all the merry-making.

I cannot recall exactly what triggered it but in the new year, very gradually, my mood turned darker. Maybe it was something inconsequential, like a neighbour assuring me that there really was no need to iron all those nappies I was having to wash. Yes, it's true – I was brandishing that iron as late as eleven o'clock at night. No wonder I was tired all the time! Or was it because we were so hard up and not able to replace that damned television set? It just sat there – mute by malice, as they say in court – but I hadn't the heart to throw it out. It had belonged to my parents, and I remember watching the 1953 Coronation on it, in black and white, along with most of the neighbours, who all crowded into our terrace house in north London.

Whatever it was, I began to feel persecuted. I had the idea that something odd was happening in the fridge after part of an interior fitting fell into a dish of prunes. To me, back then, it was nowhere near as funny as it sounds now. Was someone trying to poison me? Could it be my husband? After all, he was responsible for bringing me down to this place.

Then came the night when I awoke in high terror and ran in my night clothes to the bungalow next door. Ron only became aware of what had happened when he was awakened by the cold night air coming through our open door. He got up and was confronted in the hallway by our neighbour, Mr Woods, a retired police officer, who said, 'You'd better come with me. Your wife's with us, but she's in a hell of a state. She's not making any sense.'

Somehow, with Mrs Woods' considerable help, the three of them managed to calm me down and urged me to go and make sure the baby was all right. This got us back into our own home, but there was very little sleep during the remainder of that night.

At six o'clock, I got up and fed Sarah, then hurried round to the phone box and called the police. I told the duty sergeant that my husband was trying to poison me.

When I told Ron what I had done, he said, ashen-faced, that he would go and get some help. He went off and called my mother's eldest brother, Teddy, who lived in North London. He said he would drive down as quickly as possible.

Inevitably, after all these years some of the events of that dreadful day are hazy, but we are agreed on most of them. It took some while for CID officers to arrive from Lewes. Two of them sat with me in the lounge and, after questioning me at some length, they began the laborious process of taking a written statement. A third officer took Ron through exactly the same procedure in the kitchen. At one point I heard one of the officers saying to another, 'She's a professor of music from the Royal Academy of Music', and I stood up and said, 'No, I'm a lecturer in speech and drama from the Royal Academy of Music.' So at least part of my befuddled brain was working normally. Tea was made and served by one of the officers and then two of them went off to telephone colleagues in Lewes. When they returned they said they would take us to the hospital in Brighton. As we prepared to set off, Uncle Teddy and his wife, Aunt Florrie, arrived. It was agreed that they would accompany us to the hospital to provide support for me and to look after the baby. In the event, the hospital tests proved negative, but one of the officers contacted our local GP to tell her what had happened and to request that she should keep a close eye on me. Then the police zoomed off back to Lewes, though not before – as Ron was to tell me later – one of them had taken him to one side and said, sotto voce: 'Now listen to me, you've gotta stop chasing after these women.'

We learned later, in chatting to Mr and Mrs Woods, that that had been one of the complaints I had made to them in the wee small hours. Mrs Woods had said, 'But we see him running for that bus every morning at half-six and he's back by half-past three.' Ron, ever the joker, said, 'I'm not sure that's a complete defence of the charge.' However, there was a depressive edge to his character, and we were to live under considerable strain in the weeks ahead.

One of the problems was that I was never given a complete diagnosis of what had gone wrong. Maybe such a diagnosis was impossible to make. The family medical books went on about post-natal depression (that was certainly part of it) and puerperal fever, but my local doctor seemed reluctant to be specific. I told her I felt tired all the time and was having difficulty getting to sleep. She tried to comfort me, saying I was trying to do too much and must slow down. I found her immensely reassuring, and she said I must keep in regular touch.

As I recall it, the prescription she gave me was for aspirin in considerable quantity – nine a day. I still felt tired but continued to breast-feed Sarah, who was growing bonnier by the day and that sustained us through some difficult weeks. We were over-protective and at nights we placed her swing cot near a smokeless-fuel fire in our sitting room. We soon abandoned the idea because we were concerned that she might be inhaling injurious fumes. What a pair! So, armed with the hand mirror we were still using for breathing checks, we all moved into the second bedroom, which was the smaller of the two but warmer.

Then, another little drama we could have done without. Running like mad one morning to catch that first bus into Brighton, Ron went base over apex and ended up on the green near the bus stop with a badly sprained ankle, as the 12B departed down the hill. The sprain took some time to heal and left us regretting – not for the first time – the decision to leave dear old London Town.

A few days later I felt the need for more wise counsel and thought it might be forthcoming from Dick Moody – Uncle Dick, as I knew him. My father, Reginald Moody, was the grandson of a stone-mason who became rich through his involvement in the construction of many of the principal buildings in the seaside town of Folkestone. When his first wife died, he married the housekeeper, an attractive woman from Ireland, who was addressed as 'Mater' by every one in the family. The marriage produced two sons. One of them was Dick Moody.

Over the years, my paternal grandmother became very close to Mater, who was both engaging and enormously industrious. In the First World War she had actually managed to increase the Moody fortune by organising, in another of the family's properties, a billet for army officers engaged in the coastal defence of the seaside town. Years later, such was the bond between Mater and my grandmother that my father used to drive us down to Folkestone on weekend trips to Mater's imposing home. It was full of the works of art, antiques and other treasures that she and her husband had gathered on their frequent trips to Europe.

For me as a child, and much more so as an impressionable teenager, that house brought to life all the romance and grandeur I had previously experienced only at the cinema watching those black-and-white movies set in the Edwardian era. To my childhood eye, Uncle Dick seemed perfectly at place in the gracious setting of the Folkestone home. He was handsome and cultured and, as an only child, I found him easy to talk to. As I grew up we became quite close, exchanging letters, as well as birthday and Christmas cards and gifts. It was obvious to me that the gifts I received were selected, with Mater's approval, from among the more modest items in the family's continental treasure trove. Perhaps not surprisingly, although Uncle Dick had trained as an architect, he told me that, though fully qualified, he had never worked as such – or as anything else. I recall being enormously impressed by this – a gentleman of leisure and all that! In due course he married but he did not look for a new home. The new bride simply moved into the Moody family home alongside Uncle Dick and Mater. There were no children from this marriage and his wife died at a relatively young age. He did not marry again.

I learned all this many years later when it was once again possible to visit coastal towns like Folkestone that had been no-go areas during World War II. In my mid-teens, Uncle Dick had been enormously supportive of my hopes and aspirations as I pursued my career, so it was perhaps inevitable that my thoughts turned to him during that period after Sarah's birth rather than to other close relatives. It reached the point where I decided I must visit him, perhaps spend some time with him in Folkestone.

So, one morning, after Ron had gone to work, I bundled Sarah into her pushchair, caught the bus to Brighton station and bought a rail ticket to Folkestone. I had not warned Uncle Dick that I was on my way, but he was at home, and from his muted reaction to my sudden arrival, I sensed he had quickly picked up my underlying distress. I had intended to ask him if Sarah and I could spend some time with him in Folkestone, but as the awkward conversation continued I abandoned the idea and just sat there, dejected, as he stressed the importance of me being with my family in my new home at what he said was clearly a difficult time for me. I got the message, and Sarah and I got the next train back to Brighton. At home, Ron was somewhat distraught, not knowing where the hell I was and having called the *Argus* to say he had to take some time off to go and find me.

After this episode, and still feeling low, I made one last cry for help in the form of a telegram in Spanish to a school friend, Joan Mayhew. Fifteen years earlier, Joan had sat beside me in the same Spanish class. Even so, why write the telegram in Spanish? Because I was embarrassed at the prospect that it would be read by anyone other than Joan. The telegram was basically a desperate plea that she should come down to Saltdean as soon as possible. Next morning she rang the front doorbell.

The day went well. She listened patiently to my tale of woe and, like Uncle Dick, she obviously detected my underlying stress, but she eventually responded by listing what she called all the plus points in my life – a superb new home with a lovely garden (it had been much improved since our first day there when Georgie the cat had disappeared into the thicket that existed back then), and a perfect sea-and-country location in which to bring up a beautiful baby daughter. We spent a happy hour reminiscing about earlier times and got the giggles over the fact that she had married a man whose surname was Haddock and my man was Onions. Afterwards she took Sarah and me down the hill for lunch at a seafront restaurant. As we watched the sun glinting on the incoming tide her tone hardened a little. It was not quite the voice of the dreaded matron, but even as she insisted that we must keep in regular touch, she made it clear that she did not expect to receive any more emergency calls summoning her to Saltdean. By this time I had relaxed to the point that I knew she was saying all the right things to me.

As the days lengthened towards high summer, several positive events helped steer me out of the gloom. My young cousins, Carole and Julie – Uncle George's children – came down from Blackpool to spend the school holidays with us and help look after Sarah. On Ron's days off we caught a bus and explored all the highways and byways of East Sussex. I found this a blissful experience, echoing the time a few years earlier when the two girls had joined us on a similar escapade in the Lake District. It got even better when the news staff at the *Argus* were called out on strike over some long-forgotten dispute, but continued to have their salaries paid by the

National Union of Journalists. This meant that Ron was available full time to direct our summer safaris.

When the strike ended, Ron began to earn extra money at the *Argus* by writing a series of articles about Sussex in bygone days, and his salary was bumped up by an additional ten shillings a week when he was invited to replace the newspaper's fortune-teller – an event my beloved had failed to foresee! Yet in a town not short of fortune-tellers, he managed not merely to survive, but to receive fan letters. One reader wrote: 'You said last Friday I should expect surprise visitors over the weekend. You were right. The burglars broke in late Saturday night.'

Ron

By now, I was enjoying life at the *Argus* after the difficulties we had experienced back in the spring. These were the days before newspaper production was taken over by computers, and the process then in use involved linotype operators who, using molten metal, converted the journalists' typewritten copy into rows of hard type-face. It was a hot and noisy procedure compared with modern methods, and at the *Argus* it was overseen by a fearsome individual, the head printer, whose name was Percy. It was Percy's job to liaise between the printing technicians and the journalists to ensure that all five editions of the paper went out of the building on time.

Percy wore an impressive long grey overall coat, and several times a day he would advance slowly towards the large table around which sat the editor and all his sub-editors. The routine never varied. 'And who,' he would ask, brandishing a single sheet of A4 paper high above his head, 'is the owner of this pretty thing?' 'This pretty thing' was the work of an individual sub-editor responsible for a particular page of the *Argus*, and it illustrated in diagrammatic form how that page should be made up – where the headlines should be and the location of the various news and feature stories, as well as the photo blocks and any advertisements. The hapless sub responsible for this particular 'pretty thing' would own up, and from Percy came his traditional response: 'Well, it don't fit.' So the hapless sub would have to hurry out to the large metal table where the various pages were assembled by a team of compositors and make some quick adjustments. Keeping an eye on the clock was critical if the editions were to hit the streets on time. Somehow they invariably did.

Percy had another routine – one which occasionally almost brought the house down. Like many printers, he took snuff. It was traditional within the industry, maybe to cope with the rather fumey atmosphere that, in those days, was part of the newspaper environment. Percy's tin of snuff contained a potent mixture that seemed powerful enough to blow your head off. Sometimes he would offer a pinch of the stuff around the newsroom, and occasionally to a sub-editor who had just joined the *Argus*. One newcomer, uncertain about accepting but not wishing to reject what seemed like a friendly gesture, took a pinch of the stuff and, with all eyes on him, desperately sniffed it up his nose, with shattering results. A huge cheer broke out as the poor guy struggled to recover, with Percy shouting, 'You didn't do it right!'

The *Argus* editorial team were a talented bunch. Several of them went on to distinguished careers in Fleet Street. Two of them, Walter Clapham and Keith Colquhoun, were authors, writing their novels at home between their shifts as reporter and sub-editor respectively, Clapham's *Night Be My Witness* being a fine evocation of Royal Air Force bombing raids on Germany in World War II. Keith's first book, *The Money Tree*, came out soon after I arrived at the *Argus*, but the boss – a bit churlishly, we thought – refused to review it.

Brighton was a great town to work in and we made many friends. Some, like ourselves, were young parents just starting their families, and we exchanged home visits. It was all part of the recovery process from the difficult days of the recent past. One of the *Argus* sub-editors, Gwyn Scourfield, and his wife, Iris, were aware of what we had been through and were enormously supportive, taking us out on trips in their car. They had just adopted a baby daughter, Anne, so we had a great deal in common. Gwyn, a Welshman, was a prominent participant in the *Argus* sub-editors' impromptu choir which occasionally went into action in the newsroom towards the end of the shift or on slow news days. Much of the repertoire was from the barrack room, but we also created some local variations on hit songs from the Broadway musicals of the day. 'Take My Hand, I'm a Stranger in Rottingdean' was one of the more repeatable examples.

Come the end of the summer, when my holiday relief contract came to an end, I was offered a permanent staff job and accepted it. We were not very happy about the continuing shift pattern, which still did not give me two consecutive days off, but we were by now happy enough with our new life on the coast.

Then everything changed. I received a call from Terry Johnston, a former *Argus* reporter who had left to join the newsroom at Southern Television in Southampton. This was one of the new ITV companies set up to provide opposition to the BBC. Terry said they were recruiting more journalists and asked me if I would be interested. Doris and I decided to take a couple of days off and booked a hotel room for the three of us in the centre of Southampton so we could see what the famous seaport had to offer. At the Southern TV building, a converted cinema on the bank of the River Itchen, the Head of News, Dick Clark, with very little preamble, offered me £1,000 a year to join them in the new year. I accepted, and we headed back to Saltdean clutching an armful of pamphlets from Southampton estate agents. We had to sell the bungalow and find a new home.

Over the Christmas holidays my mother and father came down to join us for the family feast on the big day. I doubt that they had any inkling of the difficult year we had gone through, though my mother had a sensitive antenna when it came to tuning in to the emotional problems of others. Anyway, they both shared our excitement over the new job and 'We'll Take a Cup of Kindness Yet' was sung rather more fervently than usual as we welcomed in the new year.

We had put the bungalow up for sale two months earlier as soon as we returned from Southampton, but thus far there were no takers despite the fact that we had not upped the original price that we paid when we bought it eighteen months earlier. The estate agent talked about the 'wrong time of year'. Later he told us of other stumbling blocks – there was no garage, there were only two bedrooms, the solid fuel cooker was a turn-off for some prospective buyers. Meanwhile Southern TV was pressing me for a starting date, so we decided to let the bungalow fully furnished, and found a tenant living locally who was prepared to pay a rent that just about covered our mortgage commitment and the agent's fees.

That left us to find somewhere to live near Southern TV as soon as possible. As a temporary solution, we booked into a hotel on the outskirts of Southampton which seemed to be primarily a retirement home for elderly ladies, but also accommodated travelling salesmen and skilled tradesmen from a building development nearby. For us, the hotel provided a family room and three nice meals a day, and the cheerful staff were kind enough to serve a late dinner to me if I was delayed getting back from Southern. Some of them seemed to watch the station partly in the expectation that this humble scribe might suddenly appear. Aaah, the glamour of showbiz . . .

After a couple of weeks we found a place of our own just a short distance away. It was a big new bungalow, fully furnished and tucked away down a rocky lane in a rural district of Southampton called Hedge End. The owner was away in Kenya and he had named the bungalow 'Kimoyomoyo'. He said we could rent it until he came back to Blighty. So we moved in, having collected some bits and pieces from Saltdean and not forgetting the cat, Georgie, who had been looked after by some friends.

Southern TV was to prove the ideal place to learn the basics of writing for – and appearing on – television. Each script had to be timed exactly – three words a second was the rule of the thumb – so that the full bulletin would not run short of the time allotted to it or, worse, crash into the following programme. The other main aim was to avoid elephant traps for the presenter – no complicated adjectival phrases ('the missing sixty-six-year-old Mississippi skipper'. . .) that would plunge them into disaster – and to be especially careful with the weather forecast: there's a danger in 'scattered showers'.

My principal mentor in all this was a newsroom character named Terry Carroll. He was a few years older than me, with a background in print journalism, but with additional skills as an author and a guitarist, mixing jazz and Spanish style in his repertoire. He had spent some while living in Spain, and subsequently presented a special series on Channel Four titled 'Spain Is Different'. He had also written a novel called *Copy Boy*, which related to an earlier period in his career in journalism. According to his partner during his time at Southern TV, *Copy Boy* had to be rescued from under the kitchen sink, where it had languished for some while before being refurbished and sent off to a publisher. The publisher said yes.

I saw Terry only once in later years, when he was involved in horse racing, and the last I heard of him was when he took part in a discussion on BBC Radio 4 as the author of a much grander work than *Copy Boy*, on the subject of horse racing.

There was another man at Southern who was to have an even greater impact on the way my career was developing. Someone said to me, 'If you want to learn more about the basics of television, go and sit behind the guy who edits the film shot by our cameramen.' He was then at the very beginning of a distinguished international career and was to go on to direct a number of award-winning movies, notably *Point Blank*, starring Lee Marvin, *Deliverance* (Jon Voight and Burt Reynolds) and *The General* (Jon Voight again). His name was John Boorman.

Looking over Boorman's shoulder, I picked up some basics of film editing, such as cutting the cameraman's shots at a point of movement to sustain the momentum of a particular sequence, thus sharpening the dramatic impact. Occasionally, after concluding a few seconds that gave him extra satisfaction, he would mutter, 'Ridiculous, isn't it?'

Eventually, Boorman left Southern to join BBC West Region in Bristol. There he produced a successful weekly regional programme, 'Points West', introducing a number of innovative ideas and notably transposing one of the Top Ten musical hits of the time, 'Stranger on the Shore', featuring clarinetist Acker Bilk, into a dazzling sequence of film.

Shortly after I, too, had joined the BBC – though in Southampton, not Bristol – John rang me to ask if I would like to do something for 'Points West'. We agreed on a satirical piece centred on the fact that Brighton was under fire for spending too much money on events in and around the town's Regency landmark, the Royal Pavilion. This had once been the home of the Prince Regent, later George III, whose extravagance and profligacy were a matter of historical record. So I went for 'Prinny', perhaps too vigorously. Boorman rang me after the programme went out and said, 'The older guys here think it was immature to take such a destructive view of a historical figure.' Then he added, in his wry way: 'I think you've got a future on the television if that's what you want.'

After less than a year at Southern, I took a call from a man named Peter Marshall, who was a successful freelance journalist in the South of England. He said he would like me to join him in setting up one of the new BBC local television and radio operations. These were in areas of the United Kingdom where ITV's new out-of-London ventures, including Southern, were beginning to prosper. BBC Southampton would be based near the docks, just a short distance from Southern.

I was apprehensive about Marshall's call. Sometime earlier, when I was still at the *Argus*, I had gone for an interview at Broadcasting House, the BBC headquarters in central London, about a sub-editor's job in the radio newsroom. I was unsuccessful. I wondered whether this had been because, when the interview ended, I stood up and turned around to leave the room, only to be confronted by two doors. Which was the exit? I chose the wrong one and stepped into the cleaner's cupboard, triggering a slapstick sequence of falling brooms and clattering buckets.

Marshall was reassuring, saying if I wanted the job, it was mine. I decided to take it, though not as a member of staff but as a free-lance, because that gave me the opportunity to work in radio as well as television – and at £27 a week it also paid better. So, after less than a year at ITV, I joined the British Broadcorping Castration, as the jokers at Southern referred to the BBC. Another sub-editor at Southern, Gordon Randall, made the same short journey across town. So did their principal newscaster, Martin Muncaster. When told that half his news staff were departing to the BBC, Southern's managing director, Roy Rich, who had himself worked for the Corporation in both radio and television, could only comment, 'Why can't they pick on someone their own size?'

There was a time, still remembered by older staff at BBC Southampton, when London newsreaders wore evening dress while addressing the national radio audience. Certainly the dignity and formality of the newsreader's task hung heavily in the acoustics of that little news studio in Southampton. Fortunately I was not invited to do my first live radio broadcast without a lot of dummy runs. Eventually it was suggested that, for my debut, I should simply read the weather forecast for southern counties at the end of a ten-minute bulletin presented by Martin Muncaster. He said to me, 'I'll come to you thirty seconds before we have to switch back to the national network'. So I rehearsed my piece, which ran a little under thirty seconds. It was one of those forecasts with a little bit of everything but sunshine – rain, wind, low temperatures, and even a hint of snow over higher ground. As Martin delivered the main bulletin in impec-cable style I became increasingly nervous, and when he gave me the cue – 'Now the weather forecast for the south' – I froze, looking desperately up at the clock as the seconds ticked by, and then down at what seemed like a morass of words, finally alighting on just one of them, which I almost bellowed into the microphone: 'SNOW!'

This became a bit of a folk legend in the history of BBC West Region, and I was very much happier when, a few months later, the new evening television programme for the south of England got under way from an adjoining television studio.

These were pioneering days out there in the BBC regions, much more so than at Southern TV, which, by comparison, was relatively sophisticated. There was none of the dazzling electronic armoury that exists today and, indeed, no videotape machines that enabled the producer to pre-record some items. There was not even a teleprompter – the device that rolls the script alongside the camera so that you can address the viewer at eye-level rather than moving your eyes up and down from the typewritten script on the desk in front of you. Sometimes you wrote key phrases in large black capitals on a cue sheet, a large piece of paper which you hung near the camera you were addressing. Sod's Law said these would fall down at critical moments, leaving the presenter to vamp his or her way through as best they could.

This was also a time of primitive communication during live transmission between the presenter and whoever was directing the programme from the production gallery attached to the studio. Much later it was achieved more effectively through a small earpiece worn by presenters. In Southampton it was done via one of the bulky telephones of yesteryear which sat prominently in front of the presenter and rang at moments of crisis to inform him or her, as the audience looked on expectantly, of what had gone wrong and how the hell he or she might get out of it.

On one occasion at BBC Southampton the telephone rang in the middle of a news bulletin and the presenter reached forward to pick it up and hear the worst. Unfortunately, though he could hear it ringing, it wasn't where it should have been – on the desk. So the audience was confronted with the hilarious spectacle of a perplexed presenter trying to locate the wretched phone, standing up from his chair and looking on the floor and elsewhere around the studio. He found it after beguiling moments for the viewers, but agony for himself, by opening a drawer in the presentation desk from which it then rang out louder than ever as he reached down to answer the crisis call. Questions were asked after the show and, conveniently, a cleaner was blamed for the mishap. Some of us, though, with suspicious minds, suspected malevolence on somebody's part.

The American writer and broadcaster Garrison Keillor has written about a radio station in Minneapolis with a 'snakebite studio', as he called it, where bad things happened to people who went in there. I wondered sometimes whether that Southampton studio was similarly afflicted. There was, for instance, the time I was presenting the 'South At Six' programme when, as the seconds counted down to the opening titles, the pile of scripts I had mounted as usual on a small sloping lectern on the presenter's desk decided to slide off, very slowly, ending up around my feet on the floor and totally out of sequence. I scrambled under the desk to retrieve the scripts and shuffle them into some sort of order. So what the viewer saw, as the signature tune and opening titles came to an end, was just an empty desk. Then, gradually, the head of a dishevelled presenter arose from the far side of the desk, rather like one of those old-time cinema organists coming up out of the orchestra pit, except – unlike them – I was neither waving nor smiling.

You can imagine the rest. When I read the script about the Queen Mother visiting Portsmouth, up came a still of Barbara Windsor opening a fete. A little later, the story of an old-age pensioner's arrest for shoplifting was illustrated by the smiling face of the Queen Mother. John Logie Baird, up there in heaven, must have been weeping with laughter.

Sometimes things went wrong even after meticulous preparation. There was the time when one of the television sports producers in London asked me to do a live report from the Southampton studio for the BBC's national Saturday afternoon sports programme. The event was a powerboat race in the English Channel. There were two or three calls between engineers to establish that the television link between London and Southampton had been booked and was working satisfactorily. Then there were further calls involving production assistants at both ends to check on the spelling of my name because the studio director in London wanted to superimpose a name caption at the bottom of the screen immediately after the London presenter, David Coleman, handed over to me. The phone exchanges went something like this: 'So that's O-N-I-

O-N then, like the vegetable? Very unusual name . . .' 'Yes but it's O-N-I-ON-S with an S on the end . . .' 'OK – and is it RON or RONALD?' 'Make it RON . . .'

So finally the moment came for my live report after the London presenter's handover cue, which ran as follows: 'So over to Southampton and REX Onions . . .' Whereupon up came the caption at the bottom of the screen insisting that Rex was indeed my first name. My mother – watching with my father in London – was most upset at what they'd done to her son, but the Southampton staff thought it was a hoot and I had to put up with references to 'Sexy Rexy' for some weeks afterwards.

There were two other memorable examples of snakebite during those pioneering days of black-and-white television, and the first involved a colleague who was presenting the news. In mid-bulletin, the heavy studio camera started to creak a bit and then fell slowly to the floor and came apart. The poor guy said afterwards he wondered whether he should have followed the example set by sea captains by going down to the floor with the sinking camera so as to stay in vision and complete the script.

The second incident happened at Southern TV during the enthronement of a new Suffragan Bishop at Portsmouth Cathedral. It had been decided to cover the event live, which meant that Southern had to opt out of the networked programme that all the other ITV stations were transmitting at the time. This happened to be 'Popeye, the Sailor Man'. Unfortunately, somewhere along the connecting line that linked Southern's transmission studio to the outside broadcast vehicle in Portsmouth, someone hit the wrong button. As a result, the solemn music accompanying the new bishop's procession into the cathedral was suddenly interrupted and replaced by a perky burst of the Popeye theme tune.

Some two years after joining the BBC, I went on a short attachment to BBC Bristol, headquarters of West Region and home of the outstanding Natural History Unit. It was an opportunity to look at a much bigger operation than Southampton and also to make a contribution by preparing news reports for the main evening radio bulletin. I was taken aback to discover that the reports were not recorded on quarter-inch audio tape, as was the standard practice in those days, but instead you actually had to make an old-fashioned gramophone record. It was important to get it right first time, otherwise the 12-inch vinyl disc would have to be junked and the whole nerve-making process repeated. If you got it right, a green-and-white BBC label would be placed on the centre of the disc ready for playback into the big bulletin later on. I recounted all this much later on to my daughter Sarah when she was working as a programme producer at BBC Bristol. She didn't believe it then – and I'm not sure she does even now.

At the end of that visit to Bristol I had a chat with John Boorman, who said he was looking for an additional producer on 'Points West' and asked if I would be interested. Well, of course I would – but, back in Southampton, when I talked it over with Doris, we decided against it. I was fairly relaxed about the decision, feeling that if we were to make a move, it ought to be to London. She took the view that moving anywhere at this time would be a move too many. In ten years of marriage, for one reason or another, we had packed up for somewhere else no less than nine times. Even so, she wrote to Boorman, feeling that she had to explain why we could not take what was clearly an exciting opportunity. He sent a gracious reply and we were left with a feeling of 'What if . . .' that was to stay with us for many years.

Such is life – or, more specifically, such were our lives – that, just a few weeks later, we had no choice but to move. 'Mr Kimoyomoyo' decided that it was time to come home from Kenya and resume residence in his bungalow.

Our next home was waiting for us a short distance away at Locks Heath, halfway between Southampton and Portsmouth. It was a graceful – if slightly faded – Victorian house, fully furnished and with an imposing gravel drive linking two entrances from the road. To the right there were stables and, on the other side, a fig tree yielding excellent fruit; nearby, there was a plentiful supply of strawberries. There was that faint smell from the Fawley oil refinery, but the place was immediately available and the rent was £4 a week.

By this time, 'South At Six' was running like clockwork – well, almost. We had recruited extra staff, two of whom were new to television but went on to enjoy considerable success. Hugh Scully was to become the presenter for many years of one of the BBC's most popular programmes, 'Antiques Roadshow', and Roger Mills, after a period with BBC News in London and Paris, set up his own production company whose documentary and current affairs programmes became a distinguished part of television output. We also had, covering sport, the doyen of cricket commentators, John Arlott. In the bar after the programme he would tell hilarious tales of his life and times in newspapers and broadcasting. Then there was Oz. He was the cartoonist from the local evening newspaper, and in the space of about a minute he created, live on air, a topical cartoon with a balloon caption read by someone off-screen. It sounds old hat nowadays, and we could not claim credit for great innovation, simply because it was the only way of doing it. We had no videotape machine and therefore could not take the much less risky option of recording Oz before the programme went out. Still, the kids loved it, which meant much more fan mail for Oz than for anyone else on the programme, and a huge increase in young viewers.

The area served by the 'South At Six' transmitters included the homes of such distinguished people as Field Marshall Montgomery, Britain's Supreme Commander in World War II. I rang his home on one occasion to see if we could come and interview him to mark the anniversary of the D-Day landing in June, 1944. The phone was answered promptly and someone said 'Yes'. I explained why I was calling, and the voice at the other end again responded 'Yes'. Then there was a long silence, during which I assumed that Monty was being summoned to the phone by the butler or whoever it was who had picked up my call in the first place. It finally dawned on me that the celebrated Field Marshall might be in the habit of answering the phone himself. This was confirmed when, in a tone that suggested he was dealing with a clown at the other end of the line, he began asking when and where the interview might take place. I stumbled and bumbled a bit, and he interrupted with: 'Were you a soldier?' I died the death at this point. I said: 'No, sir. I was in the Royal Air Force.' His voice perked up: 'Oh really,' he said. 'I worked with your chaps.' He obviously had in mind such heroic pilots as Guy Gibson of Bouncing Bomb fame and the legless hero Douglas Bader – not forgetting those of higher rank who directed the RAF strategy that proved vital in bringing the Allies to victory.

I did not reveal that I had been a mere Aircraftsman First Class during the years of compulsory National Service after World War II had ended. I was a clerk in Equipment Accounts at RAF Abingdon, and the only time I flew over Germany was on a cricket tour playing service teams in the Hamburg area. In the event, the interview with Monty was done by someone on the 'South At Six' team who had seen active service with the army in World War II, reporter Johnny Johnston. He and Monty got on famously.

Doris

In the high summer of 1961 I realised that I was pregnant again. We had a momentary mental wobble when, inevitably, our thoughts turned back to the events surrounding Sarah's birth, but that passed quickly and we looked forward eagerly to the arrival of a son. He would be called Louis after one of our jazz heroes. Sarah had been named after another jazz immortal, Sarah Vaughan. Both names would be a nostalgic reminder that we had spent much of our courtship, as it was called in those days, in the basement of 100 Oxford Street jiving to the music of Humphrey Lyttleton and his band, and had seen both Armstrong and Vaughan in action at their concerts in Britain.

The only sad note at this time was that Georgie, the cat who came to us from that graveyard in Tottenham, became seriously ill. He had survived the journey from London to the Sussex coast and then the moves to Hedge End and Locks Heath in Hampshire, but not his final one to nearby Fareham, where a vet diagnosed a fatal liver condition.

In the wider world, there was much anguish at this time over the terrible effects of a drug called Thalidomide. It came onto the market in the late fifties as a treatment for insomnia and morning sickness in mothers-to-be. It was withdrawn a few years later after a vigorous campaign by the *Sunday Times* which established that Thalidomide had killed 100,000 babies in the womb. A further 10,000 were born with major disabilities and deformities. Many had hands shaped like fins growing directly from the shoulders. Others had deformed eyes and ears or were without a kidney or lung. As the *Sunday Times* reported, many of them died shortly after birth or were stillborn. By the time I became pregnant all of the horrible facts about Thalidomide were only too well known and I vowed to myself that I would try and steer clear of any kind of medication, including even aspirin, until after the arrival of our second child.

It was at this point that friends suggested, in view of what had happened at the time of Sarah's birth, that we should arrange for pre-natal care and delivery at the maternity unit run by Dr Scott and his wife in the Southampton suburb of Bassett and near to the General Hospital. It was not the easiest of journeys on public transport, especially as I had to take Sarah with me, but whenever he could, Ron drove me there and back. For a woman of modest build, I knew that I was carrying a formidable baby, and it showed.

It was also increasingly tiring just getting around, and to my great relief, during yet another Thursday visit, Dr Scott recommended that I stay in the maternity unit over the weekend. I did so, whereupon my second daughter decided to emerge soon after midnight on the Sunday morning. It was a long and slow process. As dawn broke, Dr Scott tried to cheer and hurry me up: 'Come on, Mrs Onions, I shall be wanting to get away to the church.' He made it there on time. Staff and visitors were captivated by our new daughter. So, too, were Ron and Sarah when they came in later in the day.

We spent a couple more days in the maternity unit before going home, where our new babe showed no sign of the problems that were to confront us four months later, after we went to the village fete. Following the diagnosis then of the thyroid condition, there were regular visits to the children's unit at Southampton General Hospital. Also, the local district nurse came to our house regularly to see how we were getting on. She was a kindly woman and revealed that in recent years there had been two births in the families who had been previous tenants of the house we were now living in. The first of these babies was fine. The second, a boy, had thyroid problems. Now Lulu was similarly afflicted.

We discussed the fact that the original lead piping that supplied water throughout the house was still in use. Over the years lead piping had come under suspicion as a health risk, and copper piping was gradually replacing it. We also wondered about that oil refinery at nearby Fawley. There was that faintly sinister smell. In summer, sitting out in the garden, sometimes I felt slightly sick. Might there be toxic elements in the discharge from Fawley that could be injurious to health, especially to babies in the womb? This anxiety was spurred by the increasing public concern about the significantly higher incidence of fatalities in communities living within the shadow of atomic power stations.

It was during one of these visits by the district nurse that I suddenly recalled that before becoming pregnant with Lulu I had consulted a local doctor because I was experiencing mild depression and insomnia during my monthly periods. He prescribed tablets but I could not remember what they were. I told the district nurse that I had stopped taking them as soon as I realised I was pregnant. Well before then the appalling effects of Thalidomide had been widely publicised so I ruled out any possibility that the tablets I had taken were in fact the drug that had caused so much misery. Even so, the district nurse suggested I go back to the doctor in question and seek total reassurance on this point. I did so and asked him the name of the tablets he had prescribed. He said he was sorry but the relevant records had since been mislaid.

Much less welcome than the district nurse was the strange man who came up the drive one morning and battered away with the huge brass knocker on the front door. Thinking there might be some kind of emergency, I rushed downstairs, to be confronted by an extremely angry-looking individual. He launched into a long tirade, the gist of which was that I had no right to be living in the house. It emerged that he had been a previous occupant but there had been some kind of dispute and he had been evicted. I managed to get rid of him eventually, but later in the day I called on my nearest neighbour – a school teacher – to see if she could throw any light on the incident. She said, 'Ah, that's the mad scientist' – but I could get little else out of her. The hostile visitor, who had come while Lulu and I were alone in the house, had left me a bit shaken. Was it time yet again to move on?

Ron

A few weeks later, my parents came down from London to see how we were getting on. Although they had seen Lulu on our occasional visits to their home in London, we had yet to tell them about her thyroid problem. We did so after lunch, repeating to them the assurances about her future that we had been given.

We were interrupted by the telephone ringing. It was someone from the BBC TV newsroom in London. He said Marilyn Monroe had just died and they would like to get a reaction from Laurence Olivier. Five years earlier, he had co-starred with her in a film called *The Prince and the Showgirl*, which he also directed. London had called me because at weekends the journalists in the BBC South newsroom took it in turn to be on call at home for any requests to cover news stories in our area. That area included Brighton, where Sir Laurence lived in one of the imposing Regency buildings on the seafront.

I said the distinguished actor was unlikely to say anything at all. It was an open secret that during and after the making of the movie he was on strained terms with Monroe, to say the least. However, I promised to call a couple of contacts who were close to Sir Laurence and see if he could be persuaded. He couldn't. The response from London was that they would call one of their own contacts. I said it might be better to approach Frankie Vaughan, a top-of-the-bill singer and entertainer of the time who had worked with Marilyn two years earlier in a film called *Let's Make Love*. I said that I knew that Vaughan was in London and provided them with a contact number. This idea was not well received, however.

A few hours later we watched the BBC national news. There was no contribution from Sir Laurence in the coverage of Monroe's death. Later we switched to ITN. There, live, sitting right next to the newscaster, was Frankie Vaughan. Ah well, that's showbiz.

My parents had just sat there totally bewildered from the moment the London newsroom had called. They were still trying to take in the news about Lulu and what it might portend.

Doris

As the weeks went by, looking after the two children on my own throughout the working week began to be more than I could cope with, not least because of the regular expeditions by bus into Southampton and back for Lulu's hospital visits. A friend told me of an excellent nursery school for Sarah close to the hospital and, as luck would have it, she mentioned that nearby there was an empty ground-floor apartment with two bedrooms. We made our minds up swiftly. Yet again we would move. It was a good move. We were close to friends and colleagues and there was a big improvement in our social life, not least because we were able to find some reliable baby-sitters, something that hadn't been easy in Locks Heath.

Sarah prospered at the school, but come Easter both the kids caught the measles. Still, there was consolation in the profusion of chocolate eggs that well-wishers sent round to the apartment. They were not quite what the doctor would have ordered, but they got us through a difficult period.

Ron

After three and a half years in Southampton, we felt it was time to do what we had always intended and get back to London. Fortuitously, we were helped on our way after a chat I had with a distinguished BBC man from Bristol, Frank Gillard. He had been an outstanding war correspondent for the BBC during World War II and was now Controller of West Region. Part of the job involved occasional visits to Southampton and Plymouth to rally his broadcasting troops in the area studios there. Over a drink he asked me: 'How do you see your future?' It was one of those BBC questions. It would have made some people nervous. For me, though, it resulted in an invitation to go up to town and talk to Alasdair Milne, later to become Director-General of the BBC, but at the time one of the principals of BBC TV current affairs and the top man on the successful early evening programme 'Tonight'. The following week I was offered a job on the 'Tonight' production staff.

Shortly before Christmas, Doris and the two children said farewell to Southampton and moved into our new home, a rented apartment we had discovered near the entrance to Kew Gardens and a short distance on the Tube to the 'Tonight' studios at Shepherds Bush. I remained in Southampton for about three months, since it had been agreed that the 'Tonight' job would commence in late February to allow for a period of continuity with my successor at BBC South. I was able to get up to Kew at weekends, though I had the bad luck one stormy night to be forced off the A3 by a vehicle that swerved suddenly in front of me as it left a garage forecourt. My faithful Ford ended up embedded in a farm gate as the other vehicle disappeared into the darkness.

I started the 'Tonight' job in late February. The programme was based in the old Lime Grove Film Studios at Shepherd's Bush and most of the production staff worked in small rooms that had once been part of an adjoining house. I found it a bit claustrophobic. It provided none of the stimulating cut-and-thrust that I was used to in the open-plan production areas and newsrooms of my previous jobs. That said, the early-evening programme, going out five nights a week, was then at the top of its form. I soon got the chance to produce a number of studio-based items for its principal presenter, Cliff Michelmore, and to venture out on film location with another radio and TV favourite, Brian Redhead. This led to the idea that I should accompany one of the programme's experienced film directors on an extended tour of the Midlands with the aim of putting several 'Tonight'-style features in the can for subsequent transmission. The presenters would be athlete and broadcaster Chris Brasher and another Tonight regular, MacDonald Hastings, father of Sir Max, the newspaper editor and author.

The tour did not go well. I rang home on my first night away to discover that Doris had had a difficult day with Louise, who was coming up to her second birthday but had yet to start walking. Lulu got around by scraping along on her bottom, propelling herself forward with her feet, but she had become increasingly unsettled since moving from Southampton. The two-bedroom flat we had rented near Kew Gardens was on the second floor of a smart apartment block, but unfortunately there was no lift. This meant that we had to hump a pushchair up and down the stairs whenever we went out. We also had to check that the front door of the flat was firmly shut when Louise was moving around to ensure that she did not tip herself down the stairs. I blamed myself for not anticipating the problems that had arisen in the flat and which Doris was having to cope with on her own. It came increasingly obvious as that first week of the Midlands tour went by that I must return home.

I had learned, however, that there was a 'Tonight' plan to recreate on film the Grand Tour of Europe undertaken by the nobility in the nineteenth century, and it had been proposed that I should join the team. That would keep me away for several weeks. That obviously could not happen, and an appointment with Alasdair Milne was arranged to discuss my situation. He was sympathetic, but asked me how I saw my future. I said maybe I should sound out the editor of BBC Television News, Desmond Taylor, to see if there was an empty seat on the sub-editors' desk. That would mean working long shifts, but there would be days off and I would be home every night. Alasdair kindly offered to ring Taylor on my behalf and explain the situation.

The following week I drove to Alexandra Palace on the first leg of a journey that would take us around the world. Ally Pally was – and remains – a landmark in the history of television in Great Britain and, indeed, the world. It was from Ally Pally, in the mid-1930s, that the BBC began transmitting a limited programme service to a small audience and on one channel only. During the years of World War II, the service was suspended. When it resumed only the news department was to remain at the Palace, other national programme departments moving elsewhere in London.

Alexandra Palace was also a geographical landmark. It was opened in 1873 to provide Victorians with an entertainment and recreation centre. After only a couple of weeks there was a fire in the dome and the place had to be rebuilt. It reopened two years later. The Palace stood at the top of a hill in attractive parkland between the north London suburbs of Wood Green and Muswell Hill, with spectacular views of the capital stretching far to the south. During the time I worked at the Palace there was, at the foot of the hill, a racetrack which featured regular evening meetings and that was clearly visible from the newsroom and something of a distraction for those journalists who fancied the occasional flutter.

On that first day, I entered Ally Pally reluctantly. I felt like a kid who had been about to win a game of Snakes and Ladders only to find himself on the head of a snake on what he hoped was the last throw of the dice and zooming all the way back down to the start of the game. It sounds like self-pity – and it was. I had met Desmond Taylor previously over a drink in the BBC Club bar in Southampton, and now he greeted me warmly and accompanied me on a tour of the Palace.

I soon realised that the times they were a-changing. When BBC Television News began, it was regarded by some as the poor relation of the long-established Radio News operation at Broadcasting

House in central London. There some unkind souls referred to Ally Pally as Monkey Hill. The TV news had started life as little more than a newsreel following the style that British Movietone News and its rivals presented to cinema audiences. There was, in fact, a reluctance in those early TV news presentations to allow the newsreader to be seen, lest the merest hint of a raised eyebrow or the pursed lips might be interpreted by viewers as an adverse comment on stories that must be presented with strict impartiality. Some claimed that the running order for the television bulletin was dictated by the radio newsroom. Others ignored that kind of speculation and the banter that went with it, preferring to look at the developments that lay ahead. These included the imminent launch of BBC2 in April 1964, and the government's go-ahead for live broadcasting from the Houses of Parliament and the arrival of colour television on BBC2 in 1967. BBC1 went into colour two years later. There was also a leap forward in the transmission of news by satellite, which enabled flow of news twenty-four hours a day between Britain and America, and subsequently between Britain and the rest of the world. Previously, the satellite system had provided only a ten-minute window twice a day to transmit breaking stories before the satellite went whizzing off into orbit and reappeared twelve hours later – so you had better be on the ball.

Meanwhile, substantial competition had arrived on independent television in the shape of ITN, with its new Editor-in-Chief, Sir Geoffrey Cox.

Gradually, I settled into the sub-editing routine at Ally Pally and we were now coping reasonably well with Lulu in the Kew flat, but, without telling me, my number one fan – my wife – had written to Granada Television in Manchester saying I was just the man they ought to employ. The first I knew was when a fellow sub-editor at Alexandra Palace shouted across the newsroom, 'Ron, there's a call for you over here – it's Granada Television.' I tried – and failed – to look nonchalant. On the line was Sir Denis Forman and, referring to the secret letter, he invited me to come and see him at Granada's London base in Golden Square. Apparently they wanted to appoint a second London-based journalist to chase after stories suited to their successful five-nights-a-week 'Look North' programme. Sir Denis arranged for me to go up to Manchester to meet David Plowright, brother of the distinguished actress Joan Plowright. David was one of Granada's programme dynamos and he said he would like me to interview Anthony Haden-Guest about his life and times as a bon viveur and columnist, just to see if I might fit into Granada's talented 'Look North' team. I was introduced to several of the team, including Michael Parkinson, who quizzed me at some length about life at Lime Grove working on the 'Tonight' programme. Not long after, Michael joined 'Tonight' as a presenter. Several years later, when I was editor-in-chief at the London radio station LBC, I employed him as a phone-in host and presenter of a weekly film review programme.

The interview with Haden-Guest took place at the Granada studios in Chelsea. It failed to take off. If I had been too hard on the Prince Regent in the piece I did for John Boorman, this time I pussyfooted my way through an interview that must have looked as dull as it felt. I knew immediately that I had blown any chance of joining Granada.

Back at Alexandra Palace, there was quite a bit of excitement over the impending arrival of the new channel, BBC2, but the scheduled opening night – 20 April 1964 – had to be abandoned because of a power failure.

By this time, several extra staff had been taken on to cover expanding programme commitments which, in addition to news bulletins on both channels, included a nightly news magazine for the Greater London area called 'Town and Around', with Michael Aspel among the presenters. Then there was 'Westminster at Work', a weekly review of what was going on in Parliament. Among the new faces at Alexandra Palace were several Fleet Street reporters, including Tom Mangold, who was to become a distinguished presenter and investigative reporter in current affairs programming and also the author of several highly acclaimed books. Other recruits included Martin Bell, from the BBC's Eastern Region, subsequently famous as 'The Man in the White Suit' and an Independent MP. I was to be closely associated with him in future overseas coverage.

The all-round skills I had acquired outside London, with both the BBC and ITV, soon opened the way to a variety of roles at Alexandra Palace, including presenter of BBC2 early evening news and also studio reporter on the channel's new half-hour programme, 'Newsroom', later in the evening. I also had an assignment as film director of key constituency reports during the first elections of the newly created Greater London Council in 1965, and I played the same role, out there on the stump, in the marginal constituencies in the following year's general election.

In my second year at Ally Pally I was posted to Broadcasting House and the 'Westminster at Work' programme. This Friday night special was presented by Ian Trethowan, who had been political editor of ITN in earlier years and was also a regular presenter on their nightly 'News At Ten'. It was the only television programme to come out of Broadcasting House, from a small studio used at other times by visiting journalists to send reports back to the television regions. I had used it myself in earlier years to file live reports down to Southampton's 'South At Six'. The main aim of the programme was to provide a rundown of the key events of the parliamentary week. My job was to take the programme out of the Westminster village and show an individual MP on the stump in his or her constituency trying to tackle local problems which had national implications. It took me all over the United Kingdom. During the parliamentary recesses, I became part of the BBC News team covering the annual party conferences.

Doris

Back home in Kew, I was finding it increasingly difficult to cope with Lulu in that small flat. When she finally started to walk, at two years and four months, I hoped her occasional bouts of frustration would fade away but, in fact, they got gradually worse. She would lie on the floor in a rigid posture and just scream. Later she added to the routine, kicking and throwing everything in sight. It was bad enough when it happened at home, but imagine what it was like when we had to deal with it out there in public, on the pavement or on the floor of the supermarket.

Every three months we took her to the Great Ormond Street Hospital for Sick Children in central London, but we heard little to comfort us from the various specialists we met. Thyroid deficiency, if untreated, results in cretinism. We were a long way from that. Lulu was alert and hyperactive. She was tall and strong, with excellent teeth, all of them arriving on time. However, we worried about the future.

With Ron now able to spend more consecutive days at home, we decided it might be a good idea to break out of the flat in Kew and head back to the coast, where the Saltdean bungalow was unoccupied but, in my vivid imagination, full of sunshine.

There were three other pluses: much more room for the four of us; an excellent primary school for Sarah, just down the hill in Saltdean Vale; and within a few yards of our home a little nursery school in a hall adjoining the local Congregational church. We had checked out that they would be able to look after Lulu each morning, Monday to Friday. I looked forward to a whole fifteen hours' weekly respite. Sadly, this arrangement soon fell apart. Lulu found it difficult to relate to the other kids and she proved too much of a handful for the hard-working staff. They provided me with a weekly written report. So many years later, they still make desperately sad reading, particularly the instances of physical assault on some of the other kids, but, in her defence, I ought to point out that Lulu was beginning to suffer from constipation at this stage of her life, which had a consequent effect on her moods and well-being. Just one piece of paper from this unhappy period brought some comfort. It has a large yellow star at the top and the following inscription: 'For improvement in speech and really trying'. Reading it so many years later still brings us to tears.

With the help of the nursery school staff, we managed eventually to get Lulu enrolled in the starter class of a training school for 'mentally handicapped' children as they were designated in those days. It was in an impressive building on the edge of the Sussex Downs, but she was transferred after a few weeks to the nursery class of Hillside School at Portslade on the other side of Brighton. Lulu was picked up each morning to be taken there in a bus which had been specially adapted to cope with various disabilities. She set off happily enough most days, but she had the occasional tantrum en route and the drivers took the precaution of strapping her securely into her seat to ensure everyone's safety on the way to school.

After a while it was obvious that she was responding reasonably well to Hillside's regime, and her attendance a full five days a week took some of the pressure off the rest of the family at home. One of the problems was that Lulu was still not fully toilet-trained, and this imposed an additional burden on the hard-working staff at Hillside, who also had to deal with several non-ambulant children. Still, there were from time to time heartening signs of progress, and we were encouraged by the occasional written reports we received.

When, from time to time, I reviewed Lulu's situation with the head teacher, she began to express the view that it would be better for everyone, including our daughter, if she were placed in residential care. Looking back now I can see that she was right, but in those early years I resisted the idea. I told myself that I had been fully trained as a teacher, and therefore I was better equipped than most mothers to cope with someone like Lulu. It was bad reasoning, of course, but pride was mixed up in it. Gradually, as I registered the strain that all of us were under – and not least Sarah – we decided to try and find a residential home for Lulu. What triggered this was a distressing incident one wet weekend when we were unable to go out and Lulu was throwing a wobbly.

Lunch was often a fraught experience, and on this occasion she scrambled out of her chair and ended up on the floor, lying there rigid and screaming. It was just too much, and finally Ron lost the last of his cool and slapped Lulu vigorously on the legs. Over the years friends and family have observed that there existed a very close bond between the two of them, and this was totally out of character; he has regretted it ever since.

The search for a residential home turned out to be long and frustrating. Suitable places were rare. The best of them invariably had a waiting list or charged higher fees than we could afford – or both. Some were just too far away.

Standards in care homes have improved immeasurably over the years, as has the support for parents, financial and otherwise, but back then very little was on offer and it was always a battle to ensure that Lulu got the best of what was available. Later, the problem would be resolved in a way we could not possibly have foreseen but, for the time being, she continued at Hillside five days a week.

Ron

Each summer we faced the problem of how we were going to cope during the school holiday. One year we put the car on the ferry at Newhaven and the four of us set off for a week on the Belgian coast at Knokke. It worked out fine. There were no problems in the hotel dining room and Lulu was a happy participant in fun and games on the beach with Sarah and some Belgian kids.

The following year, our destination was Cornwall, camping en route without any trouble and then heading for a farmhouse near the sea just outside Penzance. It had been highly recommended in a Sunday newspaper and the Matthews family proved to be terrific hosts. They insisted, when we suggested it might be better if Lulu took her meals in our room so as not to disturb the other guests, that she should sit with us all in the farmhouse dining room. It worked. We did it again the following year, but it was less successful. Lulu was going through a difficult period, triggered – or so we believed – by her continuing problems with constipation. There was one unhappy morning when she lay in the incoming tide screaming her head off. Fortunately, the beach was deserted, but even so, it didn't seem much better than when she went into the same routine on the floor in Sainsbury's. So the following year Ron's parents came down to Saltdean to look after Lulu – without too much trouble as it turned out – while we took Sarah down to Cornwall for the third year in a row.

Sarah

Despite all the problems with Louise, I had a very happy time in those early years of my life. Once we moved back down to Saltdean from posh Kew, I was able to go out and play on my bike for hours. We lived in a quiet and safe community with little traffic. I roamed up and down among the bungalows for hours and then headed down to the prom by the sea before going up again to the wild area of downland known as Telscombe Tye, where building was not permitted.

Louise and I would often play happily on the strips of sand near the distinctive white rock pools which fringe the coast from Brighton to Newhaven and beyond. Sometimes special friends from school would join me and we re-enacted wild stories. We had whole days by the sea, using our beach hut as a base, and if I had to answer that standard journalist's question, 'Where and when were you most happy?', the answer would be on a long summer day on Saltdean beach with the tide further out than usual and the sun at peak strength. It's a cliché, but that day never seemed to end.

My mother was delighted with the beach hut she rented from Brighton council for about £20 a year. There was a regular routine when we arrived at hut number 6, having turned left out of the tunnel which connected the prom to the coastal road. Two striped cloth windbreaks were put up first, slotted into the silver-coloured brackets on the bottom of the beach hut doors. These were to keep out the wind and also to provide a screen between Louise and people in the neighbouring hut if she was having a scream-

46

up. We usually knew it was coming because of an anxious facial expression and her mouth shaped as if to pronounce 'ick'.

There was a long storage box built into the back of the hut which smelled of the sea and housed interesting bits and pieces, including old 'cossies' stiff with salt. Any visitor who tried to get out of swimming because he or she did not have the right attire was promptly provided with some form of bathing apparel. Tea was made on a camping gas stove and the water came from a lone tap at the end of the row of huts.

There's a sunny snap of my paternal grandfather on a visit to the hut talking to Louise, who was wearing a towelling tunic with fashionable yellow and black blocks. She was still in nappies. My mother talked about having trained Louise to use a potty and then described her despair when she went back to nappies once she started school at Hillside.

I was not a big fan of school, though the presence of interesting characters in the playground made up for some uninspiring female teachers. Home always seemed more exciting – I had a clever father who revelled in his various broadcasting ventures, and a quixotic mother who was a careful and talented cook, steering her way through the seasons with the appropriate meal.

My mother seemed to have a wide range of interests, with her love of Spanish, her training in drama and dancing, as well as her studies in art. Spanish was a lifelong interest for her: I remember her watching a drama on television in Spanish that was all shady interiors and meaningful looks, even though it had been produced specifically for viewers wishing to learn the language. As it turned out, her passion for Spain and all things Spanish hooked three generations of our family, I and my son both studying Spanish as an extra language at grammar school.

Then there was her ability to fantasise wildly about people and their motives. Many years later, she identified a similar trait in my husband, describing him as a real 'tootsie tarler', a phrase from Robert Louis Stevenson indicating an effective story-teller or, depending on your mood, a neurotic fantasist. She once tried to convince me that Dad was a spy and, as evidence, showed me a revolver she said he had hidden away. It turned out to be a cigarette lighter which ignited when you pulled the trigger.

Even on a cloudy summer's day, Mum would sometimes take us down to the promenade. Our hut was sheltered, tucked in against the base of the towering white cliffs. She would stretch out blissfully on her sunbed while I played with Lulu down on the rocky beach. There was no one around to be disturbed when my sister shrieked occasionally and chucked a few pebbles in frustration. Moments later she would place her hand stiffly near her face in a gesture that was both intense and gleeful. One of our favourite moments was when the tide went right out, allowing us to explore more and more pools. These contained tiny shrimps and crabs, glistening brown sea anemones and stubborn limpets which we tried to prise off the rocks with limited success. Both Lulu and I were aware of possible danger – we'd seen the angry waves approaching in the winter and heard the huge slapping sound as they hit the prom.

Mum and Dad took lots of snaps with an old-fashioned box camera. There's a sweet picture of myself and a beach-hut friend, Cathy Vance, both wearing blue and white swimming costumes, or 'cossies', as Mum called them. Mine had a sailor-style stripey V neck. 'Is that a damp cossie you're wearing?' Mum would ask, insisting on a change. By the late sixties, the costumes were made out of man-made fibre as cotton got left behind.

If it was hot and we got bored with the hut and the sea, we'd lobby for a lolly – a Fab or a Zoom or a Mivvi – from the Whitecliffs Café at the top of the stairs which led up from the promenade. Outside the café there were glass panels through which we observed holidaymakers walking down a tunnel beneath us towards the sea. Sometimes we would call to them through a broken panel into the echoing space beneath us, pretending to be ghosts and making an eerie woo-hoo noise.

Ron

At work, I had left the Westminster job and was back at Alexandra Palace, working on BBC2's nightly news summary, 'Newsroom'. This was pioneering stuff in that it was substantially longer than previous news output, and that gave us the opportunity to change the way major news stories were presented. Wherever possible, we took viewers to the heart of a story by telling it through the reactions of a single individual – an old woman facing a change in pension payments, a young mother on improvements in the health service or a long-distance lorry driver reacting to an increase in road accident figures. It happens all the time now, but in those days, with the arrival of colour television, it represented a big leap forward in the way the news of the day reached television screens.

I was lucky enough to be in the thick of these changes thanks to the experience I had had elsewhere, and spent a lot of my time away from the office working on the extended news reports required for the new format. It was during this period that I became involved in the most heart-rending story of my whole career, the Aberfan disaster. This occurred on 21 October 1966, when a mountain of coal waste suddenly slid down onto a school and some houses in the heart of a Welsh mining village. The children had just arrived for morning assembly. Some were pulled out alive during the course of a horrific day, but 116 children, as well as 28 adults, were to lose their lives.

Early film coverage from BBC Wales revealed the appalling scale of the disaster, and a fast car was laid on to take reporter Robert Williams and myself to the stricken village. We were accompanied by the deputy editor of BBC TV News, Andrew Todd. The film crew arrived separately and we based ourselves in the miners' social centre, as well as we could. There was mud and slime everywhere, but at least we had somewhere to prepare updated film reports as we worked through the night and following day.

Our film coverage was edited in Cardiff and transmitted to London for inclusion in all bulletins on both BBC channels. Inevitably the scenes from the stricken village had a huge impact all over the world. On the day of the funeral, I felt that adding words to our film of what was about to take place in Aberfan's hillside cemetery would be superfluous – not to say intrusive in some way and that the cameras should just record the natural sound of the vast burial ceremony. In the event, as the hundreds of mourners came slowly to the gravesides of their loved ones, the film on its own, without commentary, said everything that could possibly be said about this devastating moment in the history of Wales.

Later, the National Coal Board tried to blame excessive rain for the disaster, but an official inquiry pinned sole responsibility for what had happened on the Board itself.

When I got back from Aberfan, the newsroom was buzzing with a rumour that someone was to be appointed to a new post with the title of News Organiser, New York. I soon learned of the reasoning behind this: America was an increasingly important news source for us and all of its coverage was now in colour; improvements in technology meant that satellite transmission from the States was now available round the clock; and Alexandra Palace was hungry for an increased supply of material to fill the considerable increased time allotted to its news programming.

When I told Doris about this, we exchanged glances but didn't say anything immediately; exactly the same thought was in our minds, however – namely: this job had my name written all over it.

A few days later there was an official announcement inviting applications for the New York job. Two of the men who responded had spent much longer in the BBC newsroom than I had and I rated them highly. In the event, the decision by the interviewing board went to me. Now my wife and I faced the obvious question: What about Lulu? There was never any doubt in our minds. She was coming with us.

The TS *Bremen* left Southampton on a cold and drizzly day in the middle of November 1967. We had let our bungalow in Saltdean to a Canadian professor and his family, and it would subsequently be let to a young journalist and his wife. It had been let previously, too, during our four years in Southampton.

The family car was given to my sister in Hertfordshire and she learned to drive and passed her test in it. It was a white 1961 Ford Popular with only three forward gears, but it was a reliable runner on petrol, costing 4 shillings and tuppence a gallon (about 22 pence in today's money). At the quayside in Southampton a forlorn-looking trio waited to see us off – my parents, Ben and Elizabeth Onions, and a friend from Doris's schooldays, Audrey Nottage, who lived nearby in Chandler's Ford and was still there more than forty years later. They came aboard with us for half an hour, and there were a few tears during the slightly stilted snatches of conversation that, inevitably, mark such moments of farewell.

Lulu was good as gold through all this, and when the 'All Visitors Ashore' announcement boomed out she came with us to the rail of the fourth deck, where we had our cabin, and we all waved to our visitors who were now back down on the quayside and suddenly looked a million miles away. It was one of those moments that stay with you for the rest of your life.

Excitement took over as we explored our cabin, with its double bed for Mum and Dad and bunk beds for the children. When the departure sirens sounded, we went back on deck and the *Bremen* edged out into the Solent, heading slowly past the Isle of Wight. This was to be our last sight of land before the Statue of Liberty came into view, five days and more than three thousand miles later.

During our years living and working in Southampton we had had quite a lot to do with the docks. For one thing, the BBC studios were on the fourth floor of the old South Western Hotel, which stood immediately facing the station at the end of the rail line from London and just across the road from the dock gates.

Though jet planes were soon to dominate holiday and business travel, the famous transatlantic liners were still working a regular schedule back and forth to New York – the old *Queen Mary* before the *QEII* succeeded her, as well as the American liner *United States* and French, German and other competitors. So the docks were rewarding territory for journalists, providing regular opportunities to interview movie stars and other personalities in addition to VIPs from the business and political worlds as they came and went.

Then there were the social occasions. We remember – hazily – a great night on the stylish *Canberra* shortly before she was launched. We had managed by this time to find a babysitter who was happy to look after both Sarah and Louise.

Doris

As the *Bremen* moved out into the Atlantic, it was a time to think about the friends and family we had left behind. My father was now living in the north of England, having married for a second time, and he and his wife were among the many people we would not see again for some while. They included someone I had only just met, at – of all places – the local family planning clinic in Hove. When I told the supervisor there that I would soon be going to live in America, she said I must meet the young woman who was about to leave the consulting room, because she had just returned from Chicago. So I was promptly introduced to Jenny Lucas and we were to become lifelong friends. Her husband, Mike, had taken a job at the University of Chicago, and the pair of them briefed us on the highs and lows of life in America. Clearly they had enjoyed being there, and everything they said convinced us we were making the right move. However, first we had to get there. Only a day out of Southampton there was a serious deterioration in the weather, and it stayed rough for most of the voyage. Its effect on board was obvious from the number of people not showing up at mealtimes.

Sarah

I was fascinated by some of the German dishes listed on what was basically an international menu but, like Lulu, I was so badly affected by the continuous rocking of the vessel that I was unable to savour such dessert temptations as 'warmer, schockoladen mit mackronen und west Falische' and 'Quarkspeise'. The only food I could manage was a superb platter of thinly sliced ham. It was irresistible.

After several years of living by the sea I finally learned how to float properly in the *Bremen*'s indoor swimming pool. I went there every day. I wore an orange life jacket, and after a few days, when I took it off, I found that at last I could survive in the deep end.

Ron

Mid-Atlantic, after a particularly wild night, the captain reported that he had had to give the order to hove-to and switch off the engines for a brief period. In these circumstances, it was difficult to stroll along the decks and talk to other voyagers, but we did make friends with an American woman who had had experience of the Lulus of this world. She said, prophetically, 'What I think you will find, all of you, is that your lives will be fundamentally changed by the years you spend in the United States.' It sounded a bit spooky at the time, but she was right.

As Dorothy Parker once said to the captain of one of the transatlantic superliners, 'What time does this place get to New York?' Our 'place' arrived there just about on time, and now we all went out on the chilly deck to take in that overwhelming view fronted by the Statue of Liberty and with the celebrated skyline in the background – the Empire State and General Electric buildings, the Art Deco Chrysler Building and all the rest. This was before they added the ill-fated World Trade Center. On subsequent arrivals and before the terrorist attack in 2001 that destroyed it, we thought the centre's soaring twin towers gave Manhattan Island a lopsided look which, in our macabre fantasy, threatened to send the tip of the Big Apple into the Hudson River.

Then came the climactic moment of our journey when every vessel in port sounded off with a symphony of sirens and hooters by way of greeting to the *Bremen*. She trumped the lot by sounding off with her own Big Bertha. Lulu was in her element. She had always reacted enthusiastically to anything noisy, notably vacuum cleaners, motorbikes, barking dogs and honking traffic, and she cheered and waved with the rest of us.

Meanwhile, the press photographers had boarded and were bowled over by Sarah's trendy trouser suit which she was now wearing against the cold. They seemed undeterred that it was the wrong colour – orange! – in this markedly Irish city. However, within a few minutes we were to come down to earth, both figuratively and literally.

When we descended the gangplank and entered the reception hall of the US Immigration Service, we were informed by an official that there was a taxi strike. 'Not a single yellow cab running anywhere in the five boroughs. Welcome to the Big Apple!' he said by way of greeting, managing to sound kind of friendly. We laughed – nervously.

The BBC administration in London had arranged for us to be met by Audrey Wigan, whose husband, Tony, was the Corporation's veteran correspondent at the United Nations. The plan was that Audrey would meet us at the immigration hall exit and accompany us in a yellow cab to a nearby hotel. We crossed our fingers.

It felt like years later that we were greeted by Mrs Wigan, whose face showed all the stress and strain of waiting for nearly three hours without having a clear idea of what had happened to us. She had rung Tony at the UN and also the BBC office on Fifth Avenue, and between them they managed to find out not much more than that there was a 'problem' in the immigration hall.

The problem was Lulu.

All four passports had been stamped at the United States Embassy in London with an 'I' visa. 'I' stood for 'Information' and authorised foreign journalists and their families to live and work in the United States for a period of four years. The first three passports presented no problems for the immigration officers. The fourth one did.

It was obvious to them that Lulu was 'mentally handicapped' – the phrase used then for individuals now described as having 'special needs'. In London, officials at the United States embassy were well aware of Lulu's mental condition, having received from the BBC an explanatory letter supporting her admission to America. We had been assured at the embassy that New York would be informed officially of the reasons for admitting Lulu with the rest of her family, and indeed they went further, extolling the 'cultural importance' of the BBC's 'innovation' in creating the post of News Organiser, New York.

At the time it had made us feel rather grand, but in that bleak immigration hall the feeling faded fast. The staff there claimed that they had no record of any communication from London supporting the granting of a visa to Lulu and said that anyway the visa itself, stamped on page four of her passport, did not contain enough information. They seemed preoccupied with a document they kept consulting that listed reasons for barring entry into the United States. Apparently these included people with a history of active support for Communism, those with a criminal record and those likely to be a charge on federal funds. Ah! That last one, they indicated, nodding towards her, included Lulu. We tried to assure them, with less than total conviction, that any such charges would be covered by the BBC under the terms of the News Organiser's contract, but they were not having that and went off, they said, to make some phone calls.

In the circumstances, Lulu was bearing up remarkably well. So was Sarah. Doris and I looked at each other and began humming a snatch of a favourite tune: 'You can bring Pearl, she's a darned nice girl, but don't bring Lulu . . .'

After an interminable forty-five minutes, the immigration squad reappeared. The consultations seemed to have worked in our favour. We think that the British Consulate in New York may have been involved, but when we asked Tony Wigan about it sometime later, he said nothing, though his smile suggested least said, soonest mended.

Anyway, back at the immigration hall, the head honcho opened Lulu's passport and began writing three or four lines of hieroglyphics in it, mostly comprising numbers in brackets. As he did so, an older officer who had just come on duty smiled at us and, with a nod towards Lulu – who was sporting a somewhat spartan hairdo – said: 'Say, you got the next heavyweight champion of the world there.' We laughed, mainly at his Brooklyn accent, and then responded: 'But she's a girl!' Back he came, quick as a flash: 'So dat's an even bigger stoy-ree!' After everything that had happened, we left that immigration hall laughing out loud. Welcome to the Big Apple, indeed.

We spotted Audrey Wigan immediately, waving at us through the glass exit doors. She raised her arms and clasped her hands together in celebration. There was no sign of a cab, but as we exchanged greetings the longest limousine we had ever seen slid across from the other side of the road. It was a stretched-out Chrysler, hired from a company called London Town Cars and big enough to take all five of us and quite a lot of luggage to the Bedford Hotel, in a street close to United Nations headquarters.

Audrey explained that the BBC hired London Town regularly to meet distinguished visitors from the UK and elsewhere. At short notice and on a very busy day for them – they were not affected by the strike – London Town had rolled out the biggest car in their fleet for us. We began to feel much better.

It was almost dark when we moved off through the Lower West Side and the skyscrapers lit our way through somewhat dingy streets to the Bedford. On our arrival, two porters came running and whisked our luggage up four floors in an economy-sized elevator. We checked in and thanked the redoubtable Audrey, who promised to call us in the morning.

Upstairs, the porters had distributed our luggage round a family room, which was a bit on the small side but comfortable enough. Negotiating the porters' payment was the final stress point of the day. They had a scale which seemed to depend on the size of each piece of luggage. Then there was the tip! Oh yes! Twice! We surrendered and handed over what felt like ransom money.

It had been a rollercoaster of a day, and down we went again when we discovered, in our tired and hungry state, that there was no restaurant in the hotel, only room service. We couldn't face venturing out to find somewhere to eat, so we settled for tea and toast. The tea was luke warm, but the toast was so good we called down for more. Hello and goodnight, New York.

After a good night's sleep for all of us, room-service breakfast impressed those of us who had been wartime kids with its jug of fresh-squeezed orange juice. Audrey Wigan rang as promised and said she would be arriving shortly with a friend, Isabel Shaw, who might prove helpful in coping with the immediate problems of settling in, with particular reference to Lulu.

This was reassuring. When, some months earlier, I had been appointed to the New York job and said the family, including Lulu, would accompany me, there was understandable concern within the BBC administration. Staff there had almost no experience of dealing with the financial and welfare considerations of someone like Lulu. For normal BBC children, the cost of private education, if need be, was fully covered, but in the case of our second daughter, nobody could foresee what costs might arise, to say nothing of other problems, such as the previous day's drama down at the dockside.

We learned later that these concerns voiced in London had been discussed with the senior BBC staff in New York, including Tony Wigan. Among Tony's contacts in the UN building was John Shaw, who had been one of the principals of the British Trade Mission at the UN before moving on to an ambassadorial career. John and his wife, Isabel, had two sons, Christopher and Alastair. Alastair was a Down's syndrome child, and was being looked after in England at an excellent residential facility in the West Country. When the Wigans told the Shaws of our situation, Isabel had grabbed hold of the problem with all the determination and resilience that had enabled her, a Jewess, to survive in a Nazi concentration camp in World War II. On that second day in New York, she brought to our hotel a list she had compiled of potentially helpful organisations in the city, plus details of all the residential homes and schools in the rest of New York State. She also insisted that if we found somewhere suitable we must call City Hall and tell them what we had done. It was the beginning of a friendship that would last to the end of her life.

There was much else to do. Fortunately we did not have to hunt for accommodation for the rest of us. It was waiting for us a few blocks away on the eighteenth floor of an apartment building called Sutton Manor. The only problem was that it was unfurnished. There was a generous budget available, however, so somehow we had to find time for a substantial shopping expedition in between sorting out Lulu as well as settling into the new job, coming to terms with the pace of life in the city that never sleeps and, not least, finding a school for Sarah.

More immediately, I had to find my way to the BBC New York office at 630 Fifth Avenue and make our safe arrival known on the daily communication circuit linking us with Washington and Broadcasting House in London. I was greeted by Leonard Miall, an avuncular figure with a marked resemblance to Alastair Sim, whose St Trinian epics from the 1940s and 1950s and many other films were still to be seen on television well into this century. Earlier in his career, Leonard had been the BBC's man in Washington and was now, in Corporation parlance, BBC Representative, New York, which meant that he ran the New York office but also looked after the BBC's broader interests throughout the United States.

Leonard was well up to speed on the Lulu situation and assured me that everything possible would be done to help us settle and that I was not expected to start the new job until we had resolved our various problems. There were similar words of comfort from both the editorial and the administration departments when I sat in on the morning conference circuit to London.

As I left the building, Leonard said, 'By the way, I've arranged a party for you in a week's time so you can meet the key players from the three main television networks, and various other useful contacts will be there too.'

Back at the Bedford, the mood was less exuberant. The rest of the family – unlike lucky old me – were showing the effects of the cocktail of innoculations we had all received in London to fight off any hostile bugs we might encounter in North and South America. Flu-like symptoms had begun to appear mid-Atlantic, but the three of them were now exhibiting a variety of bumps and blemishes.

To take their minds off the irritation, they had ventured out into downtown Manhattan on a short journey of discovery and to buy some essential bits and pieces. They noted Tad's Steak Bar, which was to stand us in good stead over the next couple of weeks, as did the Chinese and Italian takeaways in this part of town. They also came across Horn & Hardart. In those days, H & H was an institution across America, a bit old-fashioned and evoking the 1920s and the paintings of Edward Hopper. It had a style and status that echoed the Lyons Corner Houses and tea rooms of that period in Great Britain. It also had the longest steel and chrome self-service counter in the world. Like the Lyons tea rooms, H & H is now no more, but on that first day in New York, Doris and the kids ran into their first experience of what George Bernard Shaw described as two nations divided by the same language. The children wanted some biscuits with their drinks. They should have asked for cookies. 'Biscuits' in American English means small cakes of shortened bread leavened with baking powder or soda. It was only the first of many such dilemmas in those early weeks in Manhattan.

There was much to do. We had to find a residential school for Lulu as soon as possible, as well as a day school for Sarah. We also had some serious shopping ahead so as to furnish that empty apartment waiting for us at the corner of East 53rd Street and 1st Avenue.

Somehow we survived those first few hectic weeks. Several stressful days were spent in a hire car visiting a number of places on Isabel Shaw's list of homes and institutions for 'the handicapped'. We began to despair after seeing too many places that reminded us of the forlorn institutions that we had seen in Britain in the mid-sixties. After one particularly depressing trip, we looked again at Isabel's list and noted again, right at the bottom, a place called Cobb Memorial School. We had ruled it out previously because, though it was still in New York State, it was four hundred miles away.

I picked up the phone in that cluttered hotel room and dialled the number of the school in Altamont. Sister Vincentia answered in what I came to know as a Boston Irish accent. I explained our circumstances at some length. She listened patiently, but then said, 'I'm sorry to say we have no vacancies at the moment.' There was an awkward pause. She must have sensed my disappointment and said, 'Look, would it be possible to visit with us in the near future?' This response threw me a bit and I blurted out, 'I should tell you right away that we are not Roman Catholics.' It must have sounded absurdly pompous. Sister Vincentia laughed gently and said, 'Oh dear man, don't you worry about that!'

Whereupon it was agreed that the family would drive up to Altamont in a couple of days' time. Hiring an Oldsmobile for a day at that time in America was easy and relatively cheap, and so we set off a few blocks uptown before crossing the Hudson River and heading north in the direction of the state capital, Albany, as we had done several times already in the search for somewhere for Lulu in the communities closer to New York City.

Lulu was in good form, though she had to be restrained from pressing the dazzling array of shiny buttons within reach of rear-seat passengers. Doris and I shared a fantasy that one of them might launch us into vertical take-off. There was the car radio to keep us all amused with its bewildering array of stations, from the classical music station run by the *New York Times* newspaper via the all-jazz WLIB (the Voice of the Black Experience) and on through the various Country and Western outfits to the children's favourite, WABC New York, and our introduction to the Jackson 5, including a very young Michael Jackson.

Hearing them was a major moment in Lulu's life, and she went on singing all the early Jackson 5 hits, along with those of the Carpenters and the other chart-busters of that time. It was in fact one of the principal ways she developed a limited vocabulary. More intriguing was the way she responded to the rather more challenging harmonic structure of the hit songs written at this time by Burt Bacharach and his lyricist, Hal David. This ability – though we were not aware of the fact at the time – was not uncommon in some autistic children and adults and, indeed, some possessed it to a remarkable degree. Lulu was never to achieve the mystifying abilities displayed by some autistic performers in the concert hall and elsewhere, but the Bacharach melodies, as performed by his regular singer, Dionne Warwick, became part of her repertoire and CD collection. Many years later, this hint of autism in Lulu's mental and physical make-up was formally noted, though the entry in her file referred only to 'autistic traits', adding: 'some of her behaviours are similar to those on the autistic spectrum although there was no formal diagnosis of autism'.

The hits of the sixties continued to rock and roll us up the New York State Thruway until, about eighty miles south of Albany, we stopped for a comfort break at a drive-in Dairy Burger. This was a new and fascinating experience. The widespread burger chains of today were yet to reach Blighty, with the possible pioneering exception of the Wimpy organisation, so the meal and drinks ordered at one window and collected and paid for at the next without getting out of the car were voted a hit by the family. Along the way, we learned that 'chips' in this foreign country were 'fries', as in French fries. 'Chips' were something you used in a gambling joint, and 'potato chips' were what we call 'crisps'. It was another lesson in learning how to speak American after the initial skirmish over biscuits and cookies in Horn & Hardart.

After another half-hour on the thruway, we turned off to take a minor road to Altamont and the mountainous region beyond. Along the way, we noticed a Catholic seminary and stopped to ask if we were heading in the right direction. In fact, Cobb Memorial School was just a few hundred yards away on the left. It stood on a pine-covered slope, a majestic wooden building with a high-pitched roof and a vast porch running all along one side. As we walked towards the front door it swung open and Sister Vincentia came out to greet us. She was exactly as she had sounded when I spoke to her on the telephone from New York City – lively and caring. Several other sisters were waiting behind her in the hall. They greeted us quietly over refreshments and accompanied us on a tour of the building. There was the sweet smell of polish as we were shown the living and bedroom accommodation. Our spirits lifted. The place was immaculate. In the main schoolroom we were greeted cheerfully by children with a wide range of learning difficulties. They were enthusiastic and obviously well cared for, in marked contrast to those we had seen recently in some of the institutions nearer to New York City.

Next, we were introduced to Reverend Mother Immaculata. She was tall and gregarious. She wanted to know all about us before giving us a lively rundown on Cobb Memorial School. Bernard Cobb, who founded it, was not an American, as we had supposed, but a Scotsman who had come to America to make his fortune. She added, wryly, he was not even a Catholic but an Episcopalian. He had purchased the building at Altamont as his summer home. Cobb had three daughters. One of them had a baby girl with Down's syndrome, and when the old man died, his capacious summer home was made available to the Sisters of the Presentation on the understanding that it might be possible to convert it into a residential school for children with learning difficulties. The sisters moved swiftly. Cobb's summer home had to be 'winterised', among other essential modifications. The money was raised, and Cobb Memorial School opened in 1957.

It was time to head back to 'that wicked city', as Reverend Mother jokingly referred to New York, but not before she had introduced Lulu to her dog, which was called Tammy. It was the high point of the day for Lulu, who had a great affinity with dogs, especially noisy ones. We set off on the long journey south in high spirits. As we said goodbye, Sister Vincentia said they would come to a decision in the next few days about Louise's possible admission to Cobb.

Dusk was falling, and Manhattan had started its spectacular lighting-up routine as we came off the thruway and down the west side of the city. The car radio was playing a pop hit with the refrain 'It's Christmas time in the city'. Lulu sang it sweetly and with great enthusiasm. It was one of those inconsequential moments that somehow just stick in your mind.

The following night we were due at the party organised by Leonard Miall at the BBC offices at 630 Fifth Avenue. It was a flop. This was certainly not Leonard's fault. All of the key players from the news divisions of the Big Three television networks arrived some time between six and six-thirty. So did representatives from United Nations TV and Visnews, part-owned by the BBC and based in the nearby NBC newsroom. Alistair Cooke was there, already well established on both sides of the Atlantic for his weekly 'Letter from America' on radio as well as a number of award-winning television programmes. Also present were all the BBC office staff – British and American – who had stayed on at the end of their working day.

So where were the new arrivals from London? They were standing in the pouring rain outside the Bedford Hotel trying to hail a yellow cab. New York Cab Rule 1: Avoid the rush hour (it was the height of the rush hour). Rule 2: The rush hour's especially difficult in the area around the UN Building (that's exactly where we were). Rule 3: In a downpour, forget it. The new kids on the block had ignored all three.

An SOS call to the BBC office finally brought Tony Wigan to the Bedford in a yellow cab. After several years at the UN, this quintessential Englishman was by now a veteran New Yorker. He was also very tall and had developed the fearsome technique of striding boldly from the sidewalk brandishing a rolled umbrella and shouting 'Cab' at the top of his voice.

So, bedraggled and shame-faced, we arrived at the welcome party – or what was left of it. The invitation had said five-thirty for six. It was now after seven. Many of the departed guests lived outside Manhattan, in one of the adjoining boroughs or somewhere upstate or in New Jersey. They had trains to catch, dinners going cold – and it was raining like hell.

The guests who had hung on did their best to console us. A couple of drinks helped. They seemed stronger than their equivalents in London. They were. All newcomers to the Big Apple, beware . . .

Doris

In America, in late November, there's Thanksgiving Day. In the nineteenth century, President Lincoln proclaimed the fourth Thursday in November a national holiday to take place annually in celebration of the survival of the early English settlers at Plymouth, Massachusetts, thanks to the help they were given by native Americans, during the harsh winter of 1621.

In Manhattan, the celebration begins with a rumbustious parade of marching bands, massive helium-filled balloons and spectacular floats depicting key moments of the nation's history and its major achievements. It starts from the west side of Central Park and takes three hours to proceed along New York's famous thoroughfares. The four of us, including Lulu, had found a good place to watch outside Macy's, the famous department store that had organised and sponsored the parade since it began in the late 1920s. It still is, some forty years after we watched it for the first time. Santa Claus makes an appearance in the parade at some point, and his presence marks the start of the Christmas season in New York City.

The other big event on this day, right across America, is the traditional Thanksgiving feast. As we were still in the hotel, we were wondering how to celebrate this aspect of the day, and were delighted to receive an invitation from a kindly woman on the British consulate staff who knew of our situation and wanted us to come to her apartment as guests at her Thanksgiving table. Isabel kindly offered to look after the children, and so Ron and I were duly introduced to the delights of roast turkey, sweet potato, squash, cranberries and pumpkin pie.

The following day, for the first time, we were able to take a quick look round our new home at Sutton Manor. We were greeted by, as it were, the front-of-house staff, Marcel and Harold, who had two or three younger assistants. These guys would be key players in our daily lives over the next five years, giving helpful advice, sorting out problems such as lost keys and unwelcome visitors, and taking deliveries of furniture and other items. We found them a bit nosy at first, but one or other of them would always be there in their braided uniforms looking out from the foyer through the huge glass doors that led out to East 53rd Street. One of the first things Harold told us was that, if we took just a short walk along 53rd, sooner or later we would bump into Greta Garbo or Ingrid Bergman. I did spot Bergman once, and we came across many other famous faces, both inside and outside Sutton Manor, but Greta ('I want to be alone') Garbo lived up to her elusive reputation.

From our apartment high up on the eighteenth floor, looking south to the United Nations complex and the Staten Island ferry, and with the East River to our left, we had spectacular views of many of the famous landmarks, including the Empire State, Chrysler and General Electric buildings. At night that last one seemed to win the competition for the highest consumption of electricity. We never tired of the magical view that began to develop as dusk fell, and it was always a delight to see the awestruck way our visitors reacted to it.

We had two bedrooms, two bathrooms and a huge lounge incorporating a dining space. The apartment had smooth wooden floors and there were metallic white blinds at the windows. As for the galley kitchen, it was the smallest I have ever seen. It seemed to have been designed for people who ate out most of the time – not an inspiring sight for a keen cook. Still, somehow they had managed to squeeze in the world's biggest refrigerator.

We also had two balconies, which we used rarely because of the noise and dust from the traffic on First Avenue. After she had grown up, Sarah made the startling revelation that she had once attempted to climb over one of the balcony railings. Fortunately she was spotted by Luis, one of the doormen, from the sidewalk below. His horrified expression was enough. It said 'What the hell do you think you're doing?' Sarah promptly scrambled back to safety.

Now we had to furnish the place. First we had to resist the temptation to snaffle up what New Yorkers call 'sidewalk furniture'. This is stuff that is left over and no longer wanted when occupants move out of an apartment. It had become the tradition to leave it outside for the possible use of incoming residents rather than simply dumping it. Down there on the sidewalk, much of it looked new and of considerable value, but we anticipated the glares of disapproval from Marcel and Harold and their mates should we attempt to get it humped through Sutton Manor's elegant glass doors. So we set off for Macy's to start spending the furnishing budget provided by the BBC. Leonard Miall's wife had told us there were sales all the time, so we also went to places like the elegant Bloomingdale's and some of the cheaper places downtown near Greenwich Village. Getting exactly what we wanted turned out to be both very much easier and much quicker than we had expected. Shop staff were invariably helpful, many asking – maybe because of our London accents – whether we were Australians. The Australians were highly popular in America at the time, having sent troops into South Vietnam to support the United States' controversial campaign against the communist Vietcong guerrillas.

Delivery of our purchases was swift and, in one instance, brought us much more than we had expected. An elegant set of dinner crockery came twice. Getting the store to retrieve one of the sets took forever. The store clerk declared that getting the paperwork right would be more trouble than it was worth. However, we insisted that they come and collect the surplus delivery, and that's what happened – eventually.

At this busy period, I was determined to find time to sit down and write a letter to a woman named Doctor Margaret Giannini.

This was at Isabel Shaw's suggestion. She had heard from one of her contacts at the UN building that the doctor was an authority on disability and was based in New York at the Flower and Fifth Avenue Hospital. I thought she might be able to give us some helpful advice about Louise. The doctor replied promptly, and I took Louise to see her. After a brief examination of the child, Dr Giannini asked me if Lulu had ever had an EEG – an electronic examination of the brain. When I said no, she was surprised, to say the least, saying she thought the British had invented it. Certainly, we discovered later, there had been British involvement in its early development. Anyway, an EEG was promptly arranged. This, nearly six years after she was born, swiftly established that Louise was suffering from an area of brain damage.

Next we had to sort out Sarah's education. Isabel Shaw advised us there was a Rudolf Steiner school only a few blocks away from our apartment, and although some aspects of its education system were controversial, it had a strong international base and she thought it might be a good choice in our particular circumstances. So we went off to meet the staff, liked what we saw and heard, and enrolled Sarah to start in the new year. The cost would be covered by the BBC.

There was more good news just a few days later in the shape of a letter from Cobb Memorial School saying they would be happy to provide a place for Lulu at the start of the spring term in a few weeks' time. Meanwhile, they had taken the opportunity to enclose the first bill. Seeing it reminded us of Isabel Shaw's insistence that we must inform City Hall if we found a private place for Lulu outside the New York State system. Ron took a deep breath and picked up the phone, while I listened on the extension. The man at City Hall sounded formidable, but he listened patiently as Ron explained what we had done. Then he said, 'OK, I'll send you a form. Fill it in and get your employers to authorise it and then send it back to me with a copy of the bill.' I expected my beloved to quit while he was ahead, but instead, he blurted out, 'But we're English!' To which City Hall's response was: 'So? You pay all your taxes here, don'tcha?'

Ron assured him that indeed we did. The outcome was that, to everyone's relief, and not least that of BBC administration in London, New York State covered the major portion of Lulu's care and education at Cobb.

Sarah

After the first month I began to realise that I had said goodbye to the carefree and low-key life I had enjoyed in Sussex. The three of us had left a bungalow plus coal bunker in Sussex to live in a swish air-conditioned apartment in Manhattan. We were now Number 18B Sutton Manor in a smart clutch of high-rise blocks near the East River. There were trendy gift shops nearby like the Pink Balloon and Pier 51. It was all so new to me. I loved the varying character of the different avenues which ran from uptown to downtown. Lexington Avenue seemed busy, and there were lots of drugstores. Park Avenue was grander, and Fifth Avenue was the big star where the frequent parades took place. The variety kindled a lifelong love of this great city and it took me a long while to appreciate that there were other attractive places in the world besides New York.

Doris

Suddenly, we were aware that Christmas had crept up on us. I was determined that after all the ups and downs since we arrived in New York, we deserved to do it in style, and we worked hard preparing to celebrate in the traditional way.

Two big food stores were close at hand. Just round the corner from our apartment building was the Atlantic and Pacific (A&P) supermarket. Nearby was an upmarket rival, Dagostinos, where you went if you wanted to feel superior. Noisy old A&P, with its distinctive aroma, was where the bargains were. One time I went there having asked the family if there was anything they missed from our food menu in London. Ron said brawn. There's no accounting for taste but, in fact, I had spotted brawn on a previous visit to the store. This time, however, I couldn't find it. I asked the manager, who said: 'Brawn, ma'am, we don't do brawn. What's brawn?' He walked round the store with me and eventually I spotted some hiding away in a corner and pointed it out to the baffled manager. He put his hands on his hips and said, 'You mean head cheese!' I eventually worked it out. The French for brawn is fromage de tête. I rather overdid my thanks to the manager and he looked at me suspiciously and said, 'Say, are you putting me on?' We came to understand this forthright manner was just their way in this go-getting city. The niceties of English courtesy were not a noticeable part of their make-up, but generally they responded enthusiastically to the English accent and most went out of their way to assist us and make us feel welcome.

Then there was the time I thanked the checkout assistant for her help in loading the brown paper shopping bags provided by the store. She laughed and said, 'Hey, you sound just like The Late, Late Show.' She was referring to one of the many television channels there which often, in the wee small hours of the morning, ran ancient British movies full of phrases like: 'I say, you chaps, that was absolutely spiffing.'

Ron

I woke up on Boxing Day morning wondering what the hell was causing all that noise down there on First Avenue when everyone should have been having a lie-in. It turned out to be New York going to work. Just another bit of the learning curve: there is no Boxing Day in America. Soon, though, there would the New Year celebrations. That was the big event, a much grander affair than the rather dismal festivities we recalled watching in black and white on television in Britain.

As it turned out, New Year's Day was to be my first day at work in America. The president, Lyndon Baines Johnson (LBJ, as he was known) had decided to go on television and deliver a New Year's Day message to the nation. I had a call from the TV newsroom in London asking for coverage of the event from the NBC studios just off Fifth Avenue. I suspect that, the day being a public holiday in Britain, the London newsroom was facing what we call a slow news day and, without knowing exactly what he was going to say, the guys were looking to LBJ to help them out. Anyway, Gerald Priestland, one of the two BBC correspondents in Washington (the other was Charles Wheeler), would soon be on the Eastern Airlines shuttle service to New York to present an edited report of the presidential address for transmission to London and to be broadcast in BBC TV bulletins later that same day.

It's routine stuff nowadays, but back then we kidded ourselves that we were pioneers, flying by the seat of our pants. In the event, LBJ's holiday address was not exactly world-shattering, but a friendly NBC producer offered me a couple of showbizzy items from that day's schedule. They certainly added a festive touch and also helped to fatten up the package that went off to London without a hitch. At this point I said to the American technicians around me in the transmission gallery, 'OK chaps, stand down.' There was a moment's silence before one of them stood up and said, 'You mean that's a wrap?' There we were again with another example of two nations being divided by the same language!

Shortly we received from London the 'herogram' – our cheerfully cynical term for the message of thanks and congratulations that arrived after completing a successful assignment. There would be many more in the year ahead, which would turn out to be perhaps the most challenging in the history of the United States.

Gerry came back to our apartment – our very first visitor – for a drink before catching the late shuttle back to Washington. I already knew him quite well from the early days of BBC2. He was the presenter on the opening night of the channel when a power cut made an absolute mess of the main news show. Gerry was not your average news reporter. He was a scholarly man at one level and an excellent interpreter of the American scene, but he had a quixotic streak, and this was reflected in the wide range of books he wrote, ranging from *America, The Changing Nation* via several on religion to *Frying Tonight, The Saga of Fish and Chips*.

As the director of a number of news stories for BBC2, I had worked with him when we were both based at Alexandra Palace. On one occasion we went to a big military base just outside London where the army was showing off some of its latest hardware. I drove him there in, of all things, an East German vehicle I had acquired at the time – a two-stroke Wartburg. East Germany was then still part of the Soviet bloc. Gerry was fascinated by the car, and it became an alien extra in our film as it puttered around the edges of the showground.

Gerry and Charles were chalk and cheese. Charles had started in newspapers – at the old *Daily Sketch* – before World War II, and after service with the Royal Marines he was eventually to become the most outstanding of a talented team of reporters and correspondents who came to the fore on television in the 1960s. Some, like Tom Mangold, came from Fleet Street. Others, like Martin Bell, had been recruited from the BBC's regional news teams.

Shortly after Sarah started school in New York, we faced the long journey north for Lulu's first term at Cobb Memorial School. We knew the way from that first visit, but this time, as we left the thruway, the last stretch of roadway had been transformed into a wonderland of ice and snow. Families were out skiing and tobogganing beyond the great walls of snow that had been piled up at each side of the road to keep it clear for traffic.

The sisters greeted us quietly. One took Lulu's hand and led her away to be with the other children. The three of us exchanged glances, knowing how important it was that her time here would prove to be happy and peaceful. Sister Vincentia said we were not to worry. We said we would call when we got back home to see that all was well.

Three weeks into the new year, I found myself on an Air Canada flight heading for Montreal. In the middle of the night I had had a call from the BBC's foreign editor at Alexandra Palace informing me that one of the Great Train Robbers, Charlie Wilson, had been picked up by police in a small community in Quebec where he had been hiding out for nearly four years. The Canadian Broadcasting Company (CBC) had film coverage of the story which they would make available to me at their Montreal studios for inclusion in my own updated account of Wilson's capture. This was to be transmitted live via satellite during the BBC's main evening news.

The Great Train Robbery took place in the summer of 1963. A gang of fifteen men had contrived to bring a Glasgow-to-London train to a red-light halt at 3 a.m. by tampering with the signals. After threatening and then injuring the driver, they unloaded banknotes and registered packages worth more than two and a half million pounds at the time, though today's value would be much higher. When, eventually, they were caught and put on trial, Wilson was sentenced to thirty years in jail.

I arrived in Montreal ill prepared for the Canadian winter, wearing a flimsy pair of shoes rather than the obligatory snow boots. My footwear was to be the least of my problems. These were the pioneering days of satellite transmission. Things could – and frequently did – go wrong. My live broadcast across the Atlantic started well enough, but halfway through we lost sound. Was there a fault on the transmitter or did the problem lie in the CBC studio? I never found out, and was not at all pleased to overhear studio staff totting up the bill they proposed to send to the BBC administration in London. I made a mental to note to try out CBC's commercial television rival, CFCF (Canada's First, Canada's Finest) on any future satellite transmissions out of Montreal. We did, several times, and always successfully.

As for Charlie Wilson, he was put back in prison and released after ten years. Twelve years later he was shot dead at his villa in Marbella.

By early January, we had assembled all the bits and pieces we needed to turn our spacious apartment into a home and settle into some kind of domestic routine, though that was not easy, what with the phone ringing off the hook when a major news story was breaking at all hours of the day and night. During nearly five years in America, it was with Charles Wheeler whom I worked most of the time, covering so many of the dramatic events that marked that turbulent decade the sixties.

If the decision to set up the post of News Organiser, New York, needed any justification, it came in our very first year. One dramatic event after another, both in America and abroad, kept all of us at full stretch and the new satellite links around the world in high demand. This was a time when the Vietnam war was at its bloodiest, and American citizens were now deeply divided over its involvement there. In the USA itself, the assassination of some of the country's most distinguished citizens further horrified the nation.

Early on I directed satellite feeds from New York to London of such shocking events as the assassination on camera of a Vietcong officer by a senior South Vietnamese police officer. This was one of a number of similar images that were to turn US public opinion against the war in Vietnam. Later, an event that had a particular impact, because it happened in America itself, took place at Kent State University in Ohio, where students were protesting against the US invasion of Cambodia. The Ohio National Guard opened fire on them, killing four and wounding several others. Then there was the My Lai massacre in Vietnam, which happened when, during a search-and-destroy mission, American troops opened fire on a village suspected of being a Vietcong stronghold. This time several hundred people were killed. Later came film coverage from Vietnam of a little girl, Kim Phuc, running naked from a napalm bombing. This horrifying image triggered a huge worldwide reaction, and members of my family as well as many friends were among those registering their protest with the United Nations and other organisations.

Early on in my first year in New York I found myself directing satellite transmissions to Europe on behalf of all the countries belonging to the European Broadcasting Union, including the United Kingdom. This was a rotating assignment I shared with two other news producers, who were from mainland Europe but who were now, like me, based in New York.

Some days were long and hectic because of the five-hour time difference between London and New York. One night Doris and I had dozed off after dinner in the apartment with the television on at low level. Suddenly we were aware that the president, Lyndon Johnson, was on the screen and halfway through a major announcement. We exchanged glances. Had he said what we, only half awake, thought he had said? He had. He would not be standing for re-election later that year. The telephone began to ring off the hook and within half an hour I was in the NBC studios arranging a satellite transmission to London.

Such was the pattern of our first year in New York City. The following month the civil rights leader Martin Luther King was shot dead at the Lorraine Motel in Memphis, Tennessee. Then there were the tornadoes that caused so much death and destruction in Iowa and Kansas, followed by the assassination of presidential candidate Robert Kennedy in a Los Angeles hotel. A little later, Richard Nixon was nominated as the Republican party candidate for the presidency. In Chicago the Democratic party chose Hubert Humphrey as their candidate at a convention overshadowed by anti-war riots in the city.

Amid all the drama of that first year, we gradually came to terms with the city that never sleeps. The main problem was that it was not a place designed for kids. In the midtown area where we lived, there were no back gardens for them to play in. Getting together with their friends after school or at weekends meant a great deal of ferrying them to and from other apartment blocks. Still, gradually we came to realise that the city did have its attractions for an English family living eighteen floors up in a skyscraper apartment – not least because we were in the very heart of the city. That meant that we were within walking distance of all the big stores, like Macy's, Bloomingdales and the rest, as well as the major attractions, such as the Empire State building, the United Nations complex, Carnegie Hall and Madison Square Garden. Also nearby were

Broadway and the theatre district, plus museums such as the Guggenheim and the Museum of Modern Art. We were right in the middle of the action. Then there was Central Park, just a short walk away, where the three of us went ice-skating on winter weekends. If we got bored with that rink, there was a smaller one, the Rockefeller rink, even closer to home and just across Fifth Avenue from St. Patrick's Cathedral. In the summer this one disappeared under a smooth red cover and you could sit there sipping cocktails. This was very near the BBC office. It was the only job I ever had where I could walk to and from work, just a few hundred yards from home.

Sarah

One of the striking memories of my years in Manhattan was the school playground. There was no room to play behind the doomy Steiner building, so for half an hour each morning the teachers took us just across the road to Manhattan's iconic green space, Central Park. It was quite a change from my school in England – Telscombe Cliffs Junior. There, we had a huge field to ourselves. It sloped down towards the cliff top and the sea, but there was a formidable fence to keep us all safe. In contrast, in New York, the corner of Central Park that we used for 'recess' was open to everyone. The teachers kept an eye on us and we weren't normally disturbed by the New Yorkers passing by. I can remember only two occasions when our playtime was interrupted. The first was when it was decided to change our regular location and move half a block uptown but still in the park. The attraction here was a children's playground with a slide and swings. This was nearer to the Guggenheim Museum at 81st street and next door to the Museum of Modern Art. The move was short-lived because a flasher positioned himself in bushes near the steps leading up to the slide. I wasn't frightened, as the girls in the fourth grade had warned me about him. I noticed his distorted face and a bit later I saw him saunter away wearing a shirt and trousers but no jacket, and trying to look innocent.

The second interruption was much happier. We spotted the singer Art Garfunkel strolling with a friend. When the boys ran up to confront him he inclined his head and smiled in a way that suggested he was not who we thought he was. We all knew better. This was the right place to spot a strolling star, not far from where Lennon walked with Yoko in his last video.

So many years later, I often see the distinctive pattern of the low outer wall of the park running along Fifth Avenue featured in films. Recently I spotted our playground entrance in the film *Tadpole* with Sigourney Weaver. When we lived in Manhattan, Mum and I went to see the *The Out of Towners*, in which Sandy Dennis and Jack Lemmon were mugged in the park in the dark. It never happened to us.

When it snowed we went to Central Park and starred in our own family pictures. We took a huge metal tray inscribed with the words 'Kaffee Klatsch' and we used it as a sledge on a slope. Dad took a photo of Mum on the tray wearing her 'Russian' winter coat, with her legs in the air and an expression of pure joy on her face. I wallowed in nostalgia many years later when I watched *Love Story* with Ali McGraw and Ryan O'Neal. There's a scene where he skates on the Central Park rink and waves back at his love through the fence. I can still remember discovering the taste of pizza we bought from a hot food kiosk adjoining that fence.

I did not miss Louise in Manhattan. I had never been to the same school as her and I had developed ways of playing on my own because of her limited ability to participate in childhood games. However, my dad recalls one of Lulu's visits to our apartment at Easter when I managed to involve her in a little playlet I had constructed and which we performed for Mum and Dad in our bedroom. Apparently I had cast her in the role of someone called Little Ben and she made the gestures and said the words – more or less on cue – that I had prepared for her. It was a moment to treasure and Dad said, rather grandly, that it was the beginning of Lulu's international dramatic career which also saw her performing at Cobb and taking part some years later in a Dickensian panto.

When I talked to the kids at school about my sister, it was often more fantasy than fact. In a conversation with Gaby Selz, one of the fourth graders, I can recall emphasising the strangeness of Lulu's handicap and repeated my mother's assertion that she had not taken any drugs during her second pregnancy, not even an aspirin. I had a wild imagination, and remember my father having to cover for me when he picked me up from a 'playdate', at which I had told the Akeret family all about a non-existent menagerie back home in Saltdean.

I took for granted the monthly drives upstate New York to visit Lulu in Altamont. The three of us regarded the long drive – a return trip of four hundred miles – as something we must do for her out of our feelings of love and compassion. During the journey I amused myself by making a list of all the strange place names in New York State, including Schenectady and Poughkeepsie.

Many of the teachers at Steiner were German or Dutch, and they had surnames like Harrer, Koppel and Zonnenfeld. Another fascinating name was that of the school accountant, Charity Navarette. Certainly Steiner was out of the ordinary.

Back in the city, I noticed that the young women in high school wore their hair long in the hippy style, and later on I was not surprised to see a yearbook picture of Grade 10 in the radical feminist self-help book *Our Bodies, Ourselves*. Telscombe Cliffs Junior School had been so different. There, lunch was often spam fritters and the girls sang old-fashioned rhymes while turning the skipping rope. There was no spam on the menu in New York, and neither was there religious instruction. Rudolf Steiner was a secular school. Many years later, my husband intrigued me by referring to the garden of Gethsemane. I didn't know what he was talking about.

Doris

We kept in frequent touch with Lulu during her first term at Cobb, and the sisters assured us she had settled in well. Sarah, too, was making good progress. I think the fact that so many of the pupils were from other countries helped her to settle in, though she had a rocky moment when, during a history lesson, the teacher mentioned that, in earlier times, the British had burned down the White House and the rest of the class glared at Sarah as though she had been personally responsible.

As to my husband, he seemed to be revelling in his new role of international news whizz kid. What about me? At first I felt homesick, so I determined to carve out a role for myself that was more than wife and mother waiting for the rest of the family to come back to the apartment.

Back home, I had done several radio broadcasts, beginning with one for BBC Radio 4s 'Woman's Hour' on Lulu's birth and subsequent progress. Others followed, for the BBC local station in London and, when we moved to the south coast, for BBC Brighton. Picking up the threads in Manhattan was easy. The BBC studios were close by and there was a producer there who was happy to advise, as well as a high-quality circuit to transmit my efforts back to Britain. One of my best moments was persuading one of the movie-star heroines of my youth, Joan Crawford, to be interviewed while she was doing her Christmas shopping in Macy's department store.

I had kept up an exchange of letters with several people in England, including Joyce McCulloch, who was head teacher at the day school Louise had attended at Portslade, just outside Brighton. On one occasion, she wrote: 'One of my staff is reading your letter and seeing the snaps now. It takes a little time to circulate as the Newhaven ambulance drivers – those who remember Louise – like to read the letters, too. Of course, everyone who hears your husband on television rushes to school and tells me . . .' I couldn't help shedding a tear at this glimpse of life back in Sussex.

For a few days at Easter Lulu came home to Manhattan, the sisters at Cobb having gone into 'retreat', as they called it, during this significant week in the religious calendar. Ron drove up to Altamont to collect her, and there were more tears as they came through the door of the apartment. She was beautifully dressed and wore a traditional Easter straw bonnet decorated with spring flowers. She looked as though she had stepped out of one of the striking front-page illustrations by Norman Rockwell for the *Saturday Evening Post*.

We managed to take her out and about several times that week without too many problems. One trip took in the Staten Island ferry and the Statue of Liberty, and next day, after a fall of snow, we were in Central Park, sliding down gentle slopes on our big tin trays. Then, after a good night's sleep, it was off on a short train ride to Coney Island, where the sun shone fiercely, just as if summer had suddenly arrived.

You got little sense or sight of the changing seasons, living amid the tallest skyscrapers in the centre of midtown Manhattan. Suddenly summer had arrived, confirmed by the huge electronic device that registered the temperature on a building near our apartment. For those who had the money to do so, it was time to get away from the heat, to a summer retreat on Long Island or a place near the beach in New Jersey. In our case we rented a family home at Port Washington on Long Island from where Ron would be able to take the commuter train to and from the office.

Sarah

I remember that place on Long Island very clearly. It was at the end of an inlet from the Atlantic Ocean and not a bit like Saltdean, where we had a stony beach stretching out from the promenade towards the sea. In America there was strange and frightening sea life scuttling along the edge of the tide – horseshoe crabs that looked like German helmets, and with a thick green tail. Occasionally a rainstorm hit us at Port Washington, and the first time it happened everyone else on the beach ran for their cars. There were no beach huts, so we British, used to coping with plenty of rain back in Saltdean, just sat tight under an inadequate umbrella – but we learned our lesson when we saw just how fiercely it continued to tip down.

This was compensated for by lots of sunshine, a floating dock for diving and the Good Humor man who sold coconut lollies. That was a flavour new to me. My father's favourite activity was putting Lulu and myself and other kids into a blue plastic boat and launching us into the waves. Years later he would do the same for my own children, Lucy and Joe, at Pevensey in Sussex.

The thing I liked most was the floating dock. Every day I would swim out to it and jump or dive into the water, sharing the fun with the American children. We could sunbathe on the bleached surface of the dock and also hang off the side and look underneath, where it was green and cool and slimy. I was also fascinated by the hollow sucking sound underneath the dock caused by the constant to-ing and fro-ing of the sea.

Many of the people at Port Washington were affluent Americans who either owned – or rented, as we did – a summer home there. When I grew up, I often saw gossip columns referring to smart places like the Hamptons further down Long Island, and wondered if Port Washington had become equally fashionable.

Ron

Our summer retreat had enough rooms to accommodate my parents as well, so in our first full year in America we invited them to come over and spend some time with us. I had booked my own summer holiday to coincide with their visit.

We managed to take them on a trip up to Cobb Memorial School and go on a picnic with Louise and then on to Canada and Niagara Falls before travelling back south to the White House and all the other historic places in Washington. I think as much as anything they enjoyed Long Island where, on July 4, we went off to see a gigantic fireworks display marking American independence. We also took them a short distance to nearby Oyster Bay where the summer residence of former US president Teddy Roosevelt was open to visitors. They found the place of special significance for them despite the fact that they were young children during the years of his presidency. Both knew that the Teddy Bear was said to have been so named after Roosevelt's refusal to shoot one on a hunting trip, and my father came out with one of the president's sayings: 'Speak softly and carry a big stick.'

They also enjoyed the time we spent together on the Port Washington beach. It was a safe place to swim and there was a jetty from which we tried to catch eels. Local fishermen took pity on us, and for my father at least the highlight of the holiday came when we carried several eels back to the bungalow and Doris cooked them for supper. My father was a Cockney, born within the sound of Bow Bells, in a district of London where eels, especially the jellied variety, were a regular treat.

Doris

Gradually celebrity spotting turned into something of a competition between Ron, Sarah and me. It started on our first Halloween when we were about to take the lift to a party up on the twelfth floor of our apartment block. Sarah was all done up in an appropriately scary costume. When the lift door opened at ground level, we were taken aback, to say the least, when Hermione Gingold began to emerge. Ms Gingold was an English stage and screen actress living in New York, who had starred alongside Leslie Caron and Maurice Chevalier in one of our favourite films, *Gigi*. What made that film special for us was that in it, Chevalier sang one of his big hits, with the devastating opening line 'Every little breeze seems to whisper Louise'.

Hermione Gilgold had an eccentric manner and a strange, husky voice which made her seem a bit spooky, just the person to encounter stepping out of an elevator on this of all nights. She paused for a short while when she realised that we were English and made a great fuss of Sarah and her Halloween get-up.

Ron's entry in our celebrity contest did not impress us at all. Apparently he had stepped into a lift on Fifth Avenue, to be confronted with Tiny Tim. This was the stage name of a bizarre individual who had made an impact on the music charts and also on television by singing in a wavering falsetto voice a song called 'Tiptoe Thru' The Tulips'. He had a white face and long, straggly hair and accompanied himself on a ukulele. Sarah and I thought he was awful.

In the event I proved to be the winner of our celebrity contest. One morning the elevator brought me up from our basement laundry clutching a pile of clothes and heading for our apartment on the eighteenth floor. The elevator stopped at ground level and in stepped Frank Sinatra, accompanied by another man. I just had to say something, so I said, 'Excuse me, but I think your record of "That's Life" is marvellous.' Then I reached out to touch Sinatra. I guess the other man was a bodyguard, as he tried to deflect my hand, but the singer just beamed and said, 'Well thank you, ma'am,' in a booming voice that made me go a bit weak at the knees.

Ron

In the spring, and especially in the autumn – and when it was quiet on the news front – we tried to get out of town as often as possible. We visited Lulu once a month and took the opportunity to spend the rest of the weekend exploring upstate New York and the adjoining New England states, which were all at their most beguiling in the fall, as we learned to call it. One time we took Louise with us for an overnight stay in a boardwalk town called Chichester, where we found a motel run by a hunter. On a nearby tree branch he had hung a young deer shot in the surrounding woods. We were a long way from New York City.

English place names were everywhere. On a subsequent weekend, we overnighted at Essex, Connecticut at the Griswold Inn, where they have been looking after guests since 1776. Essex is near New London and not far from Colchester and Norwich. We had come here to visit Mystic Seaport, an amazing reconstruction of coastal life in the nineteenth century when thousands of seamen were involved in the whaling industry off the coast of Maine. The prime exhibit is the *Charles W. Morgan*, the last surviving wooden whaling ship, which found her final resting place at Mystic in 1941.

There are two historic trails in this part of America which came into being as trade routes used by Native Americans. One of them, the Appalachian Trail, runs for more than two thousand miles, from Maine to Georgia. You can't drive along it, so it's a favourite with hikers, despite various hazards such as black bears, mosquitoes, poison ivy and venomous snakes. So we tended to favour the Mohawk Trail. This, too, began as a trading route, but is now a motor highway with access to frequent camp sites and the chance of an encounter with bobcats and bears. We spent quite a lot of time exploring the Mohawk Trail, stopping at picturesque clapboard hotels.

At one of them, the waiter announced that there was New England Boiled Dinner on the menu. It sounded like a threat, but later we learned that it's very much a part of Irish-American culture and dates from the time when Irish immigrants substituted pork with corned beef in one of their traditional meals. It's a one-pot dish. The corned beef always comes with cabbage and a variety of other vegetables, including carrots and red potatoes. The dish is a regular feature of the celebrations on St Patrick's Day and other Irish holidays. The three of us, hungry travellers on the Mohawk Trail, declared it delicious.

On another weekend, we headed westward to Lancaster County,

Pennsylvania. This is the place with the largest community of Amish people in the United States. They were driven out of Europe by religious persecution early in the eighteenth century and have continued their simple way of life ever since. They are known as the 'Plain People', and this is reflected in their dress. They do not drive cars, and the tractors they use on their farms are horse-driven. They have a horse and buggy to get around and they have become rather more of a tourist attraction than they would wish. Taking photos seemed an intrusion, but we couldn't resist it.

Lancaster County was yet another example of the enormous diversity of America. So, too, was Salem, on the coast of Massachusetts. Here, too, religious persecution played a macabre part in its early history when it was still a British colony. In 1692, nearly a hundred years before America's Declaration of Independence, a group of Puritan colonists succumbed to mass hysteria and accused 150 Salem residents of witchcraft. Nineteen of these poor people were hanged and seventeen died while awaiting trial. Later the same year, when the hysteria subsided, the trials came to an end. All those who had been formally accused of witchcraft now received official pardons. In many cases, it was too late.

Nowadays, Salem is a tourist town. It has at least four Witch Museums and attracts a huge number of visitors who – as we were – are drawn by the gruesome story of events of more than three hundred years ago.

There's no doubt in my mind that our second year in the United States was by far the most exciting for us. First, in the spring, came Anguilla. This small British colony in the Leeward Islands insisted that it wanted to remain a colony, resisting the idea of becoming the smallest member of a new federation which would also include two larger islands nearby, St Kitts and Nevis. Back in London, the government of the time, under Prime Minister Harold Wilson, was trying to put Britain's colonial past behind it, so it ignored Anguilla's view of its future. The tiny island responded by expelling six policemen to St Kitts. Later it threw out a British diplomat, Tony Lee. This triggered Britain's decision to send in paratroopers.

The soldiers were accompanied by a contingent of bobbies from the Metropolitan Police, and this brought a touch of pantomime to the proceedings that caught the imagination of news reporters from all over the world. This was added to by the fact that, as the paratroopers went ashore, they were met not by hostile gunfire but by a fusillade of flashing, and friendly, press cameras which had arrived ahead of them. Soon they would be greeted by islanders waving Union Jacks and singing 'God Save The Queen'. Yet in London there were suggestions from a government minister that this bizarre invasion was necessary because 'some rather disreputable customers' wished to use the island for 'seedy business operations from Florida'. Another minister referred to the Mafia, and there were allegations that American gambling promoters were trying to set up offshore casinos on Anguilla. Prime Minister Wilson, increasingly doubtful about the whole business, turned to his governmental colleagues and demanded: 'Where are the gangsters?'

Charles Wheeler was the first BBC man to reach the island, followed by a film crew from Alexandra Palace, Peter Matthews and sound recordist Bill Norman. They had been just about to start a three-month assignment to the United States. Wheeler called me from Miami to say it would be impossible on his own to cover the story for both radio and television in addition to shipping the film back to London and setting up any satellite transmissions. He asked me to fly out there.

I managed to get two seats on a plane to Puerto Rico leaving New York later the same day. The second seat was for my wife. I knew she would be an excellent manager and organiser for the rest of us once we arrived on Anguilla. Fortunately, by this time, Alexandra Palace had decided I was busy enough to have an assistant and had already dispatched one of their rising stars, Caroline Ellis, to carry out that role. Now, while we were away, she would cover for me in New York. She also kindly agreed to look after Sarah. So, off we went, overnighting in Puerto Rico and then boarding the first flight of the day to St. Thomas in the US Virgin Islands. There, Charles had assured us, we would be able to pick up a flight to Anguilla.

At St. Thomas airport we found the Anguilla Airways check-in desk. It was a somewhat flimsy affair resembling the kind of structure you set up for a bring-and-buy sale, with 'Anguilla Airways' running across the top. There was nobody around. Eventually somebody told us that Bevin was outside on the tarmac fixing the plane. Bevin was the pilot. We found him on his knees next to a six-seater, carrying out another of his roles – aircraft mechanic. He was also the man who sold you your ticket.

There were two other passengers, both news agency reporters. One was from Reuters, the other from United Press International. We had met them in the airport restaurant where they were tucking into a substantial breakfast, following the good old journalistic principle that you'd better eat well now because you don't know when and where you'll be getting the next meal.

The journey was uneventful up to the moment Bevin signalled to us that he was preparing to land on the dustbowl that passed for Anguilla's airport in those days. Suddenly he changed his mind. The red light showing that the plane's wheels had descended fully, ready for touchdown, had failed to come on. So Bevin promptly banked the Cessna against the sun and looked down at the plane's shadow. Fortunately it included wheels . . .

Doris

We landed smoothly enough in a cloud of dust, and as we emerged from the plane I was surprised to see a huge crowd of children running excitedly towards us. They had been taken to the airport by their parents to welcome another aircraft that touched down shortly before we arrived. On board were Lord Caradon, Britain's representative at the United Nations Assembly in New York, and various advisors who had come to try and resolve the crisis that had arisen over Anguilla's determination to remain a colony. When the children spotted me stepping down from the plane, I was wearing a large straw hat as protection against the sun as well as a large wristwatch in the shape of a Union Jack. The rumour accordingly went round, as I discovered later, that the Queen herself had also come to Anguilla. Somehow I stammered through an apology for not being the Queen, and they cheered as I explained that we were working for the BBC. Fortunately they knew about the BBC – every home on the island seemed to have the latest transistor capable of receiving BBC overseas transmissions. So one of them cried out, 'When you see the Queen, you tell her we love her,' and the rest of them jumped up and down, cheering loudly. Years later I actually got the chance to deliver that message, at a press reception I attended at Buckingham Palace.

British soldiers were in evidence as we passed through the small customs and immigration room at Anguilla airport. Waiting for us outside was one of the island's few taxi drivers, who spent most of the day scanning the skies for customers. It was Mac, as we came to know him; he had picked up Charles and the camera crew when they arrived and had driven them to the guest house towards which, down a bumpy dirt road, we were now heading. Mac said it was the very first place to be built for visitors to the island. I asked Mac for its address and he laughed and said, 'At The Top Of The Hill By The Mahogany Tree.' When Bevin prepared to take his little plane back to St. Thomas, an hour or so later, he discovered that the battery was flat. So they had to move a beaten-up Austin to the side of the plane and jump-start it with a lead from the car battery.

The guest house turned out to be a large and rambling single-storey building, the home of Mr and Mrs David Lloyd. The former was one of the island's most charismatic personalities, a building contractor and a vigorous supporter of the campaign to remain a colony of Great Britain. Charles and the camera crew came out to greet us and help with our baggage.

Charles told us later he had calculated that moving in with the

Lloyds would put us in just the right spot to stay in touch with the feelings of the vast majority of Anguillans who shared Mr Lloyd's view. So, putting aside the temptation to check in at the island's only hotel, he and the crew had opted to stay right where they were, and promptly booked an additional room for Ron and myself. We both felt that it was the right decision – not least because accommodation on Anguilla was now extremely limited, with the arrival of the British police and paratroopers and television crews from Britain, America and Jamaica. Additionally, in the absence of phones on the island, it was essential that we all stay in one place. As we arrived, a lively meeting was taking place under the mahogany tree in the yard adjoining the house and there was no doubt about the hostility towards the proposed federation with St. Kitts and Nevis.

With our arrival, the Lloyds' place was now full, ten of us sleeping on cast-iron beds draped with muslin netting to keep the mosquitoes at bay. We were very well looked after. The temperature on Anguilla averages 77 degrees Fahrenheit, and the infrequent showers had to be collected on the roof of the Lloyd building and pumped into a tank by an electric generator. Electric light came from a smaller generator which was switched on when dusk fell.

The decision was taken that I should act as a kind of general manager of the BBC operation, keeping a record of expenses and a diary of upcoming events, on Anguilla itself and on the nearby islands. Knowing everybody's whereabouts was not easy. Charles, Ron and the camera crew spent quite a lot of time away from the island and there was no way of communicating with them because of the lack of phones. Ron used to say, 'Expect me when you see me.' Mrs Lloyd had a cheeky sense of humour, saying, 'No man in your bed tonight, Mrs Onions.'

Our taxi driver, Mac, used to drop by at the Lloyds each morning to see if we wanted a ride anywhere along the dirt-track roads, perhaps for a film assignment somewhere on the island, or for me to do some shopping. Mac had black curly hair and I learned that he was the father of six children. All his front teeth were missing. He would listen to your views about the island's future and when he became excited he'd say that if things didn't calm down he would leave the island like many others before him and he'd burn his house down before he left. When I asked him who he would like to be the leader of his people, he said, 'It is in God's hands.' At the news conferences that took place outside the Lloyds' house, he would crouch under the mahogany tree with some of his mates and occasionally rebuke one of them by quoting from the Ten Commandments.

I got to know Vida Lloyd very well. She was by far the most polite person I have ever met. She was much younger than her husband, and whenever she addressed him she would begin by saying, 'Excuse me.' She told me she was a nurse and had done some of her training in London. Now she worked part time at Anguilla's only hospital. She demonstrated her skills on one of the visiting journalists right there in the guest house by removing the stitches that had been inserted after a recent tooth extraction. He had left London in a tearing hurry, leaving no time to have the job done back there.

Mrs Lloyd had two hard-working assistants, but I marvelled at how she managed the job at the clinic as well as supervising the cooking of three excellent meals a day for everyone at the guest house. She also looked after her two young children, a girl and a boy, Christine and David. They were delightful kids. Like most small girls on the island, Christine's black hair was arranged in tiny plaits all over her head. She had a blonde glamour dolly, imported from America, and I was fascinated to see that she had dressed its long blonde hair in exactly the same way.

Life at the guest house reminded me constantly of old farm-houses in the south of France where the chickens clucked their way round the garden and in and out of the house. The Lloyds grew a few vegetables, including carrots, corn and papaya fruit, but, unlike the neighbouring island of St. Kitts, the hard and rocky soil was too dry for a sugar crop.

Ron

The island's telephone system had been blown down in a hurricane several years earlier and it had not been replaced. Mobile phones had yet to be invented. So every phone call and every film assignment or radio report to London meant a plane trip for either Washington correspondent Charles Wheeler or myself. There was yet another problem. After the hurricane, Anguilla was left with no control tower and only half a runway – and that meant there were no scheduled airline services. You just had to grab whatever was going – anywhere! It might be to British Antigua in a huge RAF supply plane. That one was a free ride but there were no seats, so you had to sit on the floor strapped into the security webbing on one side of the aircraft. The crew didn't always tell you where they were going. Other than that, you had to charter one of the six-seater planes hanging around at the airport. They would take you to St. Thomas or the nearby Dutch-French island of St. Maarten, where there were phones and airline links to London.

There was one day in particular that proved hairier than usual. Charles was out with the camera crew filming an update on the negotiations between the island's leaders and the British delegation. Meanwhile, we had agreed that I would check out a tumbledown building not far from our guest house. There were rumours going round that this place was the centre of the alleged Mafia operation on the island and possibly a site for the storage and maintenance of small arms. The owner came out to greet me. He was American and he invited me to have a look round. I stepped inside what appeared to be simply a scruffy engineering workshop for the maintenance of vehicles and other basic mechanical tasks. I said hello to a couple of employees who were just hanging around. One was a shy teenage boy, the other an elderly man anxious to tell me about his brother in London. The owner agreed to let us film the place and also to be interviewed on camera.

At this point Charles and the crew turned up. They had found out from the RAF that a transport plane would be leaving for an undisclosed destination in about an hour's time. The camera crew promptly began filming the workshop and the owner and his two employees, but there was no was no time for me to write an accompanying script, so I just scribbled one or two notes and ad libbed my way through before interviewing the owner. It may not have been the finest news report for television but it must have been among the fastest. On the bumpy road to the airport, Charles pencilled a somewhat shaky script for radio, updating the current situation on Anguilla. The idea was that as soon as I found a phone box somewhere I would read it on the line to Broadcasting House for subsequent transmission in radio bulletins.

I scrambled on board the RAF supply plane clutching a bag containing the film Charles and the crew had made earlier in the day about the current situation on Anguilla plus the one we had just shot at the alleged Mafia joint. In no time at all we landed on the island of Antigua. I rang London and read the piece Charles had written for radio. Then I rang New York about the two cans of film. The solution seemed to be for me to fly to Miami and find a passenger willing to carry the cans to New York, where our shipping agent would be waiting to put them on an overnight flight to London. That would enable me to get back to Anguilla at a critical time on the island as quickly as possible – but it hinged on me finding someone at Miami airport to act as a courier and hand the films to our man waiting in the arrivals hall at New York. He would be holding up a large placard with the inscription 'BBC'. Otherwise the film would end up in a cargo shed, with the consequent delay in speeding it overnight to London.

Today you would have no chance of getting away with such a scheme. One of the main questions at check-in desks is: 'Has anyone asked you to take anything on board?' Nervously, I approached a line of passengers waiting to get on an American Airlines plane heading non-stop for New York. The first two I spoke to obviously thought I was a nut case and shook their head. The third was a tall man who gazed at me fiercely. He took in my battered straw hat and the shirt and jeans covered in the dust of Anguilla. Then he said, 'Have you any identification?' I fished out my passport and BBC identity card. He was silent for several seconds and then he said, 'I am a sergeant in the New York Police Department.' I wondered where the hell all this was heading. He turned to the woman at his side and said, 'Let's do it.' I learned later they were returning home from their honeymoon.

In New York, the police sergeant did us proud, arriving in the airport holding aloft a piece of card identifying himself and swiftly handing over the films to our shipping agent. The films arrived at Heathrow early next morning and both featured on BBC television bulletins throughout the day. The policeman and his wife were special guests at a BBC reception in the New York office later in the year.

I set off on the return journey, stopping briefly in Miami to mail picture postcards to Sarah in New York and Louise at Cobb School. It was a way of keeping in touch with the children, and some airlines made it easy by not only providing a selection of cards but also undertaking to post them on landing.

Doris

While Ron was away, the talks between the British delegation and Anguilla's leaders had run into trouble, so in an attempt to win over hearts and minds, Lord Caradon decided to throw a party for the islanders. It was the strangest party ever. It took place in the brick ruins of an old jail on a spot called Crocus Hill, overlooking a spectacular bay. The British soldiers and sailors laid on plenty of beer and lemonade, and the guest list included representatives of the Army and Navy as well as well as MI5 and other intelligence agencies, plus television and press reporters from Britain and America and several other countries. Then there were the Anguillan people themselves, young and old, in very large numbers. It was a huge success. Later our taxi driver, Mac, said to us, 'Things go good now.'

The following morning we had arranged to visit the nearby French-Dutch island of St. Maarten to have a look round and maybe buy some duty-free goodies. David Dimbleby and his production crew came with us with us in a boat provided by their hotel. They had been making a feature film for BBC TV's weekly 'Panorama' programme.

Our departure did not go unnoticed. Neither did our return. Scotland Yard men had studied the round trip through binoculars. We had departed illegally without passing through Customs or Immigration, and, what's more, we had returned illegally. All this we learned later when two senior police officers came round to see us 'in the course of certain enquiries arising out of a boat trip'. They were very understanding about it and simply passed on a request from Assistant Police Commissioner Way that he must be informed in advance if the BBC proposed to make any further illegal departures or arrivals.

We had neither the heart nor the courage to reveal our guilty secret: during the previous night's party we had told a group of friendly coppers of our plan to visit duty-free St. Maarten, and as the conversation proceeded, I had offered to bring back some goodies for the police wives and girlfriends back in London. At the end of a happy evening I had found myself with quite a long list, and on landing after the return journey from St. Maarten, I had been clutching a large bag of swag which had been distributed to the grateful bobbies later that day.

Ron

We had two weeks on Anguilla. It was always a bit hectic, but was not without its lighter moments. There was the occasion when one British policeman insufficiently known to me introduced me to a colleague as 'Mr Wheeler's sound effects man'. I think the second bobby was a wee bit disappointed when I failed to produce a pair of coconut shells and give him a quick burst of galloping hooves.

Towards the end of our stay on Anguilla, we learned that another of Britain's colonies in this part of the world had declared a state of emergency, so we had to charter a flight to the island of Montserrat. When we got there, we learned from the British consul that the previous night a hostile group of islanders had been lobbing bricks and various other missiles over the walls surrounding the consulate, but it didn't seem to add up to much more than that. Charles interviewed the consul as part of a full report on the island's recent troubles. We dashed back to the airport, hoping to ship the film back to London. There was not a direct flight, but there was one leaving shortly for Antigua, where we knew there was a BOAC plane leaving for London that evening. It was agreed that Charles would take the film to Antigua, arrange for its dispatch to Heathrow and then phone through voice reports for radio and television. The only trouble was that a flight official at Montserrat airport became stroppy at the sight of Charles charging up the gangway of the plane at the last minute, clutching the can of film. He said the flight had been closed. Our camera crew started to film the ensuing confrontation, and the enraged official came down the gangway to try and stop them. Charles grabbed the opportunity to rush up into the plane, where he found a vacant seat and refused to budge. Things eventually calmed down and the plane took off with Charles and the film.

At Antigua airport, Charles sought out the BOAC freight manager, praised him for all his recent efforts in dispatching our newsfilm to London, and said he was confident the latest package was in safe hands. The BOAC manager, a very nice man, made reassuring noises. Five minutes later, the poor chap informed Wheeler that they had had to cancel the flight to London because of 'maintenance problems in Barbados'.

It took many more months to resolve Britain's dispute with Anguilla. We had long since returned to New York when it was announced that the islanders had got what they wanted. They were allowed to secede from the proposed federation with St. Kitts and Nevis and remain a colony, though later Anguilla was designated a

'British overseas territory'. Tourism has brought greater prosperity to the island, and that dusty runway has been replaced by Clayton J. Lloyd International Airport.

Doris

The second big event of the year was when man landed on the moon for the first time, and we were lucky enough to be at Cape Kennedy to see the launch of the pioneering Apollo 11 spacecraft. Then we flew on to Mission Control in Houston to watch its safe arrival on the moon and the first historic steps of astronaut Neil Armstrong.

After that, we did not immediately head back home to New York. Instead, the three of us flew from Houston to Japan, where Ron had been given a special assignment marking the launch of a new satellite over the Indian Ocean. This would provide the first direct television link between Tokyo and London. Still more excitement followed, as we then flew from Japan to England for a fortnight's home leave, with Lulu in the continuing care of the sisters at Cobb.

Annoyingly, our marathon journey did not begin well. While we were checking in at New York's La Guardia Airport for the flight to the Kennedy Space Centre in Florida, somebody stole one of our seven suitcases. It was the only time this happened to us in all the many journeys that, together, took us all the way round the world.

Sarah

On 16 July, it was still dark when Sandi Toksvig's mother knocked on the door of our Cocoa Beach motel suite. In a couple of hours, Apollo 11 would begin its historic journey, and she felt we should set off early to ensure a good view from the Kennedy Space Centre

VIP stand reserved for families of moonshot journalists. Julie Toksvig was also concerned about the very high temperatures in the Sunshine State, and gave us all salt crackers to prevent dehydration.

I soon made friends with Sandi and her brother Nick. She and I were both ten years old. Nick was handsome and blond and very much in charge. Sandi was the little one – but years later she was to achieve great success as a presenter and comedian on radio and television in the United Kingdom. Their father, Klaus, was covering the Apollo 11 story for Danish television and radio. Mum and I accompanied the Toksvigs on the special bus to the VIP stand, and as we approached it I could hear the resonant voice of one of the support team ticking off the moments to lift-off. The reporters and camera crews were in a stand to our right. I spotted Dad wearing an orange cap presented to him for the occasion. Watching from two miles away, my overwhelming impression as Apollo left the earth was the exhilarating power of the flames spreading outwards across the launch pad. The memory of that is still intact, and I think of it as being in a special cupboard you open only now and then.

My father had filmed the lift-off on a Super 8 cine camera, but years later, when we searched through a huge box of films and photos of our life and times in America, it had gone missing. More recently, though, there was consolation of a kind when one of my radio-club students at the school I was teaching at in England presented me with a copy of the film *The Curious Case of Benjamin Button*. This featured a reconstruction of a space rocket taking off as background to Benjamin and his lover lazing on the deck of a vessel just off the Florida coast. I felt Hollywood had saluted what for me had been the most memorable event of my childhood.

Doris

Just a day after the launch of Apollo 11, I found myself at the centre of another drama on the flight from Cape Kennedy to

Houston's Mission Control complex, where we would be based in our motel until Apollo 11 returned to earth. Soon after the plane took off, I had a severe stomach pain. The pilot decided to call ahead and arrange for a doctor to be waiting for me when we touched down. He was there when we stepped into the arrivals hall, and introduced himself as 'Moses, Doctor Moses'. He led us to our motel room, and on the way we were greeted by one of Ron's journalist buddies from New York. 'Who's that?' I asked. My husband replied, 'Jesus.' He wasn't joking. Jesus – though pronounced differently – was the the name of the Spanish reporter covering the moon mission for TVE, Madrid. We both felt that meeting Moses and Jesus simultaneously at this particular moment pointed to my swift recovery and, sure enough, Doctor Moses prescribed something that had a prompt and beneficial effect.

It took four days for Apollo 11 to reach the moon. Some 500 million people heard astronaut Neil Armstrong announce, 'The Eagle has landed.' Then, after slow and meticulous preparation, he stepped onto the surface of the moon the following day with the historic announcement: 'That's one small step for a man; one giant leap for mankind.'

Sarah

The celebrations that night around the motel pool went on way past my bedtime. There was a huge barbecue and much merriment. To add to it all, it was my mother's birthday. Everyone seemed to end up in the pool, though not all of them by choice. During the preceding days, I had spent most of my time in that pool, though the weather was often overcast and muggy, with occasional thunderstorms. I remember scrambling out in a hurry on one occasion and looking back to see a flash of lightning strike the water. I kept quiet about that.

When we finally retreated to our bedroom we were able to listen to the astronauts chatting away to Mission Control on a special sound circuit. Many years later, I thought this was a compelling detail whenever I got into an argument with moonshot cynics.

When I wasn't swimming, I had the run of the Press Centre to keep me amused. There was a huge screen providing a continuous relay of what the astronauts were up to in their temporary lunar home. Sometimes I went into the hall to find it empty, usually because a press briefing was taking place elsewhere, and I kidded myself that the astronauts on the screen were chatting away just for me.

Years later, when we dug out all the keepsakes from this exciting time in my life, I noticed a press pass in Mum's name giving her accreditation as a European Broadcasting Union reporter and, indeed, she did do a number of reports for BBC radio.

I was also surprised during some recent research in the BBC' s Internet archive to discover a special report from Houston on the contrasting ways that journalists from all over the world were covering the moonshot. I was quite impressed by the reporter, and then realised I was looking at a somewhat younger version of my dad.

Ron

Because of the time difference between Houston and London, our working day seemed to go on forever, but fortunately the BBC's veteran air correspondent Reg Turnill had come over to share the reporting duties and to make his own distinguished contribution as an expert on space and the various space ventures that preceded the launch of Apollo 11.

Even with Reg on hand, it was all go. Meals came out of a vending machine, with a menu that never varied – Tex-Mex. One night it offered only peanuts and Coke. So I suggested to Charles, who had grown up in Germany, that we drive a short distance to a German restaurant I had spotted a couple of miles away. We got out of the car only to be confronted with a huge sign over the entrance: FOR ONE NITE ONLY – TEX-MEX SPECIAL. We went inside anyway, and the boss offered to prepare a special German supper, just for us. Later he asked what brought us to Texas. We said we were television reporters. He replied that he used to be in the same line of business. 'Oh really,' I said, playing the fall guy. 'What did you do?' He replied, 'I was a crap dealer.' He was just trying to be friendly.

As Charles drove us back to base we were suddenly alarmed by flashing lights and a wailing siren behind us. We were in a built-up area. I knew Charles well enough by now to anticipate what he would do. He always tried to take control of any difficult situation that we encountered, and on this occasion he brought the car to a swift halt, swung the door open and advanced briskly towards the police car with his right hand extended. I followed him nervously but the policeman, slightly bewildered, shook hands with Charles and in no time at all they were the best of friends. As soon as we told him what we were doing in Houston and he realised we were English, he took off his sunglasses and said, 'Say, do you guys know Warrington?' It turned out that, in World War II, he had been stationed in north-west England for two or three years when Warrington was the site of the largest US Air Force base outside America. Assuring the cop that we knew Warrington very well, Charles then revealed that he himself had seen wartime service with the Royal Marines, so the two of them had been comrades in arms in defeating the Germans. By now they were buddies for life. I just stood there like a lemon – a humble National Service conscript working in RAF Equipment Accounts long after the war had ended and never leaving the ground – except to play cricket against RAF teams based in peacetime Germany. Anyway, addresses and telephone numbers were exchanged and our Texan friend waved us away with the mildest admonition: 'Next time you guys come to Texas, just take it easy, OK?'

About a year later, something similar happened to me in upstate New York. Whenever the sisters at Cobb went into retreat, that meant that Lulu had to come home and spend a few days with us. We were about halfway up the motorway on the return journey when she started making the 'icking' noise, as we referred to it, that preceded a spell of restlessness, so I put my foot down. In no time at all, the police siren began wailing behind us. I couldn't leave Lulu alone in the car so I was unable to follow the Wheeler strategy and advance on the police car in friendly fashion. Fortunately the cop took in our situation quickly as I told him about Lulu and where we were heading. He was sympathetic, as he knew someone who had similar problems. The policeman was huge, towering above me as he told me off, but without giving me a ticket. Maybe Charles and I had been lucky enough to encounter the only two traffic cops in America who were just pussycats at heart . . .

As the astronauts prepared for the return to earth, we began hearing details of a dramatic story breaking several hundred miles north on Chappaquiddick Island, off the coast of Massachusetts. After a party on the island for Democratic party workers, Senator Ted Kennedy drove his car off a wooden bridge with no guardrails, into a pond. Kennedy managed to struggle out of the vehicle. His passenger, Mary Jo Kopechne, did not. The senator told police he had made several attempts to rescue her. He was charged later with leaving the scene of an accident after an injury. Subsequently he was sentenced to two months in prison, but this sentence was soon suspended. There was uproar over the decision, and Kennedy's political career never really recovered.

Down at Mission Control in Houston, we were still at full stretch covering the moonshot. The astronauts had yet to begin the trip back to earth. So another camera crew and reporter from elsewhere had to be flown to Chappaquiddick. A few days later, Apollo 11 landed safely at sea after an uneventful return journey from the moon.

We left Houston two days later on a Continental Airlines plane heading west for Los Angeles, on our way to my next assignment. The Japanese Airlines flight from LA to Tokyo was an almost mystical experience as we flew through several different time zones in what seemed to be constant daylight, and with a delightful menu of Japanese cuisine to help us while away the hours. There was just one short stop, in Hawaii, where we took the opportunity to buy a huge pineapple. That turned out to be a serious mistake, as we learned on landing in Tokyo. In the immigration hall, the pineapple was promptly confiscated after being declared an illegal import.

Outside, two short men from the Japanese broadcaster NHK were waiting to greet us. They took us to the Tokyo Prince Hotel, and on arrival presented us with identity cards printed in Japanese script. They said that Onions was pronounced 'Tam-an-Eggy' in their language. At least that's what it sounded like, and their command of English was more than good enough for them to share our laughter. Then they set off back to the NHK studios, accompanied by the sound of gongs from a nearby temple.

Sarah

I remember the temple with the gongs to this day. It was the nearest building to the hotel pool where, as in Houston, I was to spend most of my days, now kidding myself that I was on a marathon swim round the world. The bottom of the pool was covered by an ornate mosaic pattern, and I was struck by the contrast between that and the sight and sound of the monks praying in their temple, partially open to the air and surrounded by a scruffy courtyard covered by clumps of weed. My other abiding memory of the Tokyo Prince Hotel was the western influence on its breakfast menu. We were all surprised to be offered porridge.

Ron

The reporter on the Tokyo-London hook-up was to be Martin Bell, whom I knew well and who would later become an independent MP – 'the man in the white suit', as the newspapers dubbed him. The day after he arrived in Japan, the two of us sat down with our hosts to work out the details of our main mission in Tokyo. This was to produce an extended news report marking the launch of the Indian Ocean satellite providing the very first direct television link between London and Tokyo. The tricky bit was that we had been asked to do it live, to be transmitted into the main evening news on BBC1. Such a feat is old hat nowadays, but then it was pioneering stuff. The fact that the BBC News commenced at 9 p.m., when it was already 5 o'clock the following morning in Tokyo, did nothing to calm our nerves.

The Japanese production team was meticulous in its preparation. Since it was my job to direct the live transmission to London, we worked out a system of simple commands in basic English – and even more basic Japanese – that everyone could follow. We got on well with our hosts. They were fascinated by the way we used words like 'wouldst' and 'couldst' – instead of 'would you' and 'could you' – when we exchanged cablegrams with London. We had to explain this was not an addiction to the language of Shakespeare, just a way of saving money on the number of words sent to the BBC in London and elsewhere.

After that first day at the studios, we were taken out for dinner. Fish, most of it raw, was served with a considerable amount of sake – a stronger than usual wine made from rice. Then came the moment when several live fish were plonked before us and began wriggling all over the place. We were invited to swallow them in one gulp, as our hosts had done. There we were, British to the core but unable to accept the challenge. There was a great deal of laughter, and some of our hosts raised their fist and clapped their upper arm in a macho gesture, indicating that the still writhing contents of the plate were a sure-fire aphrodisiac. Japan 1, Great Britain 0.

This had been a night out for men only, but some of the Japanese journalists had worked in England and America and were well aware of the different status of women in western society at this time. Our hosts were therefore anxious that Doris and Sarah should join us on a couple of nights out. They also arranged that my wife and daughter were accompanied by a couple of Japanese women to help them deal with the complexities of shopping and sightseeing expeditions. One of them was the daughter of NHK's foreign editor. She had been to university and spoke excellent English, but sometimes expressed concern about her prospects in what was a more male-dominated society than it is today.

There was another young woman, Masano Nakamura, who was a full-time employee at NHK and whose specific task was to look after visitors from foreign broadcasting organisations. She arranged for us to be the honoured guests at a tea ceremony, served in a pagoda by waitresses in ornate costumes. At a more mundane level, her help was invaluable in unravelling the complexities of Japanese shoe and dress sizes. The only thing she could do little about was the excessive pollution in high summer and the sight of heavily masked policemen directing the traffic at fume-laden junctions. We became good friends and we have stayed in touch, though eventually she left NHK to look after her elderly parents in Osaka.

After we had resettled in England, one of Masano's friends came to spend some time with us over Christmas. We took her to see Hampton Court, but she seemed equally fascinated by the box of crackers we opened at lunchtime, with funny hats and the excruciating jokes and mottoes. This surprised us because we imagined the Japanese had invented crackers. In fact, it was the Germans.

As we continued preparing for our pioneering satellite feed to London, we encountered just one major problem. This arose from the agreement that had been reached some time earlier that there would be a special half-hour programme to which both the NHK and BBC programme divisions would contribute. It would be pre-recorded and would include items on various national cultural activities. The BBC had provided a sequence on the Royal Ballet, among other items, and the Japanese had requested that the then Director-General, Charles Curran, should contribute a short address on the cultural and historical ties between the two countries.

Now neither Martin nor myself had any responsibility for all this, which had been agreed between Japanese programme producers and a couple of BBC grandees who had spent some time visiting Tokyo, but now here were we in the NHK studios – the two guys the Japanese turned to whenever problems arose. As they did now.

The first concerned the videotape featuring Charles Curran's recorded address that had already been sent to Tokyo. Martin and I were confronted by two NHK producers, who pointed out that Mr Curran had erroneously said friendly relations between our two countries began with the Treaty of Portsmouth.

An encyclopedia was flicked open and the Japanese pointed out that the Treaty of Portsmouth was signed in Portsmouth, New Hampshire, with the US president, Theodore Roosevelt, acting as mediator. It brought to an end the Russo-Japanese war of 1904–5. There had been no British involvement. One of our hosts then rustled the pages again and found a reference to the Treaty of Alliance signed by Britain and Japan in 1902. This, they said, marked the beginning of friendship between our two countries. They then, ever so politely, rubbed it in a bit, pointing out that Mr Curran was formerly the boss of BBC World Service – with a considerable reputation in Japan as a distinguished linguist. Could he please prepare a fresh videotape? In fact, he was out of town on an official visit. We had run out of time and the offending phrase would have to be edited out. That was done, but it meant that the Japanese tape editor had to make what is known in the business as a jump cut. Unfortunately, the result was that the Director-General's head jerked forward suddenly midway through his address and emerged out of a rainbow-coloured flash. It made him look like a pantomime genie, and it was at this point that he had tried out a couple of sentences in Japanese. It looked distinctly sinister, but our hosts were far too polite to fall about laughing.

Fortunately none of this affected our news assignment on the new satellite link. Martin had been out filming news items with a Japanese crew, and these were intermixed with various items culled from NHK's own news sources. Despite the desperately early hour, everything went without a hitch and herograms flashed back and forth between London and Tokyo.

To mark this minor moment in broadcasting history, NHK was kind enough set up a special trip for us, with Masano as our guide. We boarded the fastest train in the world, the famous bullet train, and this presented us with an outstanding view of Mount Fujiyama. It also provided a trolley service with a selection of Japanese delicacies to rival the feast we had enjoyed on Japanese Airlines the previous week. Our destination was Japan's second city, Osaka, whose ancient temples were a major attraction for tourists.

As a farewell treat, our hosts in Osaka had arranged a spectacular Japanese banquet. There was no danger of us starving on this trip. Fortunately, this time live fish were not on the menu. We sat cross-legged on the floor and were served by geishas dressed in spectacular apparel. In our room, we slept comfortably on a sloping wooden structure which turned out to be far more accommodating than it looked. Nowadays these futons, as they're called, are available at furniture stores in Britain. The room also provided us with a valuable addition to our collection of funny notices in faraway places. This one said: DO NOT HANG LOATHSOME THING OUT OF WINDOW.

Doris

Our journey home with British Airways took us over the North Pole, with a brief stop in Anchorage, Alaska. Landing there, after two weeks of the stifling streets of summertime Tokyo, was an invigorating experience. The air in this mountainous and watery landscape was stimulating, cold and clear, and with the sun just coming up, there was something about the place that made you feel you were at the very beginning of time.

Sarah

After two years away, England seemed small and quiet, and I was fascinated by the corner shops everywhere. After spending time with family and friends in north London, we drove down to Cornwall for a reunion with the Matthews clan at their farm and guest house just outside Penzance. Nothing had changed. Popsy and Shane still performed their doggy marathon round and round the garden as we arrived, and Mrs Matthews and her daughters still served their prodigious Cornish cream teas when we got back from the beach.

There was one particular moment, however, that took all of us by surprise. It had become a routine to sit with the family after tea and watch the early evening news on BBC TV. On our second day at the farmhouse, the newsreader gave details of a plane crash in a mountainous region of America, and then we found ourselves looking at my father reporting on the overall safety record for American aircraft during the previous year. This was a report he had put together a little while ago. They are known as 'shelf' items in the broadcasting business, something held in reserve until a breaking news story – in this case, the crash in the mountains – provides a peg for their appearance on screen. Mr Matthews could not get over the fact that my father was on the screen and yet sitting right next to him. He kept looking at the television and then switching his gaze back to Dad. I think he felt that it had all been arranged to coincide with our visit to Poniou Farm, a guesthouse near Penzance, but we were just as taken aback as the Matthews family.

I was looking forward to seeing my Saltdean friend Lynne Montague before we flew back to America. I had wanted to show her the pretty pink bikini with daisies on it that Mum had bought for me specially for this trip back to England. Unfortunately the bikini had been in the smart grey suitcase stolen at La Guardia Airport. Fortunately the sleeveless smock which went with the bikini was in another case, and when we managed to get down to the Sussex coast I wore it proudly when I dropped in to see Lynne and her mum at their bungalow just a few doors down the road from ours. It was a happy reunion. Lynne and I had been very close in our early years at primary school, playing the games of childhood for hours on end. I looked forward to our getting together again when we returned to England.

Doris

After we flew back to Manhattan, I was determined to continue my radio reports, and did so with the help of the studio engineers and producer at the BBC studios off Fifth Avenue. I also found myself a job at the New York branch of Berlitz, the international language school, which was planning a series of cassette recordings aimed at the many Spanish and Spanish-speaking people in America who wanted to learn English, which was essential for those seeking permanent residence in the United States. Each cassette featured a family in a particular situation – in a restaurant, shopping, travelling, at the doctor's and so on. I was cast as the mother in these little playlets, which were all in English but with occasional inserts in Spanish to assist students. The added bonus was that Berlitz presented me with a work permit. Foreigners – like me – knew these were worth their weight in gold when seeking employment in America.

The other thing I was determined to do at this time was to get my weight down. I had put on quite a few pounds since moving to America, so I spent some of the Berlitz money – 87 bucks to be precise – on a course entitled 'Learning Through Movement' at a place in Greenwich Village called the Human Relations Center. The weekly exercise was vigorous and exhilarating, and it did the trick.

Ron

Soon after we returned to New York I was at home one evening watching the 11 o'clock news when Charles Wheeler phoned me from Peru. He had just arrived there with the film crew after reports of a major earthquake north of the capital, Lima, and he wanted me to join him as soon as possible, as covering the story for both radio and television and shipping reports back to London would be impossible to cope with on his own.

At some point on the journey south, I switched planes to a Canadian Pacific Air flight heading for Lima. En route the plane landed for a scheduled stop at Guayaquil in Ecuador. There passengers were asked to disembark and, ominously, given vouchers for the airport restaurant. Too much time went by. I was able to scribble cards from Ecuador and post them off to Lulu and to Sarah and Doris. Eventually I went looking for an official of the airline to find out the cause of the delay. When eventually I found him, his response was less than comforting. He said, 'You see, sir, the airplane ... she is broken.' Some time later we took off again – in another plane.

At Lima Airport, I met up with Charles and the film crew as they returned from the stricken area in a Peruvian Air Force transport plane. It was the only way of getting in and out. The earthquake had started fifteen miles out at sea, but it was powerful enough to set off a landslide and subsequent avalanche on Peru's highest peak, Mount Nevado Huascarain. This resulted in a massive torrent of rocks, ice and snow which was to leave some seventy thousand people dead and destroy close on a million homes. It was the worst ever natural disaster in North and South America, and the Peruvian Air Force worked heroically, ferrying food and other essential supplies.

Our journey from Lima was often a bumpy ride. Sometimes it was cloudy and there would be sudden glimpses of mountain peaks when you thought you were over the sea – and vice versa – but it was the only way we could obtain several dramatic reports for television, which were air-freighted from Lima Airport on the overnight flights to Heathrow. Voice reports for BBC radio arrived in London on a special audio circuit from one of Lima's radio stations.

Doris

Sarah and I were able to keep up with Ron's activities when he was out of town on a major news story because invariably it was covered by American reporters on the national news programmes we watched in Manhattan, but it was always a relief to have him back home safe and sound. By way of relaxation we tried to get up to New England for a day or two, and it was on one such trip that we found what proved to be our summer home for that year, in a place called Ogunquit on the coast of Maine.

In the Native American language, Ogunquit means 'coastal lagoon', and it's a place favoured by fishermen and artists. It has long sandy beaches and cold seas, and the lobsters we ate at Barnacle Billy's in Perkins Cove were the best we ever tasted. Our summer home was a converted barn, shaded from the hot sun by a clump of trees and just a short walk from the beach. Ron came up at the weekend, usually by Greyhound bus but occasionally he hired a car to collect Lulu from Cobb Memorial School and bring her to Ogunquit so she could spend a day or two with us at the seaside. The house was more than big enough to accommodate the four of us.

Back when we had lived in Sussex, Louise had spent some of the happiest days of her life in and out of the sea at Saltdean, but there were one or two problems on the beach in Maine. Most of the time she was happy enough swimming with Sarah and Ron and building sand castles, but occasionally she would become frustrated and start screaming at the top of her voice. Ron had to run and collect her when she went into this routine near an American picnic party. When he picked her up, she began scratching him and streaks of blood appeared on his back. It was one of those agonising moments when, once again, I had to face the fact that Louise would never be normal.

So we decided to have a day or two away from the beach and explore the countryside between Ogunquit and the Canadian border. Usually Lulu was well behaved in the car, but you needed to ensure that her favourite music cassettes were on board – the Jackson 5, Mama Cass, the Monkees, Burt Bacharach and the Carpenters. It was also essential to stop for lunch and ice cream. However, on this trip, the unfamiliar road began to twist and turn, slowing us down. Louise soon became restless, so we decided to head back to Ogunquit.

Sarah

Turning back meant we never reached the Erie Canal. It was only a few miles ahead and I was longing to get there because I had learned a fascinating song about it at school in New York. The chorus went:

Low bridge, everybody down.
Low bridge for we're coming to a town.
And you'll always know your neighbour, you'll always know your pal.
If you've ever navigated on the Erie Canal.

We did not sing hymns at Steiner. However, we did learn traditional American songs, such as 'Swanee River' and 'My Kentucky Home'. We also sang old British songs like 'Sumer Is Icumen In' and 'The Bonny, Bonny Banks of Loch Lomond'. Singing this last one in the skyscraper setting of New York's Upper East Side always struck me as a bit bizarre.

Doris

Most weekends, unless he had to cope with a breaking news story, Ron used to come up to Ogunquit, usually on the Greyhound bus. He often walked to the nearby village of Kennebunkport to get a haircut. This was the place where the Bush family had owned a property for many years, and it was to become the summer residence of George H.W. Bush. He was already a distinguished politician when we discovered Kennebunkport, and some years later when he became US president it was here that he received world

110

leaders like Margaret Thatcher and Mikhail Gorbachev. I think Ron had the mad idea that one day Bush or someone equally well known would be sitting in an adjoining chair at the barber's and they might agree to do an interview. I told my husband he was bonkers.

Ogunquit was a friendly place and people there enjoyed talking to you, especially when they discovered you were English. Sarah found an American playmate on the beach and her mother invited us round to their imposing summer home for tea. She revealed that her husband was a senior executive at the *New York Times*. When I told Ron, he sighed and said, 'There's just no escape from the news business.'

There was something special about coming back into Manhattan as summer came to an end and the kids went back to school. There were new shows to see at the theatre and we resumed various activities designed to keep us fit and active. As part of Steiner's keep-fit programme, Sarah regularly attended the 'Y' – the YMCA – where there was not only a well-equipped gym but also an indoor running track. However, she much preferred to come with me to the Turtle Bay Music School, on nearby Second Avenue, for weekly ballet lessons.

The Turtle Bay event that all three of us could enjoy was the annual celebration of the Chinese New Year. One of the highlights was a performance of Haydn's 'Toy Symphony', the one that features the sounds of the cuckoo and other special effects. On this occasion it was played by the Cham-Ber Huang harmonica orchestra conducted by Mr Huang, originally from Shanghai and now a member of the Turtle Bay faculty.

What delighted us was that he had also recorded the symphony on a long-playing disc – but without the special effects. These were provided separately in the form of a rattle and toys simulating the sounds of a trumpet, a cuckoo, a nightingale and a quail. The record, together with the toys, was on sale at the end of the concert. The idea was that at parties at home you put the record on the turntable and then five of you tried to insert the special effects at the appropriate moments. We could not resist buying it, and it was to become a hilarious feature of our Christmas parties for many years to come.

Ron

Later the same year, I made another trip to South America, this time to cover the general election in Chile. As the plane approached the capital, I was handed an immigration form, which contained another of those phrases qualifying for our collection of funny foreign English. It read: 'On arriving at Santiago, you will be required to sing three times.'

On this trip I would be working with the BBC's South American correspondent, Adrian Porter, who spoke excellent Spanish, as did the freelance camera crew, two lively lads from Britain. When the result of the election was announced, Salvadore Allende's Marxist Popular Unity party was in the lead, but without an absolute majority. Allende's appointment to the presidency was eventually ratified, but there was a great deal of hostility from the right wing of Chilean politics, supported by the CIA in Washington.

Santiago is a fine city, but tension was extremely high throughout our stay, and the situation was made worse by the amount of illegal currency exchange that was going on. Too many times I was approached by hotel staff or somebody on the street offering to swap the American dollars I was carrying for a stack of Chilean pesos at a rate of exchange far higher than the one set by the government. Obviously this had a destabilising effect on the Chilean currency, as did the CIA in its determination to bring down the new regime led by Allende. You had to be on your guard. Some of the cash exchange offers came from the agents of the new government working in plain clothes. The result was that some people found themselves in prison.

Another hazard was the presence of two or three young men in stylish suits who attached themselves to the newspaper reporters and the TV and radio journalists when we got together over a drink or two at the end of the day. These guys never took out notebooks at the regular news conferences, and the rest of us rarely saw them when we were out and about chasing the latest developments. They claimed to be working for some news agency or publication we had never heard of. They seemed interested only in what we had been doing that day and who we had spoken to. Local reporters were convinced they were working either for the CIA or for the newly elected Chilean government in its effort to keep track of what its opponents were up to. We regarded all of them as irritating spooks. As far as we could, we kept out of their way, but they added to the tense atmosphere that followed the election of President Allende.

Fortunately, some of our film reports took us out of the city and into the superb countryside lying alongside the Andes mountain range. We went to a copper mine and a nearby processing plant. Copper was then – and remained – the country's leading export, but safety standards for miners have never been good. Much later on, in 2010, television viewers all over the world saw this for themselves when thirty-three Chilean copper miners were trapped deep underground by a huge fall of rock. They were down there for several weeks while rescue teams drilled a vertical escape shaft and inserted a specially constructed elevator. One by one the trapped miners were brought to the surface. Every single one of them survived the ordeal.

Just four months after the Chilean election, we were back in South America. This time, the British ambassador to Uruguay, Geoffrey Jackson, had been kidnapped while he was on his way to work in the capital, Montevideo. Getting there was a story in itself. Charles and the crew flew down from Washington, and I agreed to meet them at the airport in Rio de Janeiro. There we all had to buy tickets for the short onward flight on a small local airline to complete our journey. So we approached the check-in desk clutching the American Express and Barclaycards we all carried. The clerk said he was sorry, but they only accepted Diners Club. Our cheeky sound recordist hardly helped matters by saying that he didn't want a meal, he wanted a plane ride. Fortunately, we had enough American dollars between us to solve the problem. However, it didn't end there. When the flight was called, we headed out to the tarmac, only to be confronted with a huge pair of plate glass doors. They were locked. A small crowd of restless passengers just had to stand there while an official went off to search for the key. It took him twenty minutes to find it.

On our first full day in Montevideo, we decided to make a film retracing the missing ambassador's daily car journey from his home in the suburbs to the British embassy. This took us past the American embassy, where we stopped for a few minutes and poked our camera through the outer railings for a few shots of the building. We should have realised that this was a foolish thing to do. Only later did we find out that we had been under close surveillance by embassy security staff.

At about six that evening, we were getting ready for dinner at the hotel when Charles rang me from his room to say that police officers had arrived in the foyer and wanted us all to come downstairs right away. We took just a couple of minutes to tell another reporter staying in the hotel what had happened. Adam Raphael was covering the kidnap story for the *Guardian* newspaper, and promptly decided to accompany us. There were three policemen waiting for us downstairs, one in plain clothes. They checked our passports, including Raphael's, and announced that Montevideo's Chief of Police wanted to question us back at headquarters.

Two large police vehicles whisked us through the evening rush-hour traffic, and the five of us soon found ourselves at police headquarters in a small room dominated by an ominous row of prison cells along one wall. A short man marched in and shook hands with each of us before sitting down and swinging his legs up on top of his desk, which was dominated by a large ashtray made from bullets. He was wearing an expensive-looking pair of cowboy boots. This was the Chief of Police – El Jefe, as he described himself. He flicked through our passports, then checked our wallets and identity cards. During this process, we looked nervously towards the row of cells. They were extremely narrow, and sitting down would be difficult.

We were able to relax a little when El Jefe discovered that Adam Raphael worked for the *Manchester Guardian*, as it was still called at this time (only later was *Manchester* dropped from the front-page title, and the newspaper became just the *Guardian*). El Jefe seemed to know quite a lot about the newspaper, and began to address Adam as 'El Manchester'. However, he said we had been extremely foolish in deciding to film outside the American embassy at a time of great tension in the city without first telling them what we were up to or advising police headquarters of our plans.

We apologised and relaxed as the conversation went on. The police chief then took a closer look at the various pieces of identification we had submitted to him. He seemed fascinated by the fact that our Barclaycards had been issued in Oxford Street. We were almost old pals by the time we were allowed to return to our hotel. The following day, Adam's report on this bizarre encounter was published on the front page of the *Guardian* under the heading 'When El Jefe Met El Manchester'.

We kept busy in Montevideo, trying to track down where Mr Jackson was being held. The organisation that kidnapped him, the Tupamaros guerrillas, were a left-wing group with a history of kidnap and murder. The prospects for Mr. Jackson's survival did not look good. For many years, Uruguay had lived under an authoritarian regime dominated by the military and with no interest in negotiation.

Not for the first time, Charles fielded several requests from the major German TV networks for coverage in their language. These included an interview with the Papal Nuncio in Montevideo. He spoke little or no English. The only phrase that we recalled him uttering in English was when we said farewell and he cried out, 'Be of good cheer, gentlemen!' It was a phrase we kept repeating to each other as the days went by without any word on what had happened to Ambassador Jackson. Between us, Charles and I managed to provide some kind of coverage for radio and television outlets over the next few days, but there was not a word about Mr Jackson's whereabouts, so eventually we flew back to the United States.

Eight long months later, the Tupamaros guerrillas released Mr Jackson. They left him, blindfolded, outside a Roman Catholic church in Montevideo. He was in reasonable shape when found there by the priest who removed the blindfold and gave him coffee. Mr Jackson then asked the priest if he would lead him into the church and hear his confession. Soon there was word from London that he was to be knighted. He would return to London as Sir Geoffrey. Later it became known that the British Prime Minister at the time, Edward Heath, had been involved in negotiating Mr Jackson's release, and that a ransom of £42,000 was paid.

Subsequent trips to South America took us to Argentina and Brazil, and to Chile again. We frequently felt that we were in some kind of time warp, in an atmosphere that was redolent of the thirties. Well, that's what Charles felt. We pulled his leg, saying only he could remember that far back. We worked in studios belonging to one of Argentina's leading broadcasters. They dated from a much earlier era of radio, heavily draped for acoustic purposes and featuring huge microphones on octagonal desks that seemed too flimsy, more like card tables. On one occasion, when Charles was midway through a live report to Broadcasting House in London, the desk began to collapse. He managed to grab the microphone and go down on his knees, supporting the mic on an upturned waste-paper basket and somehow getting through to the final word of his report.

Nearer to home, I frequently found myself on the Eastern Airlines shuttle service to Washington, where Charles Wheeler and Gerald Priestland had their base at CBS, one of the big three television networks. Most of these trips involved some aspect of the continuing war in Vietnam. America had become deeply divided over the issue. Riots and the burning of buildings were all too frequent occurrences right across the nation.

One weekend, a major demonstration was planned in Washington itself, and since the weather was set fair and the nation's capital was a great place for sightseeing, I decided to take Doris and Sarah with me. It was the wrong decision. The city was stiff with security, and my wife and daughter did not have the identification necessary to get through the network of barricades that surrounded the hotel for which we were heading and at which we had hoped to stay. We eventually reached the Wheeler home, and Charles and his wife, Dip, managed to find a room for us in a hotel nearby. In the afternoon, Doris and Sarah would be well away from the tumult that was building up in the heart of the city.

Meanwhile, Charles and I accompanied our camera crew to the area of government offices where the main body of demonstrators was in full voice. We got behind a line of police who were trying to protect one of the most important buildings. The demonstrators advanced on the police, hurling stones and other missiles, some of which whizzed over our heads, striking the stonework behind us and showering down to where we were filming. The police responded with a volley of CS gas and the protesters turned and ran, hurling rocks and explosive fireworks towards us as they made their escape. We tried to get away from the acrid fumes of the gas, but we were burdened with a heavy camera and other equipment, including a tripod. Suddenly something whizzed towards us and struck the tripod. Charles, ever the optimist, cried out, 'It's all right, chaps – it's a firecracker.' It wasn't – it was a canister of CS gas, and we resumed our cumbersome battle to get the hell out of the place and away from the smoke and stinking fumes. It was a forlorn group who arrived back at the Wheeler household, but we recovered swiftly thanks to a little care and attention from Dip, and some generous hospitality.

Next morning we set off on our sightseeing tour. There was little evidence of the events of the previous day, apart from the smell of CS gas still hanging in the trees. We went off to see some of Washington's outstanding Smithsonian museums, including our favourite, the one dedicated to Air and Space and recalling for us the exhilarating time we had spent at Mission Control in Houston during the Apollo 11 mission and man's very first steps on the moon's surface.

Some time later, a much happier trip to Washington was for the wedding of my assistant, Caroline Ellis. Several of us from the New York office went down by train, always the best way to arrive in the nation's capital. The imposing Union Station was more than a hundred years old, built out of white granite. What made the wedding extra special was that the groom was none other than the *Guardian*'s correspondent in Washington, Adam Raphael – El Manchester, as he had been nicknamed by the Montevidean chief of police.

The following year we found ourselves in a summer home at Providence in America's smallest state, Rhode Island. We were up there filming the end of a transatlantic yacht race which took the competing crews, including Great Britain's entry, from Plymouth in the English Channel to Rhode Island's Port O'Call. Doris and Sarah had come up with me, and over the weekend we stopped in a motel built right over the water's edge and at night dozed off to the gentle swishing of the incoming tide. We liked it so much we booked it for the rest of the summer, and Doris and Sarah remained there until the new term at school beckoned us back to New York. Most weekends I found myself on the Greyhound bus once again.

Port O'Call was full of characters. Many of them looked as though they had stepped off the front page of the *Saturday Evening Post*, where Norman Rockwell's creations were sometimes criticised for being too sentimental. That might have been the view of cynics in Manhattan, but up there in Port O'Call, the locals looked exactly the way Rockwell depicted them. There was Officer Kelly, swinging his truncheon and smiling broadly, and who came by our motel each morning to see that all was well. There were fishermen and a woman with a fruit stall, and others with fish for sale. Also, there were soda jerks, a dying breed belonging to an era of juke boxes and booth seating. With a touch of showbiz and a great deal of energy, they jerked the handle of the soda fountain back and forth until they obtained exactly the right mix for the particular soft drink you had ordered.

Sarah

The things I liked about Port O'Call were the swimming and the lovely waffles they served for breakfast at the Seamen's Mission. Then there was the coastal walk that took us alongside some of America's oldest and most expensive mansions built by various members of the famous Vanderbilt family along a spectacular sweep of land at the edge of the sea. There was also Doug, who had served with the US forces in Korea. He was the supervisor at Port O'Call, and with his passion for yachts and sailing, he was in exactly the right place. He wore a stylish white hat, with white jeans and canvas boat shoes. I would soon be a teenager, and he was my very first crush.

Doris

One weekend we made the short trip from Port O'Call to Festival Field, where the annual Newport Jazz Festival was taking place. This year was special because Louis Armstrong was topping the bill. Recently he had been seriously ill, so here was an opportunity to pay tribute to him for his outstanding contribution to the story of jazz since his early days in an orphanage in New Orleans. He was not yet quite well enough to play the trumpet, but he sang a selection of his hits and was then serenaded by half a dozen distinguished trumpeters led by the master of be-bop, Dizzy Gillespie. Each of them played one of Armstrong's big numbers, including my own favourite, 'Hello Dolly'. The following year Louis Armstrong died and we had the sad experience of watching his funeral procession on television as it left his home in a corner of Long Island where he had lived for many years.

We had been jazz enthusiasts since we met in our teens, so Manhattan was certainly the place to be. One night we were at Madison Square Garden for a concert by Duke Ellington and his orchestra when suddenly he came to the front of the stage to announce that he had just learned of the death that day of another jazz master, the tenor saxophonist Coleman Hawkins.

Often we took visitors from London to a jazz joint we knew, if we thought they might be up for it. One night we were in Jimmy Ryan's, listening to a group led by Jimmy McPartland. He came over to our table during an intermission, accompanied by his wife. Marian McPartland was an outstanding jazz pianist, and what's more she was English, having been born in Eastbourne, just a short distance from our British home in Saltdean.

Ron

During our last full year in America, we decided to take our annual leave in the form of a Grand Tour, heading west to the Pacific and then south to Mexico before returning to New York. We didn't make detailed plans, beyond booking a return flight to and from Denver, where we would pick up a hire car. The sisters at Cobb gave us their blessing, and we promised to keep in regular postal touch with Lulu along the trail. Leaving Denver, we felt like pioneers, heading north-west under endless blue sky and stopping alongside Native American reservations, as well as in small towns with board-walks and saloons with swing doors where they served steaks even bigger that the ones in New York.

One of our first overnight stops was at Yellowstone in Wyoming. This is the site of one of America's most exciting spectacles – the Old Faithful geyser, which emits a spectacular plume of boiling water, around a hundred and fifty feet high. On average this happens every ninety minutes. Old Faithful has been attracting visitors for 140 years. Competing with it at Yellowstone are bears, wolves, bison, cougars, moose and elk, and we were grateful for the safety, comfort and warmth of our overnight cabin. The area gets very cold at night, down to thirty degrees below in the depths of winter and, indeed, there had been light snowfall as we approached Yellowstone

– and this was in the middle of June. We recalled this a week or so later when we stopped briefly in the Nevada desert and the temperature was over 100 degrees. That – and an ominous rattling sound which we convinced ourselves was a snake – drove us back into our air-conditioned vehicle in double-quick time.

Leaving Yellowstone, we sometimes covered many miles through the creeks and the mountains without seeing another vehicle. Just us under an endless blue sky, following the route that the early explorers in America pursued in their determination to reach the Pacific Ocean. In Seattle, we stayed on Puget Sound in a hotel where, as we observed, you could fish out of your hotel window. One or two guests were actually doing it – though not with approval from the management. Seattle has its other attractions, including its elegant tower and Space Needle, and a lively night life. There are some distinguished fish restaurants, and at the time of our visit it was also the home of the mighty Boeing Aircraft Corporation.

As we resumed our journey south, we soon came upon a theatre at the side of the road in Ashland, Oregon with a billboard proclaiming that night's performance – 'Rosencrantz and Guildenstern are Dead'. This somewhat bizarre play had been written by Britain's Tom Stoppard and featured, in the principal roles, two minor characters from Shakespeare's 'Hamlet'. It had first appeared at the Edinburgh fringe festival just a few years earlier. Well, we were bound to support the old country and go in and see it. The theatre was full and the audience was enthusiastic. So were we once we had adjusted our minds a bit to what was undoubtedly an unexpected and unusual experience.

Sarah

We had a brought a stack of cassette tapes with us to while away some of the time we spent in the car. Most of them were Lulu's favourites – and mine, too – and as we bowled along we would recall the visits we had made to Cobb over the years especially in the winter when the snow piled up high. The four of us would set off to the nearby slopes with a posh toboggan, and I recall my sister crying out with delight as Dad supervised our careful descent.

Mum and Dad remembered visiting Cobb on another occasion when Lulu had caught the mumps. I remained in New York with friends but remember Mum saying, when she returned, that Louise had been sitting up in bed looking like Lady Bountiful, attended by a nurse in an impeccable white uniform. For my parents it was another heartening example of the care and attention Lulu received at Cobb. One of the sisters told them of the confusion that arose when she kept asking for Hovis at breakfast time. Though Hovis bread was sold everywhere in Britain, it was unavailable in the States. Apart from that, my sister coped well with life in another country and was soon referring to her dressing gown as a bath robe, bath being pronounced with a short 'a', as in bat.

I have one special memory of the journey south along California's Pacific coast, and it is of the sea otters. We stopped several times to watch their activities along the stretch called Big Sur. We learned that they belong to the weasel family and, unlike seals, they are covered not by blubber, but by an intensely thick furry coat to keep them warm in the cold coastal waters. After the sea otters came the swallows. As we approached a place called Capistrano, Mum and Dad began singing a favourite tune from their teenage years, 'When The Swallows Come Back to Capistrano'. It was written by a man named Leon René, and it spent several weeks at the top of the hit parade in the 1940s. The upright piano on which he composed it was eventually given pride of place in the Mission San Juan Capistrano. Meanwhile, the swallows continue to leave this beguiling little town in late October and return in late May.

Ahead of us now lay some of America's biggest tourist attractions – Disneyland, SeaWorld, and the cities of San Francisco and San Diego, and we loved 'em all. Only Hollywood disappointed us. We headed towards the huge sign stretched across a hillside proclaiming that we had reached the birthplace of the movie business and expected to see Marilyn Monroe and Paul Newman waving from their verandahs. Perhaps we were a bit travel weary, but the fact was we never really got to grips with Hollywood. Dad said we should have done it the easy way on a tourist coach tour with a guide on board to take us to the various studios and the spectacular homes of the famous. Following that, we would have been shown round one of the big movie studios. Instead we had to settle for the Hollywood Walk of Fame, where big names of today and yesterday are immortalised with a star and inscription set into the pavements of Hollywood Boulevard and Vine Street. All of this dates from the late fifties, and we were surprised to learn that Charlie Chaplin was not included to begin with because of what Dad called 'aspects of his private life'.

Doris

San Francisco was everything we had expected – after the hotel management dealt with a leaking pipe in our room. We had to be moved to another floor with a better view. In this city, there were great views in all directions. At every opportunity, we rode the historic tramcars with their distinctive clang-clang. One day we headed for a popular tourist spot known as Fisherman's Wharf, where, among the various features, was a building promoting 'Ripley's Believe It Or Not'. I knew about Ripley because it was a hugely popular feature in a New York newspaper, and Sarah and Ron were among its devotees. Its strip cartoon style dealt with weird and wonderful items, some of them downright bizarre. We agreed that we would return to Fisherman's Wharf the following day, and the other two would spend some time in Ripley's emporium while I went shopping before meeting up again in the Ripley foyer.

My only problem with the city was that the temperature there is much affected by the cool currents of the Pacific Ocean, and in high summer it has the coldest maximum and minimum temperatures of all the major US cities. Unfortunately I am someone who still feels the cold when everyone else is complaining about the heat, so after an hour or so shopping I decided to collect husband and daughter and go off with them for a hot drink. There was no sign of them at our agreed rendezvous, and mobile phones had yet to be invented. I hung about for a while feeling wretched, and finally approached the man in the Ripley pay kiosk and asked if I could pop in for a couple of minutes to collect husband and daughter. I found them totally absorbed by the oddities around them. They were not best pleased to see me, saying they were only halfway round. This was a rare moment of dissent between us. Generally we got on well together, thanks to a close bond that arose from our care and concern for Lulu. Friends and relatives were aware of it and referred to us as The Three Musketeers.

Ron

A happier day saw us driving across San Francisco's Golden Gate Bridge and heading for Muir Woods to see some of the world's tallest living things. These are the coastal redwood trees, and in this part of America they grow to more than 250 feet high. Further north they are even bigger. Fortunately, as we parked the car, Doris didn't spot a sign announcing that Muir Woods is damp and cool all year through. In fact, great shafts of golden sunlight were slanting down between the redwood branches. For about an hour we followed a nature trail led by one of the rangers employed by the National Park Service. Our man was a walking encyclopedia on every living thing in those woods, and we enjoyed our visit there as much as any of the other highlights of our years in the United States. He used a tool to test the age of the tree; he inserted it into the trunk, and when he removed it he was able to give us a complete history of the tree and its environs, going back many centuries.

Above:
Ron's radio début – 'And now the weather…SNOW!'

Above:
Sarah snapped by the New York press as the *Bremen* arrives in Manhattan.

Above:
Lulu's sixth birthday party at her American school.

RON ONIONS, Television News Organizer, New York, sends ARIEL this dispatch on the problems of getting news out of Anguilla. . . No telephone system . . . no scheduled air service . . . no control tower. . .

WE were on a six-seater plane from St Thomas in the U.S. Virgin Islands and the pilot was preparing for the descent to the dustbowl that passes for an airport on Anguilla. Then he changed his mind. The indicator light showing whether the plane wheels were down had not come on. So he banked against the sun and looked down at the plane's shadow. Thankfully, it had wheels. . .

We took off in the same plane a couple of hours later. The battery was flat and to turn the engines over they had to trundle a beaten-up Austin to the side of the plane and connect up to the car battery.

Anguilla was that kind of story. The island's telephone system was blown down in a hurricane several years ago and they had not replaced it. And, with only half a runway and no control tower, there was no scheduled air service. So every phone call, every film consignment to London, meant a plane trip for either Washington Correspondent Charles Wheeler or myself. We took whatever was going—anywhere. We flew to Antigua (British) in the huge R.A.F. supply aircraft and chartered the 'mini' to St Thomas (U.S.) or to the nearby Dutch-French island of St Maarten.

Charles Wheeler was the first of the BBC team to arrive on Anguilla. Following him soon afterwards were Alexandra Palace cameraman Peter Matthews and sound recordist Bill Norman, who had been just about to start a three-month stint as the news camera team in the United States. I joined them to make things easier for Wheeler, who had been reporting for television and sound radio, and coping with the problem of shipping film. For a few days his feet had literally barely touched the ground.

We had two weeks on Anguilla in the first instance and returned a week later, after a lull in the story, for another ten days. It was a hectic assignment, but not without its lighter moments. There was the occasion when one British policeman of my insufficient acquaintance introduced me to another as 'Mr Wheeler's sound effects man'. I think the second bobby was a wee bit disappointed when I failed to produce a pair of coconut shells and give him a quick burst of galloping hooves. Then there was the time when we scrambled off Anguilla to cover the State of Emergency on Montserrat, forty minutes

away in one of those charter planes. Waiting at Montserrat Airport after a lightning tour of the island, I said to nobody in particular: 'I wonder what's happening on Anguilla?' Cameraman Matthews had been listening to the World Service news on a transistor and the following conversation took place:

Matthews: *'Don't worry, they say Anguilla's quiet.'*
Onions: *'Who says?'*
Matthews: *'The BBC.'*
Onions: *'That was me, mate. As soon as we*

Ron Onions (*left*) and Charles Wheeler hold an impromptu script conference

got here, I *'phoned to say Anguilla was quiet.'*

Peter Matthews was unaware that on arrival in Montserrat I had managed to get a call to London via the BBC's New York office and filed a report which I had written on the plane from Anguilla.

At this point, Charles Wheeler had left Montserrat ahead of us, clutching a bag of film. At the very last minute, he had grabbed a seat on a plane bound for Antigua, where a BOAC VC-10 would be taking off shortly for London—an excellent film flight. Arriving in Antigua, Charles Wheeler sought out the BOAC freight manager, praised him for all his recent efforts in dispatching our newsfilm to London and said the BBC were confident that BOAC would not let them down now. The BOAC manager, a very nice

man, made reassuring noises. Five minutes later, the poor chap had to inform Wheeler that the flight had been cancelled. Of all things, maintenance problems in Barbados!

But generally BOAC did us proud. So did Pan Am. And so did my assistant in New York, Caroline Ellis, and the BBC's shipping agents there, Nehls and O'Connell, who frequently had to field film shipments at all sorts of odd hours and hurry them on to London. That's why we kept ahead of the opposition.

Amid all the flying, we made one boat trip—a Sunday morning excursion from Anguilla to St Maarten with the *Panorama* team (David Dimbleby, producer Barry Sales, and cameraman Eric Durschmied). It was a small craft with an outboard motor belonging to the hotel where *Panorama*

were based. Our departure did not go unnoticed. Neither did our return. Scotland Yard men studied the round trip through binoculars. We had departed illegally, without benefit of Customs or Immigration. And what's more, we were told, returned illegally. All this we learned later in the day when two senior police officers came round to see us 'in the course of certain enquiries arising out of a boat trip, etc., etc. . . '. They were very understanding about it and simply passed on the request from Assistant Police Commissioner Way that he should be informed in advance if the BBC proposed to make any further illegal departures or arrivals.

After that, we resumed our Caribbean jet set circuit in those toy planes. Whatever else was wrong with them, their arrival and departure was always strictly legal.

2

Above:

Ron and Washington correspondent Charles Wheeler hold an impromptu script conference on the rebel island of Anguilla.

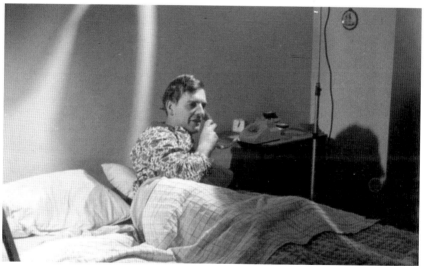

Above:
In the New York studio, with assistant Caroline Ellis, Ron links up
with London for the daily news conference.

Below:
It never ends – a 2 a.m. call from London about a breaking story in Los Angeles.

Above:
The LBC team, with Ron and
Doris (centre), line up for a relay
race from London to Windsor.
We came 24th out of 25.

Below:
Reporting for Essex Radio, Sarah
looks the part on a training
session with local firemen.

Above:
The three of us outside Buckingham Palace
after the Queen presented Ron with the OBE.

Above:
Heading from Capri (where the judging took place) to Naples for the
presentation of the annual Prix Italia broadcasting awards.
Ron was the British judge on the panel.

Below:
Lulu tries out a suitable hat for summer.

Sarah

Next stop, Mexico. Dad said it wasn't all that far away, and so we continued to head south, crossing the border at Tijuana. There were long queues in both directions at the customs and immigration checkpoint. So many poor Mexicans were trying to cross into the States to find work and a better way of life. Many died in the process, trying to sneak across Mexico's straggling and hazardous border with Arizona, New Mexico and Texas. We wandered around Tijuana for a while, but I was soon aware that my parents found it a somewhat tense experience. There was plenty of evidence of low life, including the illegal trade in drugs. The stuff was much cheaper than on the other side of the border in the States. Many Americans came to Tijuana for the nightlife, but Mum and Dad decided not to hang around.

So we bought some postcards to let everyone know we had crossed the Mexican border, not forgetting at the top of our list one for Lulu and the sisters up there near the border with Canada. We also did some souvenir shopping, and I remember going back through customs clutching a large toy donkey made from stout cardboard covered with strips of green and red paper for his coat. Mum and Dad went for a chess set made from onyx. The donkey disintegrated some years ago but the chess set – with all its pieces – is still around.

Ron

Now we were heading north, and ahead of us lay more of America's spectacular scenery and famous places. It was in California's Mojave Desert, at a place called Needles, that we experienced a temperature over 100 degrees Fahrenheit and a rattling sound coming out of a clump of cacti that convinced us we were in the presence of a snake. So, swiftly on to Las Vegas, Nevada. Here we took a short trip up to the Hoover Dam, the mighty structure built in the thirties to control flooding in the area, as well as supplying water for irrigation and hydro-electric power. More than a million people a year now visit the place. The Hoover Dam statistics are overwhelming – not least the fact that 100 men died during its construction.

That night, the three of us left our motel on the dazzling Las Vegas Strip in search of fun and games. What we found was a huge gambling casino which also catered for the younger members of the family. The place had been so constructed that parents were able to battle with the one-arm bandits and other ways to lose money on the first floor just above a huge oval-shaped ground floor reserved for kids only. It meant that children were able to spend their time playing with a huge array of games and amusements under the supervision of casino staff and in clear view of Mum and Dad just a short distance above them. Sarah got rather more out of this arrangement than her reckless father on the fruit machines, but Doris, who has a lucky streak, managed to quit at the right time and end up ahead. For all three of us it was a happy introduction to an amazing city in the middle of a desert.

Sarah

Our long and winding road now took us to places that I had studied in geography lessons at my school in Manhattan, though nothing I had learned compared to actually being right there at the Grand Canyon. Just as overwhelming was Bryce Canyon in Utah, with its extraordinary and colourful rock formations dating back thousands of years. The rangers there claimed you could see 7,500 stars at night because the sky was so dark. I soon stopped counting.

At the age of eleven, the place that captured my imagination more than any other gave me the exciting chance to be in four different states at one and the same time. This was at a remote place known as Four Corners, and it is so called because it marks the exact intersection of the rigidly straight borders of New Mexico,

Utah, Colorado and Arizona. The point where the borders criss-cross is marked by a granite and bronze disc set into the ground, and by taking up a crab-like posture, you are able to place your hands in two of the states and your feet in the remaining two. That's what I did – but unfortunately Dad's photo of this momentous event seems to have gone missing. This fascinating place is run by Native Americans from the Navajo nation, and each year visitors drive a long way off the main tourist routes to see it. The whole experience reminded me of a boxed game I had back in the apartment. It was about states and capitals. At one point in my life I could answer every single question.

Doris

Sometimes, in the car, we wondered about Lulu and how she was faring far away at Cobb School. Might it have been possible to bring her with us on this marathon trip? Sadly, we concluded probably not. However, we recalled that, one Easter, when the sisters were in retreat, we had collected her from Altamont and drove to Virginia to spend a long weekend there.

It had worked out reasonably well, and we visited some of the famous civil war battlefields and toured the Blue Ridge Mountains of Virginia, commemorated in song by everybody from Laurel and Hardy, with their 'Trail Of The Lonesome Pine', via John Denver and Earl Scruggs, to Dolly Parton. We also took in Monticello, the home of the third US president, Thomas Jefferson, author of the Declaration of Independence. It was a beautiful building which Jefferson had designed himself. It was also child-friendly, and Louise was on good form throughout. Later, Sarah looked after her at our overnight motel while we popped out to an adjoining restaurant for an excellent meal, spoiled only – according to my husband – by the wandering violinist who came to our table seeking reward for playing badly.

Ron

The last leg of our touring marathon took us through the Rocky Mountains and on our way to Denver, where it had all started, to board our jet plane back to the Big Apple. As it turned out, we were lucky to get there safe and sound. As the plane approached New York's La Guardia Airport, I was aware of a certain amount of tension among the cabin crew. I was sitting by the window seat across the aisle from Doris and Sarah, and when I looked down I could see a long row of ambulances, each displaying a rooftop red cross. Then came the announcement from the pilot's cabin. There was a problem. The nose wheel was not working properly. I learned later that its function is to prevent the plane from tipping forward when it begins its touchdown on the runway. Doris and I looked at each other. We were both thinking of that time in Anguilla when we were about to touch down not knowing if the landing wheels had descended. Yet, once again, the plane got us down safely and we stood in a long queue of thankful passengers waiting to shake the hand of our pilot.

After nearly five successful and generally happy years in the United States, we began to think about the eventual move back to England. The initial agreement with the BBC had been that the assignment to New York was for four years, subject to review at the end of the period. When the serious conversations began, they came up with the possibility of a new assignment in Tokyo. With the continuing development of satellite systems, Tokyo had become a hot spot in worldwide news communication. Well, we had enjoyed that trip to Japan two years earlier but felt there were a number of major considerations against such a move. The first was Lulu. We felt that it was unlikely that what had been achieved at Cobb Memorial School could be matched in Japan.

Then there was Sarah to consider. She had managed to do well in an unusual educational environment at the Rudolf Steiner School in New York, but by now we had developed a roses-round-the-door view of the Old Country which placed her under the Union Jack in an English grammar school and, later, at a British university. Cue 'Land of Hope and Glory'. So we said no to Tokyo.

Doris

To add to our dilemma, it was just at this point that Berlitz got in touch with me about a much bigger project than the one I had been involved in a year or so earlier. It was tempting. Ron said it could be a nice little earner. However, my mind was made up. I wanted to go home.

Ron

The next suggestion from London was much more difficult to resist. What about replacing Charles Wheeler in Washington? Charles – Sir Charles, as he became – was in the middle of a distinguished career as a reporter and correspondent in newspapers, radio and television. His return to London by the end of the year would leave a major vacancy in six months' time.

I was taken aback. I had worked with him as reporter and producer on a number of major assignments in North and South America and the Caribbean, but the idea of actually replacing him – and this isn't false modesty – was difficult to take in. Once again, though, there were the same considerations over the children. We might have found somewhere for Lulu in Washington, but we stuck rigidly to our thoughts on Sarah's future back in Blighty. To be honest, we had a growing desire to be back there ourselves. So we said no again.

Now the logistics of our return home must be sorted out. I had to remain in New York until Christmas to hand over to my successor – yet to be appointed – but Doris was anxious to get back to London by late summer so she could sort out a school for Sarah before the start of the autumn term. So it was agreed that the three of us would sail home in August with some favourite possessions from the apartment, giving me the opportunity while I was in Britain for a short time to try and sort out my future with the Beeb – though, having turned down two prestigious jobs, I felt I now had a poor hand of cards. Meanwhile, the sisters kindly agreed to continue looking after Lulu at Cobb Memorial School and I told them I would continue visiting her there on returning from London until the two of us said our final farewells and flew back home at Christmas.

With the American school year behind us, Doris and Sarah said a tearful goodbye to the Big Apple and the three of us boarded the *QEII*. The vessel had been launched only recently as a replacement for the original *Queen Elizabeth*. Close friends came on board for a farewell drink, and a formidable posse from Sarah's school gathered on the quayside to ensure that we were sent off in some style. It was a time for tears, and especially so when, as the *QEII* moved out into the Hudson River, over the intercom came the sound of 'I Am Sailing'.

With the weather on our side, this time we had a millpond crossing, leaving us to our nostalgic thoughts as we recalled the prediction of the woman on the outward journey that the years we spent in America would change our lives. She was right. Now I worried about what the return to Britain would bring. Not just for Lulu, but for the rest of us as well. In my own case, I was depressed, feeling that going home by sea was a bit of an indulgence and that I really ought to be back in London trying to resolve my future with the BBC.

The Saltdean bungalow had been let twice during our time abroad and two babies had been born there, but we gave it an energetic spring-clean and settled back in happily enough. I spent several days in London, visiting my mother and also resuming the conversations with various people in both the News and Current Affairs sections of the BBC about what I was going to do next. Unfortunately, I didn't get very far.

I flew back to New York and went up to Altamont to see how Lulu was getting on. She seemed fine. Suddenly she said in a loud voice, 'It's eighty degrees out there,' and one of the younger sisters explained that Louise picked this up from a weather forecaster on a local radio station. She had also added, 'Two Four Six Eight, Who Do We Appreciate' to her expanding vocabulary after making her modest contribution to the New York State Olympics for the Mentally Handicapped.

My last major assignment before saying farewell to New York took me back to Chile, this time for the state visit of Fidel Castro, the colourful – and controversial – leader of Cuba. It took place a year or so after the election of Allende as the Chilean president. It was not an easy assignment because of heavy security all over the place. When the two leaders paraded through the streets in an open-top car, foreign television reporters and camera crews were virtually barricaded into a small area, giving us only a brief glimpse of Castro and Allende as they drove past us. There were other frustrations. The following day I had planned to rendezvous with the BBC's South America correspondent, Adrian Porter, and film a longer report on the Chilean economy and the political divisions between left and right. Unfortunately, at such a busy time, I had not managed to book a hotel in the centre of Santiago and had to settle for a place some way out of town. Fortunately there was a taxi rank outside. Unfortunately the cab broke down after a couple of miles on a lonely road. The driver shrugged his shoulders and I had no option but to trudge the rest of the way into Santiago, feeling sorry for myself and concluding that someone up there was saying something – that it really was time to go home to Britain.

Back in New York, my successor, Denis Donovan, had arrived and the two of us shunted around town on an introductory tour for him and, for me, an opportunity to say a long, slow farewell to the contacts I had made – some of them now close friends – during the previous four years.

Soon it was time to leave New York, and the BBC sent me off in some style at a memorable party in the Fifth Avenue offices. I had a day to recover, fortunately, but then had to take a Mohawk Airlines flight up to Albany and collect Lulu from Cobb Memorial School. After picking up an airport hire car, I drove slowly through the snow to Altamont for the last time. Saying goodbye to the sisters was not easy, and the care and kindness Lulu received at Cobb would remain in our memories and help sustain us in the years ahead.

Back at the airport, we found ourselves involved in one of those unfortunate little dramas that were part of Lulu's life. We were standing in the queue waiting to settle the car-hire bill. Behind us stood a couple holding the hands of their little daughter. Suddenly the child began crying and then screaming. Lulu promptly turned round and, extending her arms rigidly towards the toddler, pushed her to the ground. Somehow I managed to apologise and explain our circumstances, but I sensed that the fact that we were foreigners was not exactly a point in our favour.

Albany was not my favourite airport. On a previous occasion, when I was waiting there with Lulu on our way home to New York for Christmas, she announced that she wanted to go to the ladies' lavatory. So, alone, in she went, but I soon sensed that too much time was going by and then became aware of an increasingly noisy banging sound coming from within. At this point a young woman emerged from the ladies' loo looking somewhat concerned, and there was nothing for it but to ask for her assistance. Would she kindly ensure that there was nobody else using the ladies' and would she then please stand on guard at the entrance while I nipped in and rescued my dear daughter? The cubicle door had been only partially locked by Lulu and somehow I managed to jiggle it open. Together we made a brisk exit, Lulu in tears and father trying not to look furtive.

We arrived back in New York to spend our very last night in the apartment and set off the following morning to catch a morning flight to Heathrow on Transworld Airlines. The cabin crew on the now sadly defunct airline rather took to Louise, making a fuss of her, and she was as good as gold throughout the journey. In London there was a car waiting to take us off to Saltdean, and when we arrived at the bungalow, Lulu advanced on the front door, clapping and cheering. It was Christmas and we were all together again.

In the new year, the BBC gave me a couple of weeks to help sort out our domestic affairs. Then it was time to report for duty in the newsroom, now relocated in the new BBC Television Centre in west London. Much had changed after the move from Alexandra Palace. Some of the principal figures had gone elsewhere, including Peter Woon, who had been appointed Editor of Radio News at Broadcasting House in Central London. The new Editor of Television News was a talented man, but somewhat eccentric.

I had first met him six years earlier during my brief spell on the 'Tonight' programme, and I had met him again only recently when, in his new role, he was chairman of a panel vetting applicants for a job which would, for me, have meant moving up a peg in the television news hierarchy. I was flown back to London for my interview. The panel chose someone else.

Six months after returning to Britain, as the family tried to readjust to life in the Old Country, my future within the BBC seemed increasingly uncertain. The trouble was that, during my last weeks in New York, one of the grandees in BBC News administration had gone over the top and assured me, in writing, that I should regard the Corporation as my oyster and that I would be given plenty of time for consultation before deciding on my next job. This was a foolish thing to put in writing, and I was foolish enough to believe it.

In the event, after a couple of weeks spent talking to the contacts I had in the Current Affairs department of the BBC, the prospects dwindled to Deputy Foreign Editor or a seat back on the sub-editors' desk. The new Editor of TV News spoke not of oysters but of the need to make my bloody mind up – and quickly. In a foolish display of petulance, I said I didn't see myself as deputy to anyone and I would go back on the subs' desk. So I took my seat there and, uncannily, almost the first story I worked on was the crash of a Fairchild Hiller aircraft at Albany airport, killing 16 passengers and one person on the ground. Soon, though, I developed that snakes-and ladders feeling I had experienced when I had first walked into the newsroom at Alexandra Palace seven years earlier.

If all this has the ring of self-indulgence in someone who was being unnecessarily bolshie, I can only point to the stressful situation that had developed at home in Saltdean during the two months since I had brought Lulu home from America and to the fact that my mother had been diagnosed with Parkinson's disease. My sister Iris had first expressed concern about her in a long telephone conversation with me during our last Christmas in New York. After our father's sudden death two years earlier, Mother had continued to live in the family home in North London where Iris and I were both born and which she now shared with an old family friend, Percy Adams. He did what he could to look after her, but while he was at work during the day she had taken to leaving the house in a distressed state and wandering off. Usually a neighbour would catch sight of her and lead her back home. Sometimes a kindly passer-by went to her assistance until a neighbour came to the rescue. Occasionally she stayed at my sister's home in Hertfordshire, where she was well looked after, but her occasional bouts of odd behaviour increased my sister's concern for her.

We managed to go and see her at the Enfield house occasionally, and I sometimes overnighted there when the shift pattern at Television Centre would have meant a long late-night train journey back to the coast. She seemed to derive some comfort from the few hours I spent with her as we talked of old times and how much the grandchildren meant to her, but whenever I rang Percy it was obvious he was finding the situation increasingly burdensome.

We had to find professional care for my mother. Eventually she was admitted to a gloomy but secure care home in Essex. She was not happy there. So they moved her to a place in Surrey which was smaller and friendlier. Finally they found a place for her at a new care home in Enfield, where at least she was close to family and friends, who were thus able to visit her regularly.

Doris

There were still two other domestic problems to resolve. The first was finding a residential home for Lulu, and the second a place for the rest of us in London so I could be close to work and Sarah could transfer to a London grammar school. When she and I had come back to Saltdean the previous autumn, Sarah had begun classes at Tideway School in Newhaven, which was part of the new – and controversial – comprehensive system.

At this time, a psychiatrist from East Sussex County Council made occasional visits to the bungalow to see how we were faring with Lulu. Invariably, she was as good as gold when he turned up. I insisted that our daughter required residential care in her own interests and in those of the rest of the family. I think he was doing his best, but nothing happened until a health visitor from the County Council called on a day when Lulu was behaving badly.

Just a few days later we heard from the County Council that they had found a possible place for Lulu in Gloucestershire. Apparently it applied some of the principles followed by Rudolf Steiner, though it was not part of that organisation that we knew of from our experience in New York, where Sarah had attended the Steiner school for normal kids.

A few days later, we drove to Gloucestershire. We had some immediate misgivings when we arrived. Few words were exchanged as the principal led us into a large conservatory serving as the reception room. It was completely shaded by venetian blinds. A group of children in uniform stood watching us. They were uncannily quiet. The principal spoke in a European accent we found it difficult to identify. She studied Lulu intently as we sat down. Our daughter was quiet but clearly confused by the situation. The principal said she wanted to see how Lulu reacted to light and shade, and adjusted the blinds accordingly. Lulu seemed not to react at all.

After an interminable period of nothing very much happening, the principal announced that she would accommodate Lulu for a trial period. She pronounced these words as though she was making a considerable concession. They did not bring us as much relief as we had anticipated, but after a tearful farewell we drove away hoping that it would work out to everybody's benefit – not least, Lulu's.

Ron

It didn't work out. A few weeks later, after several desultory telephone conversations concerning our daughter's progress – or, as we surmised, lack of it – we received a call in Saltdean as dusk was falling at the end of a golden day in late spring. The message was clear: 'We cannot cope with her. You'll have to come and collect her by next weekend.' So angry was I that I decided to drive to the wretched care home immediately. It was a foolish thing to do, but I just wanted to see our daughter back without any delay in what at least strove to be a loving and caring environment.

After a stressful drive up to London and west along the motorway, I arrived at around midnight. Lulu was awakened from her bed and struggled slowly into her clothes. I took her by the hand and led her to the car holding her small bag of belongings for the journey back to Saltdean. We arrived home at three o'clock in the morning.

Just a few hours later I was due on shift at Television Centre. The day did not start well. I just missed the first bus out of Saltdean, but managed to flag down a tourist coach and – highly irregular, this – beg a lift to a point near Brighton rail station. There I was confronted with an announcement that, because of problems on the line, trains to Victoria were being diverted through Littlehampton further down the coast.

I arrived in the newsroom an hour and a half after the shift had started. 'What time do you call this?' demanded the Editor of the

Day, as they were known, loudly. He didn't deserve an answer, and I didn't give him one, beyond saying that the trains were running late. I sensed that some instinct persuaded him to drop the matter.

Doris

A few days later we were presented with an opportunity to leave the country. If only we could have snapped it up there and then, we might never have come back. It all began with a formal dinner for TV news staff and partners to commemorate the fiftieth anniversary of the BBC at a central London hotel. Raffle tickets were on sale and the big prize was a fortnight's cruise through the Mediterranean on the *Orsova*. All you had to do was to guess the vessel's present location in terms of latitude and longitude. What we did was to base our entry on the numbers in our New York address – 411 East 53rd Street. It was the winner. The reaction in the room was one of disbelief. For goodness' sake, we were the couple who had spent the previous four years travelling extensively – mainly at work, but also on holiday – in the United States and Canada, as well as the Caribbean, Mexico and South America, and who had also had a working trip en route for home leave that took in Honolulu and Japan.

The only slight disappointment for us was that the *Orsova* was not sailing right away. Our cruise was scheduled for the summer of the following year. Still, the win was a rare and exhilarating moment in that first year back in Britain. Generally it had not gone very well for us.

Nationally, it was a time of strife and turmoil. Prime Minister Edward Heath and the Conservative government wrestled with both serious inflation and a prolonged miners' strike which had had serious consequences, including a three-day week for many employees. There were also frequent power cuts which had left us with only candlelight in the Saltdean bungalow.

When Ron was on the late shift, I used to drive to Brighton

station to pick him up, leaving the children fast asleep at home. Often there were no lights along the windy coast road into Brighton. I found it an ordeal. I had never been a confident driver – perhaps because the examiner who supervised my driving test had said afterwards, 'I'll pass you, but I never want to meet you on the road.' I try to assure myself that it was a joke . . .

One night, after parking in the dimly lit area around the station, I advanced towards a figure striding towards the exit. I assumed this was my nearest and dearest. I was wrong. It turned out to be Sir Laurence Olivier, returning to his seafront home after that night's performance in the West End. Ron was huffy about my mistake. He insisted that Sir Laurence was much older than him.

As the weeks went by, and with high summer approaching, the Lulu problem had still to be resolved. After the depressing experience with the care home in Gloucestershire, we seemed no nearer to finding a place for her. The psychiatrist from the County Council still came to the bungalow from time to time. Lulu was invariably on her best behaviour then, but I continued to insist that I was worried about the strain her continued presence was having on the rest of the family and, not least, on myself.

One day, we had a visit from a county social worker, and this time Lulu unleashed one of her terrible tantrums. The result of this was that over the next few weeks, the two of us were taken by car to visit a number of care homes in the county in the hope that somewhere suitable place would be found. For one reason or another, it was not to be. We drew a total blank.

Another frustrating experience followed when we visited friends in Southampton and took the opportunity to drive out to our former home in Locks Heath, where Lulu had spent the first months of her life. We had not forgotten the conversation we had at a party in New York with a United Nations scientist. We had told him about the births of two babies in that big old house; one of them was Louise, and both of them had thyroid problems. He had urged us to try and obtain samples of water from the building and have them analysed in a laboratory. Imagine our reaction on arriving in

Locks Heath and turning into the drive only to discover the old house no longer existed. It had been demolished to make way for an estate of new homes.

One plus factor in Saltdean at this time as the weeks went by was that, down the hill, we had retained the beach hut that we had first rented before we went to America. Lulu was never happier than when we were able to spend long sunny days down there. She would spend hours running in and out of the ocean and throwing herself without fear out of a small inflatable boat, under very close supervision. She had developed this breath-taking technique during our summers in America, where she learned how to swim, more or less – or perhaps how not to sink would be more accurate. For all of us, once more, that beach hut by the sea and the chance to sit together over a happy family picnic took a great deal of stress out of our situation.

Meanwhile, we had stepped up the search both for a house in Greater London – partly to cut out that long and sometimes hazardous journey between the Sussex coast and Television Centre – and also for a school for Sarah in London before the autumn term began. We found the right house just outside Kingston upon Thames, overlooking the river and with a walled garden at the rear. The school we had targeted was close by – Tiffin Girls' School, then, as now, a state grammar school with an outstanding reputation.

The head, Miss Weedon, was a formidable figure, to say the least. I handed her Sarah's school records from America, but she seemed less than enthusiastic about a Steiner pupil educated in, of all places, midtown Manhattan. This might be unfair on Miss Weedon, but certainly she came across as austere. In any event, Sarah spoke up well, with only occasional hints of an American accent. A week later Miss Weedon wrote to say that Sarah would be admitted to Tiffin at the start of the autumn term.

A few days later, we had a call from East Sussex County Council informing us that, following the Gloucestershire debacle, they had found a possible place for Lulu, much closer to Saltdean, at Halland, a few miles from Lewes. It was a private venture by a man who had a son with learning difficulties, and it had received formal approval from the County Council.

We took Louise to meet the principal, a young woman named Jane, who became one of the significant figures in Lulu's life at that time. Nearby, there was a day school for children with special needs, and Jane would arrange our daughter's attendance there five days a week. The date for Lulu's move to Halland was critical. It meant that we would be able to move up to our new London home just a few days before the start of the autumn term at Sarah's new school in Kingston-upon-Thames.

Ron

It was at this point, just as we seemed to be surmounting our domestic difficulties, that we were suddenly confronted with a situation involving our first-born, Sarah, which almost overwhelmed us. It began late one Sunday afternoon when, as she often did, she went off to spend a couple of hours with a friend, Lynne Montague, who lived close by. We expected her to return by eight o'clock as she always did. On this occasion, she was more than half an hour late, so I went down to Lynne's place to collect her. There was no reply. We knew Lynne's parents well – they had been guests at our homecoming party eight months earlier – so I hurried off to a favourite haunt of theirs on the coast road, where I found them having a quiet drink at the bar. Lynne was with them. She told me that Sarah had gone off with a boy who was at their school in Newhaven.

I looked up the boy's address in the phone directory and headed off down a nearby side street to a large detached bungalow. Sarah was there. I said little, just that we were getting worried about her. When we got back home, she went straight to bed. She said nothing. The following morning I went into her room and found her in a comatose state. There were several loose pills on the beds. I managed to rouse Sarah and get her on her feet. Doris was in the room by now, tearfully trying to take in what had happened. She had been worrying for some months about the possible effect of all the stress we had been enduring, and had been particularly concerned for Sarah, but this was not the time for questions. They would come soon enough. Somehow we managed to scramble into our clothes, rouse Lulu and help her to get dressed as quickly as possible.

We drove off before the rush hour had started, so there was little traffic on the coast road. Within ten minutes, we entered the Accident and Emergency Department of Brighton General Hospital. We tried to compose ourselves as the doctor carried out a meticulous examination of our daughter. Finally he said she would be OK, but they would keep her in the hospital under observation for the rest of the day. He also said we must make an immediate appointment with a counsellor at the hospital to discuss our family situation.

Years later, as we each began to write our contributions to *Don't Bring Lulu*, Sarah set down her own recollections of what had prompted the events of that awful weekend . . .

Sarah

It was a long while ago, but I can recall feeling increasingly depressed by the difficult circumstances I faced back in Britain. Very little seemed to have gone right since we returned from America. Life with Lulu in that cramped bungalow was getting too much for all of us. Dad was unhappily trying to settle down in his job, and he and Mum were frequently snapping at each other. Nanna's declining health was an additional worry.

As for me, I had become increasingly concerned about the prospect of yet another new school later on in the autumn. I worried about maths because I found it so difficult, and also about some aspects of grammar, even though I loved reading and had a wide vocabulary. I felt that Tiffin Girls' Grammar would be an academic hothouse. Also, I kept recalling the cooped-up feeling I had had in New York, where my parents insisted that I must travel to and from school on a special bus laid on for the younger kids, unlike the children of my age whose parents allowed them to travel on public transport. The other thing was I never felt completely at ease in the Steiner classroom, where the routines were so different from the junior school I had previously attended in Saltdean. Though I made some friends, too many of my Steiner classmates, all from affluent families, seemed prickly and difficult. Unlike them, I had never fussed over what clothes I wore at school. In England, everyone wore the same uniform. At Steiner, I felt there was pressure on you to look fashionable – at the age of thirteen. Even at playtime in Central Park supervising teachers would comment on what they regarded as unsuitable clothing. At least at Tideway, I was back in the old shabby but comfortable school uniform, which included an orange nylon blouse. I was also an adolescent with a developing interest in boys. In New York the boys had teased me, but now, back in Sussex, they seemed more grown up, more sexually aware.

Then something else happened that left me feeling extremely low. I had assumed that Lynne Montague and I would be just as we were in the years before America. However, though we still spent some time together, she had become close to another girl who liked the skinhead culture that was all the rage among teenagers. To some extent, the skinhead culture and pop music had an influence on us all. One day the three of us were in the playground and I was suddenly aware that Lynne was looking towards me in a way that seemed cold and indifferent. We said nothing, but in that instant I felt that the old relationship of five years earlier was no more. It was a devastating moment.

I still saw Lynne at the weekend occasionally, but it wasn't the same. I found some consolation in a wider circle of youngsters at Tideway School, including older boys. I knew, as I left the bungalow on that fateful Sunday afternoon, that Mum would stop me if she knew where I was going. I felt intense resentment when my father knocked on the door of the boy's house. When we got back home,

I went straight to my room, without saying a word. I was on the edge of puberty and desperately unhappy. Yet even though I thought I had swallowed enough pills to end it all, I can remember dutifully inserting my overnight tooth brace before lapsing into unconsciousness for more than twenty-four hours.

Doris

Many years later, we try not to dwell on what was undoubtedly the lowest point of our lives. Sarah went on to become deputy head girl at Tiffin Girls' and later completed a Master of Arts degree at London University.

At the end of that awful summer it was time to take Lulu to her new home. We worried how she would settle down at Halland after living with us for nine months in the Saltdean bungalow. The answer emerged swiftly – not very well. I suppose it was to be expected, and Jane Reynolds, the young manager, was reassuring about it, saying to us on our first two visits that we had to give our daughter time to settle down. On a third visit we were told of one or two problems arising from Lulu's continuing hyperactivity. We decided to have her home for a few days because we were concerned that the staff at Halland might not be able to continue looking after her. Such was our anxiety that we made the foolish decision to stop giving her the daily intake of thyroxine in the misguided belief that this would help her calm down. On returning Louise to Halland, we explained what we had done. We said we would come back at the weekend to review the situation. On our return, as soon as we turned into the drive at Halland, we realised we had made a foolish mistake. There was Lulu standing behind a ground-floor window, her face pale and without expression. It brought us to tears. We apologised to the carers who were on duty, and it was agreed that the thyroxine tablets would be resumed immediately.

Ron

With Christmas fast approaching, we decided to have Lulu home for the holidays. I drove down to Halland to collect her, and soon after we had arrived back at our new home in Surbiton there was a dramatic banging at the front door. It was a policeman from the nearby station in Kingston. Did we know the whereabouts of a Miss Louise Onions? He said she had been reported missing by a care home in East Sussex. It was at this point that Lulu wandered out of the sitting room to see what was going on. We introduced her to the policeman, who smiled with relief as we explained the circumstances. I then called Halland, where one of the staff explained that somebody on the earlier shift had failed to record Louise's departure in the all-important daily log book.

Doris

With Lulu beginning to settle in at Halland, we were all able to look forward to a more settled – and hopefully happier – existence at our new home overlooking the Thames.

In that first full year back home from America, Lulu was rarely out of my mind. Over breakfast I used to think about her on the school bus that took her from Halland to the special school in nearby Cuckfield and hope that everything would be all right during the journey and in the classroom. I told myself that I was worrying too much, and the first of the annual reports sent to me by the head teacher, Mrs Lyne, read: 'Louise has made good progress and her concentration has improved. Tantrums are not so easily triggered off or as severe as they used to be.'

Later there was the comment that Lulu 'has almost finished book 1a in the Ladybird series'. In our special world, that rated along-side a university degree. Sadly, subsequent reports from Court Meadow were darker in tone, regretting Lulu's total preoccupation with food. This explained her obsession with someone called Gwen whenever we visited. It turned out that Gwen was the cook at Court Meadow.

Ron

At Television Centre it was time for my annual interview. This was a Corporation ritual requiring every member of staff to sit before someone higher up the pecking order to hear a written account of his or her progress – or lack of it – during the preceding year. My interlocutor turned out to be Mr What-time-do-you-call-this? His report did me no favours. I declined the chance of reading it myself – which was an optional part of the procedure – and said I had just one request, and that was that the 'oyster' letter should be left on the top of my file when, as I intended to do, I left the Corporation in the near future. I was referring to the overblown promises I had been given in writing while I was still in New York. Of course, my request was meaningless, but I felt that it reflected my feelings about the BBC and my determination to get out.

There was more to it than that. Recently I had received a phone call from David Dimbleby, whom I had first met when we were both working in Anguilla. David was well established in the media. He presented the BBC's leading current affairs programme, 'Panorama', as well as major political and social events such as the general election, and State occasions like the commemoration of Armistice Day and the weddings and funerals of the royal family. He was also involved in the family newspaper business in Richmond. Now he was showing interest in independent radio. He had become involved in the proposals for a London seminar on this new development in broadcasting, and invited me over to his house in south-west London to talk about my possible involvement.

What emerged from a lively bit of brainstorming was a plan to recruit a small team to present hourly bulletins throughout the day-long seminar. The aim was to offer a lively alternative to the sound of BBC News on the radio. I was happy to be involved. During those years in New York, I had been a keen admirer of the all-news radio stations, CBS 88 and WINS, on the air 24 hours a day. They had a dynamic quality not yet experienced in the United Kingdom. So we signed up the major news agencies to provide a service via teleprinter – those were the days – and any sound clips that were available to embellish the written word. We also recruited a newsreader, while London's evening newspaper, the *Evening Standard*, kindly loaned us a reporter for the day. The newsreader would help me write the scripts. It worked out pretty well.

I cannot recall much about the news that was around on the day of the seminar beyond a breaking story from Washington about the death of J. Edgar Hoover, the famous – some said notorious – head of the Federal Bureau of Investigation, the FBI. Anyway, we had proved a point or two, and the following day I had a call from an Australian who was heading a group intending to apply in due course for a franchise to run one of two independent radio stations proposed for Greater London. He wondered if he could put my name down as Head of News in their application. I said yes.

Before we went to America, we were increasingly aware of the pirate radio stations broadcasting from the North Sea, some operating from forts, others from boats of one kind or another. At Saltdean, Radio Caroline came through loud and clear as an accompaniment to our beach-hut picnics, and all of them pulled in a considerable audience in opposition to the BBC's Light programme, as it was called, which sounded distinctly old-fashioned by comparison.

By the time we came home, officialdom was moving strongly against the pirates. It was claimed by the government that the signals from the North Sea had been interfering with the work of the emergency services, such as the fire brigade and the ambulance service. In due course, the campaign against the pirates led to the passing of the Marine Offences Bill which brought an end to the jolly noises from the North Sea and paved the way for legal commercial radio stations throughout the United Kingdom. There were regular radio announcements about their impending arrival by a man who, for me, in an over-the-top moment, became the Voice of Freedom.

As it turned out, the Australian group that had listed me in its application for a franchise was not successful. The winners were Capital Radio (music) and LBC (news). Capital had chosen a man named Michael Bukht as their programme chief. I knew him slightly from the time he worked for the BBC, as he came over to New York from time to time. So I rang him. He said Capital were looking for a Head of News and arranged for me to see their chairman, Richard Attenborough, and managing director, John Whitney, and they offered me the job, to start as soon as possible.

Doris

Finally the time came for us to claim the prize we had won the previous year and go cruising on the *Orsova*. We had arranged for Sarah to stay with one of the friends she had made at Tiffin and we set off for Southampton in high spirits. As we climbed aboard, a voice cried out, 'OK, Scene Two, Take Three,' and we heard the snap of a clapperboard. Ron cried out, 'Oh, no,' as he spotted a BBC crew filming an episode of a series called 'Doctor West'. As it turned out, we appeared in a number of sequences, including those involving cricket on the foredeck and dancing in the ball-room.

At the First Officer's table in the dining room, we were to meet a couple originally from Yorkshire who became two of our closest friends. Fortunately they were nothing to do with the media. Frank Proctor was a big wheel in British Rail, and he and Pam lived in a delightful home outside Reigate. The *Orsova* took us to Lisbon, Majorca, Sicily, Corfu, Crete and, finally, Athens, where we saw all the sights and then got lost, as well as sore feet, looking for a place called 'Jimmy's Bar'.

Ron

We stayed in touch with the Proctors and invited them down to Sussex for a weekend in late August. Just as I was leaving London, the phone rang. It was my sister. She had been trying to reach me at work and at home to tell me that Mother was dangerously ill. Now it was to say that she had passed away. Elizabeth Amelia Onions was 68.

I spent only six months working for Capital, but I now think of it as perhaps the happiest time of my life. It was the go-getting atmosphere set by Dickie Attenborough and John Whitney plus Michael Bukht's energy and enthusiasm that drove us through the limited time we had to get the station on air by the autumn.

I joined Capital's pioneering team in late July, just ten weeks before we were to go on air. To begin with, we were based in a former car showroom in Piccadilly, just across from Green Park, while the studios were being built in a tower block near Euston station and next door to one of the ITV pioneers, Thames Television. Immediately above us would be a no-go area housing one of Britain's security organisations.

In those few weeks in the showroom, somehow I managed to put together a team of radio journalists to run a round-the-clock radio service. Most were all-rounders, able to work as both reporters and newsreaders. Among them was one I lured from the BBC TV newsroom, as well as others with BBC experience. Also, there were two Australians, one of whom – Greg Grainger – just happened to be wandering past the car showroom during his honeymoon in London and came in to ask if there was any work going. We took him on and were very sorry to see him go when, after several months, it really was time to take his bride back to Sydney.

Shortly before Capital Radio was due to go on air, we said farewell to the car showroom and moved into our brand new home in the Euston tower. It was almost ready, though some of the carpets had still to be put down on newly laid floors. That meant a certain amount of swirling dust, and that was bad news for two reasons: it had a bad effect on broadcasting throats, as well as a possible impact on sensitive – and expensive – broadcasting equipment. In the event, the work was done very carefully and everyone – and every item of broadcasting kit – was in good shape for the big day.

On 7 November, at five o'clock in the morning, the chairman, Richard Attenborough, went into the studio and signalled the station's arrival on air with the words: 'This, for the very first time, is Capital Radio.'

It was a successful launch thanks to a line-up of presenters with experience in the BBC and pirate radio – or, in some instances, in both. They included Kenny Everett and Dave Cash, who, in due course, were to recreate the Kenny and Cash roles they had played out at sea on the pirate station, Big L (Radio London). The news, too, got off to a good start and was rounded off with a chirpy little jingle: 'Capital Radio, In Tune with London'. An old friend at BBC's Broadcasting House rang to say one of their presentation advisors hated it. I was delighted.

One week earlier, the London Broadcasting Company (LBC) had been the first of the new independent radio stations to go on air. It had a dual responsibility. The first was to operate a twenty-four-hour news and information station for the Greater London area, and the second was to provide both a national and a worldwide service of news and information for all of the independent music stations that were scheduled to come on air in the years ahead.

LBC sounded in reasonable shape on its first day, though the choice of a newscaster with a heavy Australian accent to be the first voice on air just seemed inappropriate at this significant moment in the history of broadcasting in Great Britain. John Whitney commented, somewhat cryptically: 'Well, we have sounds coming out of independent radio boxes.'

However, before too long, LBC was in trouble. Too much was going wrong on air. It reached the point where the leading Labour politician, Michael Foot, stood up during a parliamentary debate and suggested that the station 'should be put out of its misery'.

The basic problem, it seemed to me, was that there were too many journalists without any broadcasting experience at all levels of the LBC operation. Far too late in the weeks before the station was launched, several junior production staff from the BBC were signed up to provide the essential skills required to put a non-stop sequence of news and programming to air twenty-four hours a day. In fact I had applied for a job myself at LBC in those miserable weeks when I was desperate to clamber over the BBC barbed wire, but there was no response until some weeks after I had joined Capital.

While the problems at LBC were grabbing all the headlines, Capital, too, began to face problems of its own. There was concern that the station's musical mix was not luring enough listeners away from the substantial opposition coming from the BBC, and specifically from Radios 1 and 2. This was having a consequential effect on our advertising revenue. All eyes – and ears – were on Capital. It was the first and biggest of the new music stations at this early stage of the commercial radio system, and much depended on its success or failure. It had to establish itself quickly as a major force in music radio, not least to encourage the considerable number of other companies throughout the United Kingdom intending to apply for an independent radio franchise.

Michael Bukht called an urgent meeting of key programme staff at his home, and a number of changes were agreed on – notably, the breakfast reunion of Kenny Everett and Dave Cash in a revival of the Kenny and Cash show which had been so successful on the pirate broadcaster the Big L (Radio London). News bulletins were voted a hit. So, too, was London Today, an early-evening round-up of news and features produced and presented by newsroom staff – though one or two DJs were critical of the fact that some of the bulletins ended on what they called a 'downer'. They were referring to news items featuring death and disaster which left the DJ struggling to restore Capital's upbeat tone. They liked the idea of the 'And finally . . .' item which had been introduced by ITN at the end of its television bulletins to ensure a lighter tone in the handover to the succeeding programme. It was a reasonable point, and I said we would do something about it.

Capital's problems seemed manageable compared with the deteriorating situation across town at LBC. Early in the new year, I was talking on the phone to someone at the Independent Broadcasting Authority about some minor matter when he said suddenly, 'Your news operation is too good.' I asked, 'What's that supposed to mean?'

The answer came a few days later during a conversation with Richard Attenborough and John Whitney. They told me they had been talking to senior officials at the Independent Broadcasting Authority (IBA) about the situation at LBC with particular emphasis on the low quality of their news coverage compared with what they were hearing on Capital. I also learned that LBC would announce shortly the appointment of a new Editor-in-Chief, and was told I should expect a call from him.

I knew what that would be about – the obligation placed on LBC under its franchise to set up a separate news service for all the independent radio stations to come via an organisation called Independent Radio News (IRN). At Capital we had been on the receiving end since the day LBC started. IRN came to us in those days before computerisation via teleprinter and a separate audio line carrying clips of sound. It was often slow in responding to breaking news stories and occasionally it displayed a curious sense of news values. On a day when the Bank of England announced a sudden change in the bank rate, IRN seemed preoccupied with 'fears of panic food buying in Austria'.

As an additional aid to communication between Capital and LBC, an extra link was established by installing in both newsrooms an old-fashioned field telephone with a cranking handle to make the bell ring at the other end. This was not a success. The man on duty at IRN, increasingly frustrated by Capital's questions and requests, finally picked up the pesky phone and hurled it to the floor. Game, set and match – but the incident raised serious doubts about IRN's ability to provide its service to all of the commercial radio stations coming on air in the next few years.

151

IRN's basic plan was to enable customers to compile and present their own bulletins using the scripts, reports and clips of sound coming down the line from London. If they wished, they could simply transmit LBC's top-of-the-hour news bulletins reaching them via a separate audio line. They could also choose either one of these options at any time of the day or night. All of this, however, represented a formidable undertaking by IRN, which had set up in opposition to the BBC with all that organisation's sources and resources and its long-established reputation as a news provider.

The call came soon enough from the new Editor-in-Chief of LBC/IRN. He was a man named Marshall Stewart, and he had just left the editorship of the BBC's prestigious breakfast-time programme, 'Today', on Radio 4. Many regarded him as the best of all the 'Today' editors. I knew him slightly. He had rung me during my time in New York to ask if I could set up some coverage of the city's St Patrick's Day parade. He wanted a live contribution that brought 'Today' listeners all the razzamatazz of the parade passing by with an impromptu commentary over the top.

The BBC office in New York was eighteen floors up but directly overlooking St Patrick's Cathedral and Fifth Avenue, along which the parade would proceed in all its strident glory. It worked out fine, except that we had dangled an effects microphone out of one of our front windows, and this eventually caught the eye of the police, who came rushing up, suspecting that some kind of explosive device was about to be set off. Fortunately we had got what we wanted by the time they arrived, but Officer O'Brien and his buddies were not best pleased and said they would be filing an official complaint against us for infringing umpteen City regulations. Happily the complaint never materialised.

It was four years later that Marshall invited me to join him for breakfast at the Connaught Hotel. He spoke quietly and with great enthusiasm. He wanted me to become the editor of Independent Radio News and, as his deputy, to do my bit towards lifting LBC out of its current misery. He said that others joining the cavalry would include BBC production and presentation staff.

I had anticipated what Marshall was going to say long before I arrived at the Connaught, and I knew that, with some reluctance, I was going to say yes to his invitation to join the battle for survival at Communications House, the LBC/IRN base in a little square just off Fleet Street. When the formal offer came in the post, I discussed it with my wife and oldest daughter. Doris said, 'I'm afraid you have to go.' I agreed. So farewell to Cuddly Capital. They sent me off in some style, and Sir Richard wrote me a letter which sits on top of an old box file I still have marked 'Very Good Things'.

Next door to LBC/IRN was Dr Johnson's house, a handsome structure where he would have been able to work in daylight, unlike the subterranean squad now trying to do their thing in the neighbouring building. When I went down to the basement for the very first time, I spotted three or four people who had applied for a job at Capital. I had rejected them after talking to people in the business whose names they had given as references. It was an awkward moment, to say the least.

Sorting out who did what took up a lot of our time. Marshall decided that the three principals in news and programming – himself, myself and Mike Field, whom he had brought in from the BBC as LBC programme controller – should together interview all the editorial and programming staff to try and sort out who did what and whether individual talents might be better employed in a different role. This exercise resulted in many late nights as we pondered how best to use the experience and skills that became obvious during the course of the interviews. There was one memorable distraction when suddenly the door to Marshall's office crashed open to reveal a woman from Administration, swaying from side to side and showing all the signs of a heavy drinking session in the King and Keys. She stared at the three of us in turn and then, pointing a wavering arm towards Marshall, cried out, 'Oh Gawd, look at 'is face.' She left the company the following day.

There was much more to do. The early departure of the original management team – chairman, managing director, editor-in-chief and others – had left a small band of loyal and hard-working producers and duty editors to assume the day-to-day running of the radio station and the IRN service. Frequently they had to cope with the fact that nobody had turned up to replace either themselves or staff working alongside them. This frequently required them to stay on for a double shift. Sometimes, because nothing had been prepared for the following hour or two, the hapless producer had to raid the music library to ensure the station stayed on air. To some extent, the station and the IRN service owed their survival to the dedication of the senior staff and those working under them down there in the gloomy basement at this very difficult time in the station's history. All this had its effect on the holiday roster, and the company had to pay out a considerable sum to compensate for leave that just could not be taken if LBC/IRN was to get through these challenging months. Yet that was the least of our financial problems. It could not have been foreseen, but commercial radio came to the United Kingdom at the worst possible time . . .

A few weeks after LBC and Capital went on air, a three-day working week was ordered by the government because of a slowdown by coal miners and an oil embargo by Arab states. This was an echo of the serious industrial problems that confronted Britain when we had returned home from the United States, resulting at that time in widespread power cuts and serious disruption to industrial production.

The three-day week had a consequent effect on LBC advertising revenue, already depleted as a result of the bad publicity the station had suffered in the first few months after its launch. Additionally, inflation was rising fast, triggering much higher demands in pay negotiations with the trade unions. On top of all this – and to some extent because of it – the opening of further commercial stations outside London had fallen a long way behind schedule. Not until they went on air would they start paying the fee that had been agreed for receiving the IRN service from London. The fee varied according to the size of individual stations. In theory they were able to shop around for a supplier; in practice, they all signed up for the IRN service. The delay in the arrival of IRN fees from outside London put an additional burden on the increasingly serious financial situation at Gough Square.

The major shareholder of LBC/IRN was a Canadian company, Selkirk, based in Toronto. It had appointed one of its top executives, Bill Hutton, to replace the original managing director of LBC. At about the same time, Sir Gordon Newton, the former editor of the *Financial Times*, had taken over the principal hot seat as chairman. His considerable reputation was on the line. His style was slightly eccentric and he would turn up early for board meetings and call for the latest set of advertising figures. On one occasion, he stared at the dismal document set before him, sighing and harrumphing in turn. Then, addressing no one in particular, he cried out, 'Get me Speedwell!' None of us had the courage to ask him who the hell was Speedwell? Without saying a word, a secretary sitting nearby picked up the phone and quietly rang the advertising boss, Dick Seabright.

The financial situation remained grim. At its lowest point in that first full year of LBC's life, advertising revenue fell in one particularly gloomy month to just £4,000. This was for a single commercial plugging the benefits to be derived from – of all things – a bottle of babies' gripe water. Outgoings in that same month, derived from staff and running costs, totalled a quarter of a million pounds.

From Canada, Selkirk assured the broadcasting authority that it would continue to provide financial backing for the ailing company, and LBC received similar support from other shareholders, notably from the Daily Mail newspaper group. However, for those of us in senior management, it was all too obvious that we were in a critical battle for survival. There came a particularly bad week when our bank in London announced that it was no longer prepared to support us.

Sir Gordon shook his head, worried that we might be trading illegally, whereupon three members of the board promptly got on a plane to Toronto to discuss the situation with our Canadian owners. The result was the prompt appointment of Toronto Dominion as our new bankers. Conveniently they had a base in London, close to our place in Gough Square.

In the continuing review of costs that went on at this time, the company introduced a voluntary redundancy scheme. This was a high-risk strategy, the danger being that we would be stuck with the duffers who might not get a job elsewhere, even as we lost the good guys who had had enough of the aggravation of the early days and had decided to take the money and run. In the event it turned out reasonably well for us, though we had to say farewell to one or two people we rated highly.

At about the same time, there was a dramatic development involving the IBA, LBC/IRN and Capital Radio. In highly confidential discussions, Capital had agreed to close its newsroom on the understanding that its journalists would be offered a job with us. Additionally, Capital would take a live feed of the networked IRN bulletin at the top of the hour right round the clock. One or two Capital journalists decided to go elsewhere, but the rest came to Gough Square, and as a result, we gained a couple of additional newsreaders and several extra reporters. Generally the arrival of the Capital cavalry was regarded as a positive development. Just one or two people who didn't like it decided to move on.

While all this was going on, Marshall had been busy recruiting several people he had known well at the BBC during his time as editor of 'Today'. Among them were Douglas Cameron and Bob Holness, who he wanted to co-present LBC's revamped rival to 'Today'. It was called 'A.M.', and was potentially LBC's biggest money-earner. Cameron quickly established himself as the principal news voice on both LBC and the IRN service networked to other stations. In Holness, on the 'A.M.' programme, he had the perfect foil. They were to work together for some ten years and twice won the Variety Club of Great Britain's award for joint independent radio personalities of the year, in 1979 and 1984. In addition to Bob and Doug, Marshall brought in two senior producers from the BBC.

Next we lured Brian Hayes away from Capital, where he was

both a producer and a phone-in presenter. In the wrong hands phone-ins came to be regarded as a cheap and lazy way of filling airtime, but Hayes had raised the standard dramatically in favour of brisk and intelligent discussion, both with the VIP guests he attracted to the studio each morning and equally with the listeners who called in.

Doris

Already America seemed a long way behind us. I was now an LBC wife, and that meant attending official functions with Ron and helping out at various promotional events organised by the station. Each year I was part of the team at the *Daily Mail*'s Ideal Home Exhibition, where LBC set up a studio and transmitted live broadcasts each day. I welcomed the opportunity to get out and about. It helped me overcome the preoccupation we both had with Louise and how she was faring and what might become of her. Ron and I were even mad enough to become part of the LBC team in a 25-mile relay race from central London to Windsor. We finished 23rd out of 24 teams. The fact that the two of us managed to keep going during just a single lap each was thanks largely to the efforts of a famous athlete known as 'Barefoot Bruce'. His real name was Bruce Tulloh, and he often competed without running shoes. He ran alongside us shouting encouragement and keeping up a non-stop conversation to which we were able to contribute with only gasps and grunts. Still, we got there.

At home, I tried to keep up with developments in the care of people like Louise. On the BBC's 'Weekend Woman's Hour', I caught a discussion about a book raising the possibility of euthanasia in cases where a son or daughter was so handicapped that his or her life had become meaningless even as the parents struggled to sustain the child. A doctor in the studio rejected the idea of euthanasia, insisting that such children should be given the chance of developing their full potential. I was amazed that someone in the doctor's position could be so out of touch. The fact was that far too many of these children had to be kept at home because there were nowhere near enough places for them in a care home or special school. I shouted at the radio, asking what about the potential of a young parent, a virtual prisoner in their own home and struggling to keep up with the demands of a merciless regime? Over the years the press reported cases of those mothers who were unable to keep up and took both the child's life and their own.

Ron

Back in the basement, there was a small group of young presenters and producers who had been with LBC since day one and who now emerged from the early turmoil to make a distinctive contribution to the station's revival. Among them were Carol Barnes and Jon Snow. Carol stayed on for a couple of years before joining ITN as a reporter and newscaster. She came to interview me for ITN when LBC was involved in one of too many confrontations with the journalists that occurred in those years. Later in her life, she had to face up to the death of her daughter in a skydiving accident in Australia. Four years after that, Carol died in hospital after a stroke. She was 63.

We managed to hang on to Jon Snow. The only trouble was that he insisted that he wanted to stay in the studio, orchestrating the big news events of the day and adding his own distinctive gloss. Marshall was convinced that Jon could become an outstanding reporter and correspondent. We both tried to assure him that moving out of the studio and 'getting some mud on his boots' would enhance his undoubted skills as a presenter. I think I actually did a Sir Gordon and rendered the phrase as 'snow on his boots'. No matter, we managed to convince him and he covered a number of major assignments, at home and abroad, with great distinction. When he finally escaped our clutches, he went on to become ITN's correspondent in Washington and later their diplomatic correspondent before becoming the main news presenter on ITV's Channel 4.

Jon Snow was not the first IRN reporter to be sent on assignment overseas. In its first year, LBC/IRN relied on 'stringers' – journalists based abroad and sometimes working for a variety of newspapers and/or broadcasting organisations. We also took voice reports provided by the major news agencies, Reuters and United Press International. It was at Christmas time, a year after we started, that we sent one of our own reporters abroad for the first time. His name was Paul Michaels, a young Australian and one of the reporters who came to IRN when Capital Radio closed down its news operation. The story that took him off to Australia was the arrest there of a former British MP and junior minister named John Stonehouse. He was wanted in Britain in connection with a string of failed and fraudulent businesses he had set up. Before his arrest down under, he had faked his own death by leaving a pile of his clothing on a Miami beach.

Michaels did well on a story that was grabbing headlines all over the world, with a consequent uplifting effect on the state of morale down in the LBC basement. We were also getting plenty of publicity thanks to our parliamentary unit which, led by Ed Boyle, was beginning to break a number of political stories. These often made the front page in the national newspapers, crediting IRN and therefore creating good publicity for us.

Another publicity coup came our way as a result of a discussion about – of all things – gardening. We were just leaving after a board meeting and someone mentioned the fact that I grew tomatoes in my garden. Sir Gordon promptly declared that he was interested in gardening. Somehow he got the wrong idea that I was an expert on the subject and came up with the idea that I should present a weekly feature on LBC. He had a puckish sense of humour and seemed intrigued by the prospect of someone called Onions broadcasting gardening reports. Marshall Stewart was on the fringe of this conversation. He said nothing, but he had heard on his BBC grapevine that they had decided not to renew their contract with the best of the gardening broadcasters at that time, Percy Thrower. In no time at all, Marshall signed him up and the story made a splash in the newspapers the following day. I was off the hook, thank goodness.

Doris

Shortly after her sixteenth birthday, we were informed that Louise would be leaving Court Meadow School at the end of the summer term. We asked the head teacher if, in view of the progress Lulu had made there during the previous five years, she might carry on at the school for the time being. Ever so nicely, the head said no – rules are rules and all that. There was a much bigger disappointment in the offing in a letter from East Sussex County Council informing us that they intended to transfer our daughter from her care home at Halland to Laughton Lodge, near Lewes. We had visited this hospital some years earlier. It was a place from a previous era, an institution for 'the retarded', as they were then known. They were housed in what looked like barrack blocks. We appealed against the decision that she should be transferred to Laughton, but without success.

We did not let the matter rest. We were invited to Laughton to have a look round, and I took the opportunity to talk to one of the medical staff, Dr Margaret Forster. I emphasised what I saw as the advantages of Lulu staying at Halland, stressing that its family environment seemed ideally suited to her particular needs. Dr Forster wrote to me a few days later saying that, unfortunately, Louise had given the Halland staff a great deal of 'anxiety'. This suggested to us that Lulu's carers, whenever we visited her, were reluctant to burden us with any problems that had occurred since last we saw her and preferred to report just the good news. We could understand why, but it meant that usually we learned about the bad news only at Louise's formal and infrequent review meetings.

So our daughter took up residence in Alciston villa at Laughton for what was to be for her – and for us – one of the unhappiest periods. It wasn't that the staff were incompetent. Far from it. Some we rated highly, though maintaining the quality of care was not always easy, depending as it did from time to time on free-lance replacements. The main problem for us was that Lulu became more and more difficult to deal with on our regular visits to Laughton.

We managed to take her out for picnics in the summer months, and, to begin with, they were happy experiences for all three of us. There was, however, an occasion when, soon after we set off with her in the car, she went into a tantrum. Lulu was next to me in the front of the vehicle and began grabbing at various wires behind the sunshield above her. This triggered a spectacular shower of sparks and a swift and tearful return to Laughton Lodge.

Louise had also developed one or two obsessions – principally about the Laughton food menus, which she knew by heart, and the staff rotas, repeating endlessly phrases like, 'Who's on tonight, then?' and becoming increasingly agitated in the process. In the winter our get-togethers took place in a large recreation room. We had it to ourselves and we managed to play bingo and other simple card games, but too often her mood would change, particularly when she spotted members of staff either coming on or going off duty, and we would be back to Lulu's fixation with the rota.

Occasionally our visits ended when she went into a sequence of continuous screaming. Staff would appear and try to calm the situation, leaving us to head for the exit and drive home in tears, wondering how the carers managed to cope with our daughter. They had recourse in those years to a technique known as 'Time Out', during which a troubled individual would be placed in a secure room until their bad behaviour came to an end. This controversial procedure was stopped many years ago, and in Lulu's case we wondered whether it caused more problems than it solved.

Ron

Sometimes we were unable to get down to Laughton because trouble was brewing down in that claustrophobic basement at Gough Square. This was during the time of the rock-bottom relationship between the LBC management and the unions representing the staff – both the journalists and the engineers. We felt we were not helped by our proximity to Fleet Street, where industrial relations were in an even bigger mess. Our meetings to resolve some sudden crisis, usually on the eve of bank holiday weekend, invariably went on to a late hour. Marshall Stewart and I had been banging on for some while about the urgent need to take on someone to handle the problem of industrial relations. The IBA was increasingly worried about LBC going off air occasionally and the consequent inter-ruption to the Independent Radio News service supplied to the other commercial stations now on air, for which – as the recipi-ents were quick to point out – they were paying good money.

It reached the point where the managing director, Bill Hutton, decided to go home to Toronto. He was missing his family, but also I think he yearned for the relative calm he would find back at the Selkirk headquarters, where the staff regarded the turmoil in Gough Square, over in the mother country, with constant amaze-ment. He was known by LBC staff as Wild Bill. In fact he was the most laidback man you could meet. On one occasion, when the commercial radio bosses from outside London came to Gough Square to complain about interruptions in the IRN service because of strike action, Bill opened a tense meeting by placing a blank sheet of A4 on the boardroom table and saying, in his laidback way, 'OK, there's my agenda, nothing's barred, so I'm going to turn this thing over to Ron Onions . . .' Fortunately, Marshall Stewart, in his role as editor-in-chief, jumped in immediately and invited the visitors to summarise their concerns, and this, to my considerable relief, put the meeting back on an even keel. Wild Bill was succeeded as managing director by a man named Patrick Gallagher, who had been a fighter pilot in World War II before embarking on a successful business career.

In the few weeks before Bill Hutton said farewell, Patrick seemed to be establishing a good relationship with the key members of staff, especially the union representatives, but all too soon he became frustrated by the industrial problems he had inherited. He sometimes wondered whether 'these kids', as he referred to them, had all spent time on the barricades of Paris during the turbulent student protests of the sixties.

Marshall and I waited in vain for the arrival of someone to deal with industrial relations, but they never arrived. I guess we just couldn't afford it. So we soldiered on as best we could. This was at a time when inflation was rising fast, with a consequential effect on pay demands, making it more and more difficult to put LBC/IRN in the black. One pay negotiation started with the National Union of Journalists pitching for a forty per cent increase. There was a similar demand from the engineers. It reached the point where, during Marshall's temporary absence on sick leave, Sir Gordon decided to trim LBC's already meagre programme budgets. He didn't tell me about it, he just instructed the company secretary to do it.

After four years in what one newspaper described as the hottest seat in journalism, Marshall left us for what we all hoped would be a quieter life in an executive role at Central Television. I was sorry to see him go. No one could have done more to ensure LBC's survival through such a turbulent period.

Sir Gordon called me into his office and asked me to take over. I knew what Marshall had been paid and declined the chairman's lower offer. So he then offered to pay me exactly the same, and we shook hands on it. I wish I could say that, from this point, there was a dramatic improvement in LBC's fortunes. There wasn't. Still, I was pleased that Peter Thornton took over my previous job as Editor, IRN. He was a survivor from the days before LBC went on air, having been recruited from the *Daily Telegraph*. There he became a distinguished correspondent in Northern Ireland, which was then at the peak of its long turmoil involving the IRA.

So we soldiered on, still without anyone to deal specifically with industrial relations within the company, and facing increasing financial pressure. Outside London, the protracted development of commercial radio meant that income for the IRN service was now a trickle rather than a flow. This was a consequence of the worsening state of the national economy.

Still, there was some good news. In June, the Queen lit a bonfire in Windsor Great Park at the start of a week of celebrations marking her twenty-five years on the throne. To the family's delight, an envelope from Buckingham Palace fell through our letter box the following day announcing that I was among those to be presented with a Silver Jubilee medal.

I tried to follow Marshall Stewart's policy of hiring some big names to present programmes so as to attract publicity in the newspapers and push up the audience figures. It was a strain on programme budgets, but it worked. David Frost had been an early recruit, followed by Michael Parkinson, who sat in occasionally for Brian Hayes but also did a regular – and stylish – programme on the cinema. Then there was Jeffrey Archer, a controversial figure and sometime MP, still to establish himself as a highly successful novelist. He asked if he could present a night-time phone-in. We offered him a modest fee – which he accepted – and he did a very good job for us.

Then there was Carol Thatcher. Her arrival, though attracting some useful publicity, also triggered a rumpus with the National Union of Journalists, who claimed that LBC was a 'closed shop'. Here we go again. Somehow the matter was resolved at the last minute, and Carol, too did a good job for us, notably on one Christmas Day when she invited her mother into the studio for an interview, with a consequent impact on press headlines.

Doris

In the summer, Laughton Lodge organised a fete in the grounds of the hospital, and we were there most years, selling books and records that came our way after the annual clear-out of the LBC library, just as we had done at Court Meadow School. For Louise this was rarely a happy event. She expected to be driven out some-where for a picnic. One year, when Frank and Pam Proctor came to Laughton to give us a hand selling the radio station goodies, she refused to come out of her room and say hello.

The one visit to Laughton we always enjoyed was at Christmas time. The staff there invited parents and friends of the residents to a party, and it was always a happy occasion. Sarah and the grand-children, Lucy and Joe, often joined us, and there was music and dancing and a dazzling display of things to eat and drink. Lulu was at her best in the midst of the merriment, elegantly dressed and rock and rolling to the music.

It was also at this time of year that Lulu lifted our spirits with her second appearance on stage, this time in a Laughton Lodge show featuring scenes from Charles Dickens' *A Christmas Carol*, produced by Janet Loyd, who had done her training – as I had – at the Royal Academy of Music. Lulu appeared as one of the Cratchit children, and it was a joyous echo of her debut in the Christmas show at Cobb Memorial School and also of the time when she was cast as Little Ben in the playlet written by Sarah and performed by both of them in the Manhattan apartment.

Ron

The following year there was more good news coming out of the research carried out annually into audience figures on behalf of all independent stations. It revealed that we had more than two million listeners. This would not be possible today since there are many more radio stations competing for audience. Also, we were broad-casting exactly the same service on our AM and FM transmitters. Only much later would LBC be able to transmit completely sepa-rate programmes on the two wavelengths to which we had access.

When Sir Gordon retired as chairman of LBC/IRN, he was

replaced by Sir Geoffrey Cox. He was the man who, as Editor-in-Chief, took charge of Independent Television News (ITN) after its difficult start in the late fifties. Under Sir Geoffrey, ITN became an innovative rival to BBC TV News. He recruited a talented team of reporters and presenters, including Robin Day, who was to become BBC's current affairs guru. ITN's 'News At Ten', in the later years of Sir Geoffrey's editorship, was to have a considerable effect on the BBC's style of presentation.

I got on well with the new chairman, but he became increasingly concerned about industrial relations and the way disputes at Gough Square impacted on the rest of the commercial radio stations who had been encouraged by the IBA to take the IRN service from us. One morning he turned up for a board meeting to be confronted by a picket line stretched out across the main entrance. Above the door canopy the words Communications House had been amended. Someone had scrawled the word 'Non' in front of them.

The trouble was that as soon as one problem had been resolved another one took its place. The worst example took place the night everyone had just resumed work after a strike that took us off air for more than a week. It was the day the Vatican announced the death of Pope John Paul I after the shortest ever papal reign, just a few weeks. Broadcasting law at the time ruled that presenters must not voice their own opinion on politics and religion, among other topics, but LBC's night-time presenter suddenly expressed his view that the dead pope was a 'silly old fool'. I could not believe what I had heard. I tried to call LBC but the switchboard was jammed. So I set off to the studios, having asked Doris to field any calls and say I was on my way. On arrival I was given a long list of people who had rung the switchboard to demand the instant sacking of the hapless presenter. I spoke to him in my office first thing the following morning. He was in fact one of the people I had taken on as Capital Radio prepared to go on air, and was among those given a job at LBC when the Capital newsroom closed down. Sacking him seemed a high-risk strategy, given our troubled relationship with the journalists' union, and instead we agreed that he would write a letter of resignation there and then. Soon afterwards, I was pleased to hear him on another radio station, choosing his words carefully.

Meanwhile, Sir Geoffrey was as determined as ever to bring sweetness and light to Gough Square. He sought the advice of former colleagues at both ITN and Tyne Tees Television, where he had been chairman for several years. A former colleague of Sir Geoffrey's at ITN spent some time with us at Gough Square, talking to union representatives and the management team. I hoped he would stay with us for ever. He didn't. What happened next was that Sir Geoffrey asked me out for a drink one evening, and after a long preamble he said he would like to bring in one of his old buddies from ITN and Tyne Tees, a journalist and interviewer named George Ffitch. He would be appointed Editor-in-Chief. I realised immediately that this was a revival of Marshall Stewart's old title that had been abandoned when he left. I, meanwhile, was to take over Marshall's job but with a new title of Editorial Director. Any way you looked at it, I was being demoted. In a state of some confusion, I said I thought we had been trying to sort out the company's appalling industrial relations, but now I was being made the fall guy. Sir Geoffrey tried to be reassuring. He said George would sort out the unions for us.

When I got home, I was so wound up I put off telling my wife and oldest daughter what had happened until the following morning. When I told them, they found it difficult to take it all in, but Doris said I must do everything possible to hang on to my position as editorial number one. So I called various people I counted as potential allies. From the IBA I learned that they were aware of the plan to bring George Ffitch in, but were unclear about his role. I then spoke to a couple of managing directors in the commercial radio network I thought I could count on for support. One of them gave me the name and telephone number of a lawyer at a firm specialising in media cases. When I arrived at work the following morning I broke the news to Peter Thornton and several others at LBC I regarded as buddies. Then the managing director, Patrick

167

Gallagher, came on the phone. Wrongly, I had suspected that he was part of the plot to replace me and I refused to speak to him. I then took a cab round to the lawyer's office in Soho. He said the firm would be happy to represent me in what he called 'a clear case of constructive dismissal'. Then I went home.

There was a further complication in our family life at this time. We had begun to receive nuisance calls on our home telephone at all hours of the day and night. They were from a man who, in a sneering tone, addressed me as Ron. He suggested that we had known each other in the past, but when I tried to find out more he would invariably go off the line and I would find myself talking to some innocent individual whom he had hooked into the circuit in some way. Understandably, when I tried to establish who they were and where they lived, they became nervous and hung up, anxious to get rid of this apparent nutter.

Eventually British Telecom set up a screen to check on all incoming calls to our home. This deterred the nuisance caller but it also irritated genuine callers who were subjected to an interrogation process before they were put through to us. We would be asked whether or not we wished to take a call from so-and-so. Following my visit to the lawyer, both Sir Geoffrey and George Ffitch tried to call me at home in the evening. I decided not to speak to either of them until the letter from my lawyer had arrived at Gough Square. Two days later, Sir Geoffrey called me into the boardroom. He said that, after consultation with other members of the board, he had decided not to appoint George Ffitch as Editor-in-Chief, but then went on to insist that 'there would have to be changes around here'. We soon learned what they were. Patrick Gallagher would be leaving the company, and George Ffitch was to replace him as managing director. I went to Patrick's office to apologise for slamming the phone down on him when he rang a few days earlier. In fact, he had been calling me to pass on a tip from a former business colleague, now working for the IBA, to the effect that George Ffitch was about to join us at Gough Square. As we shook hands, Patrick added, 'You should know that you have friends at Court.' He was referring to the IBA.

George Ffitch embarked on a determined attempt to sort out LBC's troubled relations with the unions. He did so at a time of widespread industrial unrest. During a series of national strikes, rubbish piled up in the streets, people were turned away from hospitals, bodies remained unburied. In another dispute, *The Times* newspaper ceased publication for a whole year, and problems in the road haulage industry resulted in 150,000 people being laid off. It was against this background that George chaired boardroom discussions with the LBC unions. He showed a great deal of patience and dealt with some outstanding individual problems that had been sore points for some while. However, he was not helped by the serious financial situation gripping the country and the crippling effect it had had on LBC's finances.

In the spring of 1979, Margaret Thatcher became the country's first woman Prime Minister after the Conservatives defeated Labour in a general election. Various politicians and commentators came into the studios to contribute both to LBC's non-stop coverage and to the service provided by IRN to all the other commercial stations. Afterwards they were taken upstairs for refreshments. There they were able to watch coverage of the night's results on BBC TV. When the hard-working scribes down in the basement heard about this, they sent up a formal complaint that the boardroom guests should have been given the opportunity to follow the night's developments on LBC radio. Though I thought they were right, this grievance illustrated how carefully the management had to proceed in creating a greater sense of unity within the building.

Later that year we were among the guests at the Local Radio Association's annual dinner and awards ceremony. It was a boisterous occasion, propelled by the news editors of the two Scottish stations then on air who provided our table with a generous supply of their national medicine. Without any forewarning, the announcement was made that I had been voted commercial radio's Personality of the Year, and I walked carefully to the rostrum to receive a formidable glass trophy, inscribed accordingly. The following day, there I was in full colour occupying the front page of one of the entertainment magazines. I said to Doris and Sarah that gongs and other rewards made me nervous. Soon after the previous one, I had found myself in the lawyer's office trying to hang on to my job. My wife told me to stop being stupid. Meanwhile, various jokers at LBC derived much enjoyment by running off copies of the magazine cover and pinning them up in the newsroom. They had been embellished with biro beards, moustaches and rude comments. That put me in my place.

I looked forward to happier days ahead, but that was too much to expect. There was never a period without some new problem coming out of the woodwork. The state of the nation did nothing for our company's financial health, and we still awaited the wizard who would sort out industrial relations. Additionally, we were not helped by the fact that valuable broadcasting and office equipment was disappearing from the building overnight. The police came round to check on security procedures. All staff carried identity cards that they were required to show on arriving at the single entrance to the building. Additionally there was a logbook recording the arrival and departure times of all visitors. The system had appeared to be working well, occasionally too well. The former chairman, Sir Gordon, turned up at reception one day without any means of identifying himself and was refused entry until someone came down from the management floor to rescue him. On another occasion, Archbishop Desmond Tutu arrived for a late-night discussion on the political situation in South Africa. Unfortunately nobody had told the security guard about this, and the Archbishop, to his considerable bewilderment, was told to come back on Sunday morning when the religious programme went to air.

In addition to the vanishing equipment, we were suddenly confronted with a crisis in the accounts department. Someone working there told me that a senior colleague was falsifying expense claims purporting to have been submitted by reporters and other editorial staff. I was shown a batch of expense forms on which every signature but one – including my own – had been forged. The only genuine signature was the final one at the very bottom of the form authorising payment. The guilty man was summoned to the managing director's office and left the building immediately.

When Sir Geoffrey retired, he was succeeded by Sir Christopher Chataway, the distinguished athlete, broadcaster (ITN and BBC) and Conservative politician. There were further changes on the board. Some directors who had been with LBC since the very beginning were replaced, and the newcomers included our first woman director, Sarah Hogg, who had been, among her other accomplishments, a news presenter on Channel 4. Her arrival was timely. The changing role of women in society was one of the principal topics of discussion on radio and television and in the newspapers at this time. More than that, a high proportion of women were employed as producers and reporters on LBC in addition to those working in accounts and as secretaries. The arrival of a woman on the board of directors was long overdue.

In the spring of 1982, Britain went to war in the south Atlantic after an Argentine force invaded and captured the Falkland Islands. Mrs Thatcher promptly ordered the dispatch of a British fleet to recapture the islands, which Argentina referred to as the Malvinas and regarded as their sovereign territory. Among the reporters who went off to the south Atlantic were two from LBC/IRN, Kim Sabido and Antonia Higgs. It had been agreed that all radio coverage should be pooled and made available to all commercial radio stations in Britain as well as to all of the BBC's outlets. As a result, we began to receive letters from BBC listeners praising the reports of Sabido and Higgs that the BBC had kindly passed on to us. It also happened the other way round. We received letters from commercial radio listeners reacting to the reports of BBC staff covering the Falklands war, and we ensured that all these were passed on to Broadcasting House. It left us with the feeling that we had more than made our mark in the story of radio reporting in Great Britain. Research figures at this time showed LBC's audience to be at its highest ever.

Yet, six months later, we were down to almost our lowest ever figures, even as the music stations were reporting spectacular increases. Some of us thought it inevitable that, with the surrender of Argentinian forces, listeners would seek escape from the harrowing coverage of a faraway war that resulted in the deaths of more than 250 British military personnel and an even greater number of Argentinian troops, by tuning in to stations playing music instead. Whatever the reason for the fall in audience, George Ffitch faced the increasing concern of our sales force as the revenue from advertising dropped sharply. There followed several discussions about changing the programme format to include some music in the afternoon. We had always featured an hour or so of classical music in the early evening, but I resisted the idea of a significant change in the news-and-information structure of the station. The atmosphere on the management floor became more and more strained, taking us back to the early days and the sudden change in our banking arrangements. Then, after one particularly difficult day, I received a call at home to say that George Ffitch had been admitted to hospital with a serious heart condition and was likely to be away for some while.

What else could go wrong? In addition to the problem of falling advertising revenue and the management dispute over whether, as a consequence, there must be programme changes, there was another major hurdle just ahead. Every few years commercial radio stations had to apply to the Independent Radio Authority for the renewal of their licence to broadcast. This was a competitive process open to other applicants and called for the preparation of a detailed written submission to the Authority followed by an interview at their imposing headquarters opposite Harrods in Knightsbridge. The principal figures in each applicant group faced detailed cross examination of their proposals. For us that vital meeting was now only weeks ahead. I had written an outline of our application for consideration by the LBC board, but it now required George to make his essential contribution as managing director. He had a way with the written word, as he had demonstrated during his time on the *Economist* and in other publications. Now any contribution from him seemed unlikely.

So it was agreed that I should work on completing the final version of the application while Peter Thornton looked after the running of both the radio station and the IRN service. Fortunately Sarah Hogg was around to develop some thoughts she had expressed when she read the basic outline of the application I had written some weeks earlier. She pointed out that there would be several women on the IBA team and they would want to know what plans we had to increase our appeal to women listeners. It was a valid point, and not least because the changing role of women in society had become one of the principal topics of discussion on the radio and on television, as well as in newspapers. More than that, we employed a high proportion of women as producers and reporters, and in other roles. This was always a big point in our favour whenever Lady Plowden visited Gough Square during her five years in the chair at the IBA.

As the written application to the Authority neared completion, we had to face another hurdle, in the form of a meeting to present our case for the renewal of our franchise to the world at large. The venue was Caxton Hall, a historic building in central London in use at the time as a register office for weddings and a place for public meetings. In the chair was the IBA's head of radio, John Thompson, and the event was open to all. It was a packed house; some had just wandered in on a very cold night, but there were also representatives from a rival group seeking to take the franchise away from us. They had the backing of London's *Evening Standard* newspaper and were led by a former BBC grandee who was their chairman. They had also recruited two of our former colleagues, men who had distinguished themselves at LBC/IRN before moving on to high-profile jobs elsewhere in broadcasting. Also present were several people representing special-interest groups claiming that we broadcast too much – or too little – of this, that and the other. Most of them made a useful contribution to the discussion – even the Labour MP who stood up and, pointing to the LBC represen-tatives huddled on the rostrum, yelled out, 'You're not as good as you think you are!' This triggered a huge wave of laughter, and that cleared the increasingly tense atmosphere that had developed in a discussion on how much – or how little – we were doing on air for immigrants and minority groups.

George Ffitch came out of hospital and returned to work in time to put his stamp on our franchise renewal application. This happened shortly before we were to face the IBA panel who would decide whether or not we could carry on broadcasting. When the big day dawned, we were not in good shape. The previous night we had been kept out of our beds trying to settle some dispute raised by the unions which seemed to arise from nowhere. It was resolved at a late hour. Just imagine our having to face our masters at the IBA with an unresolved industrial dispute looming over us and the possibility that the radio station was about to go off air. Inevitably we were not on top form when, the following day, we faced the great and good sitting on the IBA's interview panel.

Somehow we battled our way through, but for me it was one of those climactic moments in life and convinced me that it was time to move on. It was ten years previously that I had joined LBC, and five of them had been in a job described in the press as 'the most difficult job in broadcasting'. I did not change my mind about moving on when, much later that same day, we learned of the IBA's decision that our franchise would be renewed.

Doris

We went down to Laughton Lodge at the weekend to visit Lulu and think about our future. During a recent holiday in the south of France, we had decided to buy a small apartment in Mougins-le-Haut, a few miles from the Mediterranean coast and with a view of the southern Alps from the bedroom. Maybe, we were thinking, the time had come to go and live there permanently in happy retirement. We decided that it was perhaps too early to do that and, anyway, we couldn't really afford it, but we were anxious to complete the house purchase and made arrangements to do just that in ten days' time. We promptly booked flights and a hotel, having decided to take a few extra days off while we were in the south of France.

Ron

It was just our luck that at this point, the Prime Minister, Mrs Thatcher decided to call a general election in the autumn. I talked it over with Peter and senior programme colleagues, and they said they would be able to cope during the short time I was away in France. On returning home – and after a hurried weekend visit to Louise – I called Peter. He told me that, in my absence, George had held several meetings with senior staff to finalise changes in the programme schedule. Peter had been unable to contact me because nobody knew where we were staying. I felt the same as I did on the night the IBA renewed our franchise within hours of our settling a sudden dispute with the LBC's unions: I wanted out of the place. I did not have to wait long.

The exit door swung open suddenly during a phone call from Peter Marshall. He was the man who had persuaded me to leave Southern Television and join the BBC in Southampton. He was now the general manager of an organisation called Visnews, the leading distributor of newsfilm to television stations all over the world. It was owned by the major Commonwealth broadcasters – the BBC, the Australian Broadcasting Corporation, CBC of Canada and NZBC.

What Peter wanted to discuss was the possibility of starting a non-stop news channel using the worldwide resources of Visnews and aimed principally at the burgeoning cable television market. It would target European cable stations to begin with, and it might be possible to fund it with pan-European advertising. Would I like to take charge of it? And could I start soon? Yes, twice.

Doris and I were lucky enough to spend my final few weeks on the LBC payroll thousands of miles away in North America. First, I had been selected as one of the British delegates at an international conference in Toronto on radio broadcasting. Doris and I decided to go the long route, flying to New York for a nostalgic forty-eight hours spent meeting old friends and then hiring a car and heading north to revisit some of our favourite haunts, notably Boston and the coast of Maine. We then shuffled off to Buffalo, where we caught a plane to Toronto for the conference. Next stop, Atlanta, where Visnews had offered to fund a visit to the capital of Georgia so that we could visit the headquarters of Ted Turner's Cable News Network. Turner was a pioneer among cable news providers, and I knew a couple of his staff from the New York days, when they worked for the television news agency UPITN.

It was difficult to guess quite what the Turner organisation thought it would derive from a visit by a potential rival. There was vague talk of synergy, to use one of the then current buzzwords. Anyway, we were well looked after during a detailed tour of Turner's pioneering venture and came away determined to set up a similar, but multilingual, operation for Europe.

One of the abiding memories of that visit to Atlanta was the number of people we spoke to who claimed some connection with the 1939 blockbuster film *Gone with the Wind*, starring Clark Gable and Vivien Leigh, which highlighted the burning of Atlanta during the American Civil War. We were assured by cabbies, bellhops, waiters and several others in the city that they had been bit part players in the award-winning film or knew people who had been, or that they had worked on the set or in the crowd scenes. Most times we didn't believe them – but the southern accent was beguiling, and they weren't all looking for tips.

We flew back to London looking forward to yet another trip abroad. I had been nominated as the British juror in one of the categories of the prestigious Prix Italia competition organised by RAI, the Italian state broadcaster, and supported by all the major radio and television broadcasters of Europe. Each year the event took place in a different Italian location. This year they had chosen Capri, the original venue for the festival when it began in 1947.

As the United Kingdom representative on the radio documentaries jury, I often found myself involved in heavily political arguments. Happily, though, choosing the winner of the Prix Italia prize for overall excellence was easy. The BBC entry took it with unanimous support from the jury. Less easy was the process of deciding the winner of the Italian Press Association prize awarded for some special quality or qualities. The Finnish entry eventually won it, but it faced a considerable challenge from a Swedish effort; the decision proved controversial enough to split the jury and involve us in a heated debate which was to take up most of the final Friday afternoon and evening.

The programme, by two young Swedish producers, was about the fortieth anniversary of the Battle of El Alamein in World War II and the reunion that took place on that occasion between troops of the British Eighth Army and some of the German soldiers commanded by Rommel. It began with music by Palestrina, swiftly proceeded to Binyon – 'They shall not grow old, as we who are left grow old' – and quotations from wartime speeches and broadcasts, and then went on to reminiscences of the kind that old soldiers indulge in, most of them unremarkable and, indeed, tending to the mundane. To some ears there was nothing special about it – it was occasionally moving, but for the most part it was a less than riveting commemoration of one of the great turning points of World War II. My view of it was shared to a lesser or greater degree by the Canadian and Australian jurors – the Commonwealth united, so to speak – but it was quickly obvious that there was a group of three or four within the jury for whom this Swedish entry was a Great Anti-War Statement, a striking condemnation of militarism and the glorification of armed conflict. There is no doubt that we – the Commonwealth – swung the Spanish and Vatican jurors our way, not out of misplaced patriotism but because we genuinely felt that this was a programme of no great merit and that if there was an ironic element in it – as was claimed subsequently – then it was so well disguised as to be not apparent at all.

The following day there was a limited replay of the argument about the Swedish programme when, at a public meeting, the jury had to justify its conclusions. We were asked why we had not selected the Swedish programme for a prize. One of its producers rose to say that it was a 'programme against war and if we failed to see that, then . . .' and he waved his hands in a despairing gesture as his supporters in the audience stood up and cheered. My response was that it was the producer's responsibility to make his meaning absolutely clear and he could not blame the audience for failing to understand a message that was too subtle or obscure.

The following night we were among the people from independent radio invited to a dinner hosted in Capri by the BBC. It was an opportunity to renew old acquaintances and, without actually naming the winning programme, which would have been against the rules, I said how much we had enjoyed the BBC entry. A colleague from the IBA asked if the producer had come to Italy for the festival, and raised his eyebrows in a significant way. The BBC took the hint and the producer was quickly flown to Naples for the following night's presentation ceremony.

We stayed on for a few days' rest and recreation and then flew home for my final week at LBC/IRN and the farewell party. The staff had bought me a huge world atlas, which was a nice touch for someone who had done so much globetrotting. I told them that nine years earlier I had not wanted to come to Gough Square. Now, fleetingly, I did not want to leave, but the reality was that it was time to go.

The Visnews building was in an industrial area of west London, not far from Heathrow Airport, where there were regular shipments of film to and from the company's clients worldwide. One of our nearest neighbours was the huge Guinness factory standing in the middle of a large paddock where a herd of cows was put out to graze. According to what sounded like a folk tale, one night towards Christmas a gang of rustlers turned up with cattle trucks in the dead of night and spirited some of the cows away.

Visnews had recruited a technical adviser, Tom Cooke, to provide expert guidance on the cable news project, and he assembled a small team of engineers and other experts to help devise the format for – as we rather grandly entitled it – World News Network. The formula that emerged after a great deal of head-banging was a single stream of images of one kind or another – newsfilm, maps, charts, still pictures, computer graphics and other illustrative images – that kept the presenter off the screen. The off-screen presenters would provide the essential verbal accompaniment, in the major European languages to begin with, adding other languages as the service developed. This would be a much cheaper way of delivering World News Network by satellite, since it would cut out the need for a conventional transmission studio equipped with cameras requiring extra staff to operate them.

The show reels put together by our team in three different languages – English, French and German – were much better than we expected. So we hawked the World News Network prototype around the English cable stations to begin with. The response was good. They could all see the merit in having a non-stop news service on top of the various services they were already offering. However, some asked how much we would pay them to be part of the package of services they were transmitting. This took us back a bit. We had seen it differently, wondering how much they would pay *us* for the opportunity to feature a reputable twenty-four-hour news service as an important part of the overall package they were selling to subscribers. So we approached a major advertising agency to look at the possibility of funding World News Network with pan-European advertising. The agency was enthusiastic about the idea, thought we had a good product, and went off to gauge reaction from its major clients across Europe.

At this point, the Visnews managing director, Brian Quinn, called for a detailed projection of the costs of providing the WNN service – 'best case and worst case', as he put it. Several of the Visnews bright young sparks were seconded to help with research and development of the project, and a senior engineer, formerly with ITV, also came on board. All this left me free to set off to the Continent clutching the European show reels. Reaction was good, especially in Germany and the Low Countries, where cable television had caught on much more quickly than in the rest of Europe.

Again, as in England, there was plenty of enthusiasm at the prospect of providing in their own language an international news service backed by reputable news providers like the BBC and Reuters. Recently Reuters had taken a stake in Visnews and was represented on the board of directors.

As word spread about World News Network, I received an invitation to present it to a morning assembly of the European Parliament in the French city of Strasbourg. I went on my own, which did nothing to calm my nerves after a sleepless night just across the border in Germany. I presented myself at the parliament building and sought out the German engineer who would be responsible for feeding the WNN show reel into a number of screens. These were strategically placed all the way round the parliamentary chamber. After a brief and nervous introduction, I gave the engineer a cue to roll the tape, which then appeared on all the screens. The only problem was the one experienced by the team of translators employed by the Parliament. Some of them found it difficult to cope with the English speed of delivery. I detected this on my headphones as I switched through the full complement of sound circuits to see how well the team of translators was getting on. Clearly it was something we had to work on.

There followed a session of questions and answers. Some members of the Parliament seemed obsessed with the idea that this was a further example of American cultural invasion, believing that Ted Turner was in some way behind it all. I assured them that he wasn't, and emphasised the considerable influence of the BBC and Reuters on World News Network. Overall, there was a lot of support for the project, and afterwards I was taken off for a splendid lunch by two veterans of the European Parliament.

Yet within Visnews itself over the next few weeks, I became aware that there were mixed feelings about the WNN project. There was increasing concern about 'all those noughts' whenever the subject was discussed at senior management meetings. Might it be possible, I was asked, to contrive a much simpler service? Oh dear . . .

The BBC, too, had its reservations when some of its principals viewed the WNN show reel. It emerged later that there was a feeling such a project should be produced by the Corporation itself, backed by its huge resources, and that Visnews should revert to its original role as an international news film agency. The BBC seconded someone to look at this possibility, and I sat in on a couple of meetings at Television Centre. Someone suggested I should 'rejoin the fold'. I said, 'No thanks,' or words to that effect.

We all cheered up late that first year at Visnews when the postman delivered a letter from the Prime Minister saying that I had been nominated to be awarded the OBE (Order of the British Empire), and that it would be presented to me by the Queen at Buckingham Palace the following spring.

Meanwhile, another organisation, the European Broadcasting Union (EBU), had begun looking at the possibility of operating a pan-European news channel. It already organised and operated daily exchanges of news film, but was – and remained – best known for running the Eurovision Song Contest as well as the New Year's Day concert from Vienna.

I think some people at the EBU regarded Visnews and UPITN, its rival in providing a worldwide service of news film for television stations, as tradespeople, only in it for the money, and not driven by loftier imperatives like cultural exchange among the nations. Like the BBC, they felt that if there was a future for a pan-European news channel then they should be doing it, not us. Some unkind individuals shared the belief that Visnews was just a retirement home for elderly BBC gentlemen.

We soldiered on with the WNN project, presenting it at several conferences around England organised by the Cable Programme Providers Group, of which we were founder members. The enthusiasm for the project was still there. One of the big three American networks, CBS, certainly liked what it saw when representatives came over to London to watch our show reel. Inevitably, though, we were always faced with two searching questions. They were first put to me by the man representing Ted Turner's Cable News Network in London. At one of our presentations he asked whether WNN was available to subscribers now? He knew the answer already: Not yet. He knew also he would get exactly the same response to the second question: Do you have a starting date in mind?

So I found myself chasing after one or two other ways of getting added value from Visnews' resources. One involved us in a competitive bid to provide news bulletins to Thames TV, which at the time was the ITV contractor for Greater London. We found ourselves up against my old firm, LBC. Neither of us was successful. Another project saw us sitting down with people from the British Medical Association to see if we could devise a 'medical' channel for transmission on cable television. We couldn't. The projected costs overwhelmed us.

Reuters was taking a close interest in the company at this time, and when our managing director, Brian Quinn, left to set up his own enterprise, he was succeeded by one of Reuters' senior employees, Julian Kerr. Soon after Kerr's arrival, Peter Marshall announced that he was off to America to take up an executive post with Intelsat, a telecommunications and satellite organisation based in Washington, DC. This left me feeling restless, not least because the Independent Broadcasting Authority had given the go-ahead for new commercial radio stations in Greater London, one of which would be devoted to jazz music. I then received a call from a man who used to present a weekly jazz hour on LBC, Keith Howell. He said he had been approached by a group who wanted to apply for the jazz franchise. I said they must be mad. Keith persuaded me to talk to them. So I had lunch with jazz pianist and composer Dave Lee and the proposed chairman of the group, Jasper Grinling, former chairman of Gordon's gin and occasional jazz drummer.

I recall saying it would all end in tears, but they persuaded me to help them prepare an application. So I sought the advice of a former senior employee of the IBA and he read through our initial draft. He liked it, commenting only that we should be careful not to 'over-egg the pudding' in our formal submission to the Authority.

There was much acclaim, in the press and elsewhere, when it was announced that the group had been awarded a licence to run a jazz radio station for Greater London. Somehow the idea had caught the public imagination. I was appointed to the board of directors, but the inevitable question arose: Did I want to go beyond that and become an employee as well? It wasn't easy, but I finally decided to leave Visnews and go back to radio. I had been a jazz enthusiast since I was fourteen, and I now looked forward to a job where every day would be Christmas. In fact, it was to prove one of the unhappiest periods of my life.

The principal problem was that I was the only member of the board who had had previous experience of the day-to-day running of a radio station. I should have sounded a warning when the decision was taken to buy in the latest technology instead of sticking with equipment that had proved to be reliable over the years. Thus, we acquired a new computerised system which selected the records to be played according to the time of day. It proved a nightmare for presenters. It was supposed to put the next disc to air by touching a screen. Too often it didn't, resulting in the presenter's arch enemy – silence, or 'dead air', as we called it. In the days before Jazz FM actually started on air, valuable time was wasted trying to put this problem right.

My main task at this time was to recruit a team of experienced radio presenters who would be heard at fixed times in Jazz FM's twenty-four-hour schedule. Each of them had sent in an audition tape illustrating how they sounded at the microphone and their skill in putting themselves to air and linking jazz records. Time was short. The station was to go on air only six months after we had won the franchise. Three members of the board, including the chairman and the vice-chairman, decided they would like to listen to the tapes and make their own judgement. I provided them with a selection which included experienced presenters I had already invited to join Jazz FM, as well as others I had rejected. The rejections included a bookmaker from Coventry and a man who was a joke within the radio business because of the large number of brief DJ appointments he had held at stations throughout the country. It was these two who were selected by my three colleagues on the board even as they rejected two people to whom I had already offered contracts.

This was ridiculous, and I just ignored it. The two the board had turned down were to become Jazz FM's outstanding presenters, Helen Mayhew and Jez Nelson. Helen went on to an award-winning career, which included a long spell on BBC Radio 2 as a jazz presenter and interviewer. Her later jobs included a two-hour jazz show each week day on the national classical music station, Classic FM. She then joined a station which revived Jazz FM on digital radio, and this brought back the nightly 'Dinner Jazz' feature that had proved so successful on the original station. Jez, too, went on to join the BBC in due course and soon began a long association with BBC Radio 3 as a producer and presenter of jazz programmes.

Before a commercial radio station begins broadcasting, engineers from the IBA spend time testing the transmission signal, checking the quality and power of reception at various points in the designated reception area. This is a simple enough process, involving regular announcements that the station will begin broadcasting on such and such a date at this point on your radio dial. Sometimes light music is transmitted between announcements. This was not meant to provide an opportunity to jump the gun and launch a new station several weeks early, but that was, in effect, what happened. Against my advice, the principal presenters were encouraged to record two-hour sequences of jazz records, linked by themselves, for transmission between the test signal messages. We were unable to prepare these sequences in the Jazz FM studios because the necessary equipment had yet to be installed. So extra costs were incurred hiring outside studios, and presenters spent valuable time away from essential preparations for the station's launch in a few weeks' time.

When the tapes went to air between the test signals, they sounded

OK, but the constant repetition began to drive us all mad. It had the same effect on potential listeners who were tuning in. So the cry went up for more tapes to be recorded. I had more than one call from the IBA asking what the hell was going on, and soon we were coping with letters and phone calls from listeners, some of whom – not all – were not impressed by what they were hearing. We tried to explain to them that when Jazz FM was launched officially, we would be using a computer to ensure that we broadcast a programme schedule that balanced the various styles of jazz that had existed since its birth at the beginning of the twentieth century. I am not sure that this was what callers wanted to hear. In the jazz world, one man's meat is another's poison. Mention of a computer as part of the process didn't help either. One caller said she didn't want a robot choosing the music. Some felt that selection of records should be left to the individual presenters, given that they knew what they were talking about.

None of this gave us much comfort. Neither did the computer, when it was eventually installed a couple of months before we were due to go on air. There were too many teething problems. Understandably, presenters became nervous about using it, and it was still playing up in the last few days before we began broadcasting. By now most of us were at the studios seven days a week to try and ensure a successful launch of Jazz FM. Newspapers and the trade press were rooting for us, and the First Lady of Jazz, as Ella Fitzgerald was known, came to London to send us on our way with a sell-out concert at the Albert Hall.

The opening day of Jazz FM did not go as smoothly as we had hoped. It had been agreed that Ella Fitzgerald would come to the station mid-morning and meet guests at a reception taking place in a large room behind one of the two studios. In due course she would be taken into the principal studio for an interview, during which several of her records would be broadcast. It all went wrong. When she arrived at the radio station, she was not taken to meet our guests and spend some time with them, as had been agreed, but instead was guided straight to the on-air studio. The waiting guests, through a large window along one side of the studio, watched the ensuing pantomime as the man who was due to do the interview was summoned from the reception party. Worse than that, all the discs to be played during the interview with Ella were in another studio which she should have been taken to some time later. So the discs had to be grabbed from there and transferred to the on-air studio in a highly embarrassing episode. Fortunately our distinguished visitor took it with her customary composure.

The rest of the day went reasonably well. We linked up with New York, where one of Jazz FM's company directors, saxophonist John Dankworth, and his wife, the singer Cleo Laine, were on a concert tour. They shared the sense of achievement we all felt on that first day, and this was reflected in the following day's newspapers, only one of which was churlish enough to comment on the moment when a microphone fell over and caused some confusion in the studio and a considerable amount of clatter on air.

In that first week, there was a celebration dinner, followed by a sizzling concert featuring Ella Fitzgerald and the Count Basie Orchestra, and the young Scottish tenor saxophonist, Tommy Smith. A few weeks later, our first set of research figures looked good. We had managed to introduce a number of specialist features for the more serious enthusiasts in our audience, and these caught the attention of the jazz writers in both the national newspapers and various entertainment magazines. They liked especially the regular live recordings from Europe and America, and a weekly twelve-part series on the Duke Ellington Orchestra, as well as weekly shows presented by leading musicians such as trombonist Campbell Burnap and guitarist, actor and former lead singer of the pop group Manfred Mann, Paul Jones. The American alto saxophonist David Sanborn had a two-hour programme on Saturday, and on Sunday we had as a presenter a man selected by the BBC as its Jazz Musician of the Year, trumpeter Digby Fairweather. He drew the biggest audience of Jazz FM's week for his two-hour special, Digby's Sunday Joint. Another popular weekend show was called Sitting-In. This was an opportunity for various personalities to present their own favourite jazz records. They included Sir David English, who was then editor of the *Daily Mail* and a regular listener to the station's Dinner Jazz programme, as well as musicians and the jazz critics from national newspapers and other publications. We also brought in three men who had built a considerable reputation as jazz presenters at the BBC – Benny Green, Charles Fox and Malcolm Laycock.

So we had something to sustain the serious jazz buffs in the audience, though they were to prove vociferous in their likes and dislikes in reacting to the various styles that had come and gone during the development of a form of music that had been around for nearly a century. What about the other potential listeners, the ones who liked the hit performances of people like Louis Armstrong, Ella Fitzgerald and a host of other jazz and blues performers who appealed to the widest possible audience? They constituted a much bigger potential audience than the jazz diehards alone could provide. Would they stay with us?

In the first year, Jazz FM failed to find the magic formula that would keep both these groups as regular listeners. Continuing problems with the computer meant that too often presenters were left to their own devices. And there was something else that also made them unhappy. I learned from my secretary that she had been asked to join a group of non-broadcasting staff who, under the chairmanship of the managing director, would prepare written reports on the on-air efforts of the presentation team. Imagine how the presenters reacted when they heard about this barmy development and the effect it had on morale generally!

Meanwhile, consultants came and went. Some knew about jazz but nothing about broadcasting. With others it was the other way round. Peter Gelardi left the company halfway through the first full year and was replaced by a man with an excellent track record in commercial radio, John Bradford, whom I knew quite well. He soon became aware of what he referred to as the poisonous atmosphere in the place. I knew what he meant, having seen copies of one or two memos critical of me which some friendly soul directed to my in-tray.

John Bradford just wanted to get through the first year with the station more or less intact, but he had ambitious plans for the future. He and I went to Paris at one stage to discuss a plan to set up a French version of Jazz FM. However, in London research showed a substantial fall in the number of listeners, to around 500,000, with a consequent impact on advertising revenue. The figures also showed that when the Gulf War started in late summer many people switched away from music stations to those that were heavy on news and current affairs.

At the end of a less than exhilarating year, Doris and I decided to take a skiing holiday in the south of France. It was terrific up to the moment I fell and hurt my back. We managed to get back home, but there was a message from John Bradford waiting for me on the answering service. He was asking me to see him urgently. I drove to the Jazz FM building and hobbled into his office. He poured me a beer and said, 'It's not good news.' Then that weasel phrase: 'I'm afraid I'm going to have to let you go.' I pointed out that there was a little matter of my three-year contract with the company. He promptly rolled out another golden cliché: 'Can't pay, won't pay!' So I responded with one of my own: 'You'll hear from my lawyers in the morning.' I then left and headed straight round to Soho Square to fix an appointment with the lawyers who, twelve years earlier, had fought off the attempt by the LBC chairman to bring in someone over my head as editorial boss.

The next day was cold and snowy, and the *Evening Standard* ran the headline 'Radio Jobs Go As Jazz Fans Tune In To War' over the following report:

The Gulf war and the recession have forced radio station Jazz FM to shed almost one-third of its staff just eleven months after its launch. Audiences have halved in three months to an average 500,000 a week, while advertising revenue has slumped. Listeners are tuning into BBC Radio Four or switching on the television for war news instead. Engineers, programme assistants and back-up staff were among the 17 to go yesterday.

Last night managing director John Bradford said: 'We have cut back overheads to a level that we can sustain through one of the most appalling advertising recessions. I am sorry to lose so many talented and loyal people.'

I am not sure that he was including me in that statement.

The following morning's post brought a legal-looking letter from the managing director accusing me of this, that and the other and a separate demand that my company car must be returned immediately. I ignored the bit about the car and sent both documents to my lawyers. It took some while, but eventually Jazz FM came up with a satisfactory financial settlement. As part of the deal I kept the car, a Citroen XM, and Doris and I made an immediate decision to celebrate by taking it across the Channel to its home country and heading south. We had overnight stops in France and Switzerland and then crossed the border into Italy and set off for Lake Maggiore and the hotel where, exactly forty years earlier, we had stayed on our honeymoon.

When we got back home, Jazz FM was still hitting controversial headlines. It had new – though temporary – owners in the form of Golden Rose Radio, run by a man named David Maker. I had known him earlier when he was one of the principals of Radio City in Liverpool before his subsequent spell running the commercial station in Preston. Now Maker had stepped in to stop Jazz FM going into receivership. He quickly became the target for jazz fans anxiously trying to preserve the station's identity. Dave Lee got into the dispute after a newspaper suggested that he had been 'edged out' of Jazz FM. He wrote a letter insisting that he was not edged out and went on to make the extraordinary claim that it was he who had insisted that I should be replaced by someone I had recruited from the BBC, Malcolm Laycock. He then went on to say that his role as director of music gave him the right to veto any record he thought unsuitable.

In reply, I wrote:

The group of jazz enthusiasts, including myself, who won the Jazz FM franchise two years ago will be astounded to learn from Dave Lee that he was employed merely to veto any unsuitable records.

In fact, as director of music, his brief was to build a comprehensive music library so as to implement the agreed policy. This called for a wide ranging mixture of jazz categories from ragtime to the present day with a high proportion of vocal performances at peak times.

The management files at Jazz FM show only too clearly that Mr Lee was constantly at odds with this policy and particularly the use of a computer to ensure a careful balance of artists and styles.

Before we went on air, as the only broadcaster on the board I argued unsuccessfully against the muddle of a dual command – Lee supervising the music, me in charge of programming and both reporting to the managing director. It was doomed to be a failure.

During a frustrating year, I still managed to air a 26-part history of jazz by Charles Fox, a 16-part Duke Ellington retrospective, major jazz concerts from around the world and record review panels and personal choices by distinguished critics. Sadly, none of these programmes or features now exist.

Doris

The opportunity to fly away from it all – up to a point – came when the Swedish government gave the go-ahead for commercial radio, and a newspaper group in Gothenburg started looking for advice on how to set up and run a station in that city. That's how we came to spend several weeks in Sweden. There were in fact three of us – Ron and myself, and a man named Keith Belcher, a journalist who had been one of the stalwarts in the early days of LBC when the station was struggling to survive. At the time, the combination of the names Onions and Belcher caused much merriment in the columns of the weekly satirical magazine *Private Eye*. Keith went on to become one of the key figures at the school established by Capital Radio for the training of would-be broadcasters, among them our daughter, Sarah, after she left university. More recently, Keith had spent a lot of time in Europe teaching the basics of radio broadcasting and advising on various projects. I went along in the role of voice coach and advisor on microphone technique, as I had done at Jazz FM and was to do later when Reuters moved into radio.

We learned a lot during our stint as instructors in Sweden. For instance, although the speed of news presentation, either at the radio microphone or in the television studio, runs at roughly three words a second in Britain, we were wrong to assume the same rough-and-ready rule in compiling news bulletins with our Swedish students. This was because many Swedish words are much longer than their English equivalents. We should have anticipated this. Anyway, we decided to go with two words a second for our Swedish students, and it worked out fine. They were a willing bunch, all with excellent English and mostly from newspapers, but including a number fresh out of college. There was one young man from England, as well as one from Norway, and a young woman from Iceland. So well did the training sessions go that we were able to set up dummy runs, as they are called, which meant using the newly built studios to work through a daily schedule of news bulletins and music programmes as though we were actually on air.

A few weeks later we were invited back when those in the Swedish group were confident they would be given licences to broadcast. It was a happy reunion, and we were able to do a little fine tuning to the excellent sound they were making. Unfortunately, though, I caught a heavy cold and croaked my way through several coaching sessions. I finally went to see a doctor, and at least I was able to experience the high quality of Swedish health care.

On our last night in Gothenburg, our hosts invited us to join them for one of Sweden's culinary traditions, the Friday-night shellfish supper, accompanied by formidable flagons of beer. At the end of it, their managing director stood up to pay tribute to us in excellent English, whereupon Ron rose to make an impromptu response though, as he admitted himself, he was a bit tired and emotional. Keith saved the day by rising to his considerable height and saying a few words in Swedish. At least, it sounded Swedish. Keith had a rare gift for mimicry and managed to bring the house down.

Ron

We had one more get-together with the Swedish radio group. This time, shortly before the Swedes went on air, they came over to London for a final spell of coaching. This took place at Spectrum Radio, which had won a commercial franchise to broadcast a variety of programmes in different languages. Keith had become programme controller and we were able to use the station's facilities, sending the Swedes out into the streets of west London to gather vox pops – the broadcasting term for brief interviews with passers-by on some topic of the day. This demonstrated not only their technical ability but also their impressive command of English.

We also organised visits to several other radio stations, including Capital and a Country and Western station, but I sensed they began to feel that if you've seen one radio station, you've see 'em all. So we took them on a pub crawl so they could sample British beer and express amazement at how cheap it was compared with the cost of a pint back home in Gothenberg. As a bonus, the very first barmaid we encountered was Swedish, and she gave them a quick rundown on where to go and what to see around town. One of the things they wanted to see – the women as much as the men – was a Premier League soccer match in London. We were happy to arrange it, and then, for the last time, we said farewell to them.

Doris

Louise was in her thirtieth year when we learned that Laughton Lodge Hospital was to be closed down. The news was welcome. This was no reflection on the dedicated and hard-working staff; however, the fifteen years she spent there were often troublesome, both for her and for us. On one of our last visits, we set off on a picnic, but suddenly Louise threw a wobbly and began ripping at the roof upholstery, pulling down several wires in the process. This triggered a shower of sparks and a speedy return back to base.

The decision to close Laughton was in line with the newly fashionable policy of 'Care in the Community'. In fact the idea had been around for some while, but it gained momentum in the 1980s. Basically it was a move against the old institutions, dating from the Victorian age, which virtually shut away people with mental or physical problems. Now the thinking was that they should be looked after in much smaller homes within the general community. So Lulu was transferred to a rambling building half a mile from the centre of Eastbourne with a great view of the open countryside and an impressive garden. Two of the other six residents at Bedfordwell Road were also from Laughton, and each had their own rooms, which were then in the process of being well furnished and newly decorated.

Louise was lucky enough to have a young woman named Anne Carroll as her 'key worker', as they were designated. Anne did her best to ensure that Lulu got the best out of life, both at work and at play. In her lively Irish accent, she announced, 'I will not have her slighted,' as she reported back on a recent trip into Eastbourne with Louise to buy fashionable clothes for her at Laura Ashley and Marks and Spencer and have lunch out at a place called Maxim's. By comparison, our own lifestyle suddenly seemed a bit humdrum.

Such was the improvement in Lulu's general behaviour at this time that Anne Carroll decided to accompany our daughter on the train for a day out in London. There were no problems, and this encouraged two other carers later in the year to accompany Louise to the Isle of Wight for a five-day holiday. This, too, saw her in top form, and she returned to Eastbourne talking of another holiday the following year. She mentioned France as a possible destination, or a return to the Isle of Wight.

Her various carers in the new home supplied us with copies of the detailed reports they compiled on Lulu's progress. These recorded that building work was still going on as she settled into her new home and that she had had to make a temporary move into another flat while her own was being renovated, along with the installation of an adjoining kitchen and dining room. There was no adverse reaction from Louise to either the upheaval caused by the building work or the arrival of two other residents who were to share the kitchen and dining room with her.

The news from Bedfordwell Road continued to cheer us up. Staff reported that Lulu's response to her new home had been very positive. When she arrived they had concentrated on the development of her social skills, and she was able to enjoy life much more than had seemed likely when she first moved there. Her behaviour remained good for a longer time than the 'honeymoon' period to be expected after a move to a new home.

A decision was made to concentrate on our daughter's social skills before looking at educational prospects. As we had become all too aware over the years, Louise could become quiet and withdrawn, resulting in limited communication with others and little eye contact. This characteristic was observed in her new home as well, and new routines to try and deal with it were introduced by the staff, with backup from specialists working for Eastbourne Council who had particular skills in looking after people with learning disabilities.

One of Lulu's subsequent key workers, Josette Davis, had a remarkable ability to tune in to Louise's wavelength. She was dedicated and painstaking, as indeed were many of the staff who looked after our daughter over the years, but she was also the owner of two dogs. They proved an immediate hit with Louise. Over the years her vocabulary had been expanded by the presence of various pooches she had met, all the way from Tammy at Cobb School, via Popsy and Shane, who lived at the Matthews' holiday farmhouse in Cornwall, and to our own English Springer spaniel, Hershey, when we returned from America.

Josette's dogs were to be a major feature of conversation with Louise whenever we visited her at Bedfordwell Road, and she regaled us with tales of what they got up to when she went on outings led by her redoubtable key worker. This may not seem all that remarkable, but in Louise's case it was another sign that she was coming out of her shell to some extent and relating well to the people around her – so much so that it became possible to enrol her on a cookery course at Eastbourne College of Arts and Technology where, accompanied by a member of staff, she went once a week.

Despite her passion for food – both the preparing and the eating of it – staff at Bedfordwell Road were successful in reducing her weight, thanks to plenty of exercise, including regular visits to Eastbourne for a boisterous half-hour in the Lido pool. She became proficient enough to achieve Grade 1 in the Amateur Swimming Association's Water Skills Award, and had a framed certificate on her bedroom wall to prove it.

Yet despite the progress that had been made after three years in her new home, there were one or two hangovers from those earlier years at Laughton Lodge. The principal one was anxiety, often arising from her obsession with future events or with the staff rota or that day's menu. She had no sense of time, so that when she was told that Mum and Dad would be coming to see her on such and such a date, she expected it to happen immediately.

Our failure to appear right away would result in a tearful outburst and a difficult day for her carers, who gradually devised various strategies to cope with the dark side of Lulu's behaviour, including giving her constant reassurance. Their patience paid off. Progress was such that they managed to enrol her on some additional courses at Eastbourne College designed for people with learning difficulties. And – always accompanied by one of her carers – off she went without any problems.

In the following couple of years, there were occasional ups and downs, but progress continued to the point where her carers began to wonder whether she might benefit by moving to a smaller home a short distance away. She was sharing her accommodation at that time with two other women in one wing of a very large building. Another wing accommodated the male residents. The new place, still to be renovated, would have room for six residents, each with their own room, but living together as a family in what one official report described as more like an 'ordinary' home than her present place. It was in an upmarket residential district known as Hampden Park near Lulu's college and Eastbourne hospital.

When we saw Park Lane for the first time, we were delighted. Inevitably, though, the building work took longer than expected, and then came the various official safety inspections, but finally she moved into her new home, shortly before the turn of the century. We were now increasingly hopeful about her future.

In the spring we went to Park Lane for our first review meeting on her progress so far. We learned that she was attending college for literacy and numeracy classes, but she was becoming increasingly anxious before and during the cookery course there, so her attendance at it was abandoned and instead she was encouraged to do more cooking back in her new home, helping to prepare the evening meal for residents on Tuesdays and Thursdays, and making her own breakfast each morning.

Socially she was having a high old time. Her recent diary dates included discos, a barn dance, bingo, and a pantomime in Hastings, and then there was the mince pie morning to which, along with other parents, we were invited at Christmas time. Later on there would be visits twice a week to Aqua Splash on Eastbourne seafront, and movement and dance classes every Friday. Then there was church on Sunday.

She also had a paid job. This involved a weekly visit to a place called the Ford Room, where she and other residents from her new home sat around a table and assembled small metal parts. The report on Lulu's efforts was that 'she works very hard and needs very little supervision'.

In May of that first year at Park Lane she went back to the Isle of Wight for a holiday, accompanied by another resident and two carers. Once again she was in great form and came home talking about Blackpool as the holiday destination for the following year. In the autumn she was back at Eastbourne College for courses in literacy and numeracy, as well as simple horticulture and sewing and knitting.

At subsequent review meetings at Park Lane we learned that on the days she attended Eastbourne College she was now able to join other students at lunch in the canteen. Meanwhile, her social life had expanded to include ten-pin bowling and visits to the cinema and theatre – but there was a mind-boggling moment when her carer reported that at the weekly meetings of Mencap's Acorn Club in nearby Hailsham, Lulu had taken up darts! We just hoped that they were the safety kind with suction pads instead of the traditional sharp points . . .

Getting the medication right was a continuing challenge at Park Lane, as it had been in Lulu's former homes. Generally she remained in good physical health, but the effects of the anti-psychotic drugs had to be carefully monitored in aiming for emotional stability. Sadly, during one unsettled period, she was unable to go on the holiday that she had been looking forward to so keenly. A subsequent review recorded two 'incidents of violence'.

Despite the occasional setbacks, we thought that Park Lane was an ideal location for Louise. There were six people with learning difficulties living there, four men and two women, including our daughter, and they sat down together for meals in a well-appointed dining room. We always had a sense of visiting a family whenever we went to see Louise, and felt that the friendly carers were very much a part of it.

Ron

Some time before Lulu settled in at Park Lane, I had a drink with one of my old buddies, Peter Thornton. He was the man who had succeeded me as editor of IRN, and when I left to join Visnews, he had taken over my role as editorial director. Some years later he had been appointed managing director of LBC/IRN, and he remained in that role when Selkirk, LBC's original owners, sold out to the Australian company Darling Downs. Peter did not get on with the new owners. They had sacked a close friend who had been recruited from the BBC in LBC's early days and was a key figure in the station's gradual revival. They also scrapped LBC's on-air identity and renamed the station Crown FM. Peter felt – as we all did – that this suggested that the station was now being run by one of Britain's leading paint manufacturers. He found himself involved in too many disputes with the Aussies. The programme changes they introduced resulted in a significant fall in audience figures, whereupon they decided to restore the original LBC identity. But by then Peter had had enough and managed to negotiate a satisfactory settlement which took him happily through the exit door.

So when we met for that drink, we asked ourselves what we were going to do now. Perhaps the answer should have been nothing. What prompted the question was the fact that soon the Australian owners would have to face the renewal of their franchise to run the LBC operation, which by now was broadcasting separate services on it its two wavelengths, AM and FM.

Franchise renewal occurred every seven years and was the opportunity for rival groups to try and take over from the sitting tenant. We were both aware that Lady Porter was now involved with LBC through a company called Chelverton Investments. Lady Porter had been the leader of Westminster City Council and was now being accused by the district auditor of selling off Westminster council homes in an attempt to buy Conservative votes. Our calculation was that the ensuing scandal would do nothing for the Australians' chances when shortly they met the IBA panel deciding who should run LBC for the next seven years. So I contacted a man named Bruce Fireman, who worked for a city bank called Guinness Mahon. He had shown interest in the World News Network during my time at Visnews. Subsequently I had an idea for a classical music and news station, based on one in America owned by the *New York Times*. I discussed this with Bruce and he took it to the editor of the *Independent* newspaper. He showed interest but the project didn't go very far. However, this time Bruce persuaded Guinness Mahon to back an application to take over the LBC franchise, and for the first – and only – time in our lives, Peter and I found ourselves working five days a week in a bank. We were joined by a couple of advisors we had known during our days in LBC's Gough Square basement. One was financial editor Douglas Moffitt and the other was a man who claimed – correctly – to have done shifts as an LBC reporter, but who then rose to dizzying heights at the top of other companies in the media. When Michael Grade quit as boss of the ITV network, this man – Roger Parry – was among those tipped to take over the job.

Then Bruce Fireman announced that John Tusa had accepted an offer to join us as chairman of what was to become London Radio. Tusa – later Sir John – had an outstanding record as a broadcaster and administrator at the BBC, and notably as managing director of the World Service. Many people thought he should have become Director-General of the BBC when the post fell vacant. He left the BBC, though continued to work for them freelance. We were delighted to have him with us, leading the charge against LBC's present owners.

So Peter and I travelled into the City five days a week and started to pound out the golden words that would form the basis of London Radio's application to take over ownership of LBC. We were joined by Roger Francis, who had been chief engineer at LBC for many years. We needed him to look after the technical side of the application. We also appointed a managing director, Graham Luff, from the *Independent* newspaper's management team. Meanwhile, Bruce and his colleagues at Guinness Mahon began raising the money that would be required, if we were successful, to get the station up and running.

By now we were getting plenty of publicity and Reuters approached us with the idea of making an investment. Money was not exactly flooding in, but Guinness Mahon resisted the Reuter approach. In the autumn of that year, six months after we started on the application, the IBA announced that we had been successful. London Radio would take over the two services run by the Australians on the AM and FM frequencies. We would move into their premises in west London in about a year, and begin broadcasting the new services soon afterwards.

We celebrated our success with dinner at the Savoy Hotel, but we were only too aware that there were important matters still to be resolved. Like money. We were struggling to raise enough of it to deliver everything we had promised. Eventually negotiations with Reuters were resumed and, with months still to go before we went on air, the decision was taken to sell the franchise to them for £5 million. Some of us felt we sold out too cheaply. Still, at least under Reuter's ownership we were now able to push ahead in setting up the two new stations that had formed the basis of our successful application.

So we moved into the Hammersmith building, where broadcasting would continue under the existing regime until we launched our new services in the autumn. We interviewed the editorial staff – we knew many of them from the old days and were happy for them to stay on. One or two people decided to leave – or were asked to leave. Several former members of the staff came back, including Brian Hayes, programme controller Robin Malcolm, and Keith Belcher, who had been involved in several broadcasting projects, including the setting up of Southern Sound, the commercial radio station for the Brighton area. Keith helped us in signing up extra staff, especially those required for the new non-stop news channel.

Several months before we were due to launch the new services, Reuters took formal control of the London Radio franchise. The following week came the unsettling announcement that Graham Luff, the man we had appointed to be managing director, would be leaving us. When Guinness Mahon sold out to Reuters for £5 million, it was Graham who had negotiated so fiercely on behalf of the directors who came from outside the bank, including Peter Thornton and myself, to ensure that they all got their fair share.

The trade press speculated variously that Graham would be succeeded by someone with a background in marketing or maybe an existing Reuters employee. *Broadcast* magazine referred to speculation 'over the future of key London Radio figures Peter Thornton and Ron Onions'. That sent us into fits of laughter. We both knew exactly what was going to happen to us. Peter had been through major heart surgery only recently and, with his partner, Lesley Judd, he intended to head to France and into happy retirement as soon possible after the launch of the two new stations. Doris and I had exactly the same aim. I was older than Peter, and, for me, thirty-five years in the rough and tumble of broadcasting, BBC and commercial, home and abroad, was more than enough.

Still, Graham's departure and continuing guesswork in the press about the future of London Radio under its new owners led to a tense atmosphere as the arrival of the two new stations drew near in the autumn. What made it worse was a decision by the new regime to replace the secretary who had worked for me and then for Peter in the early days at Gough Square, and who had come with us on the present move to Hammersmith.

Then came the announcement from Reuters that they had chosen a man named Rory Macleod as managing director. We knew Rory well. In the early days of LBC, we had recruited him to the IRN news desk from one of the Scottish radio stations. He left us after deciding to make a bid to the Broadcasting Authority to run a new franchise in Brighton. He was successful, and asked me to join him down on the coast as managing director of Southern Sound, as it was called. Later it became part of the Heart FM chain of commercial stations. I was tempted by Rory's offer, but in the end it was Keith Belcher who took the job.

Very early in October, the two new radio stations went to air and there was a spectacular launch party at a place called Imagination. Reaction in the press and elsewhere was low key, and we were taken aback by some hostile comments by a senior figure in the IBA hierarchy. It was felt that the new non-stop news channel should be going out on the AM frequency. It had a smaller audience than the original programme service provided by LBC. This, over more than twenty years, had provided a mixture of news and discussion, with some music in the evening. Critics argued that it should have stayed just where it was on the higher-quality FM wavelength, which was more attractive to advertisers. Eventually this transition took place. By that time, Peter and I were gone, happily settled with our partners in France.

As for Independent Radio News, its previous vitality just drained away. Its clients around the country decided they no longer wanted to hear from reporters. Instead they preferred a do-it-yourself service which provided written accounts of the news stories of the day plus what the trade referred to as 'actuality'. These are short clips of sound taking listeners to the heart of the story.

Reuters did not hang around all that long, and the London Radio stations were sold on to another organisation, Global Radio, for a much higher figure than Guinness Mahon received from Reuters. There followed a period when the stations were sold on at a higher and higher price, losing much of their original identity in the process. Eventually the FM Channel gave itself a new title, which retained the same company initials, but now LBC stood for London's Biggest Conversation. For some of us it stood for London's Biggest Cop-out. Phone-ins were king, and this name change marked the end of any successful attempt to establish a high-quality news and current affairs service strong enough to rival the BBC's output.

Many reporters and correspondents from LBC/IRN now went on to work for BBC television and radio or ITN, at home and abroad. Others found jobs with Channel 4 News or Sky News. Sadly, ITN and, later, Sky News became the principal source of news for the IRN service, and eventually IRN was of less consequence.

Doris

Many of these changes happened long after we had gone off to France. Peter Thornton and his partner, Lesley, beat us by several weeks, having found a temporary place in Dieppe before moving to an imposing building right on the front overlooking the English Channel. We wondered whether the sound of ships departing back to Blighty might bring on too much nostalgic longing. Not a bit of it, they said. In due course they moved a long way south to a glorious retreat, complete with swimming pool.

It took us longer to make the move to France. We already had somewhere to go – the small apartment at Mougins-le-Haut, not far from the Mediterranean coastline, that we had bought some ten years earlier as a holiday home. However, our departure was delayed while we discussed our move to France with the rest of the family and, equally importantly, with Lulu's carers back in Eastbourne. We finally worked out a schedule which would bring us back to England for a few days every month. This would enable us to get down to Sussex to spend some time with Louise as well as check on our home in London and see Sarah, her husband Christopher and the grandchildren, Lucy and Joe. Reassuringly, Sarah said they would manage to spend some time with Lulu in the midst of their busy lives. The staff at Park Lane gave their blessing to our plan and we finally flew off to Mougins-le-Haut in the early spring.

It was a huge relief to get away to France. At last we could put some of the grisly experiences of the past few years behind us and just think about the good times we had also had. There had been a lot of those. Even so, Ron needed plenty of reassurance about making this drastic change of lifestyle. I jollied him along, and told him there were several more formalities we had to go before we could settle down and enjoy our new life.

Ron

First we had to acquire a car. We did this at the Avis depot at Nice Airport, where the policy is to replace rental cars when they are still young and lively. The one we bought from them was an automatic, a Renault Clio with about 6,000 miles on the clock. It was to take us all over the place, including two trips to London and back and many happy journeys throughout southern France and northern Italy. Fifteen years after we bought it, the car was still ready and willing to go.

Most of the early trips were on formal business, such as obtaining a resident's permit for each of us. Essentially this is an identity card displaying one's photo and establishing one's rights and benefits as a taxpayer in France. We had to fill in a formidable document at a customs and immigration unit just outside Nice. This place had an air of 'Abandon Hope All Ye Who Enter Here' that recalled the day of our dismal arrival in New York City so many years previously. During a long wait we started talking to a Dutch couple who revealed that they had, in fact, lost the permits that had been issued to them, along with their Dutch passports. When we asked what had happened, they told us they had been cruising to South Africa on a ship called the *Achille Lauro* when, fifteen miles off the coast of Somalia, she caught fire. Passengers and crew had to take to the lifeboats, and in the process the Dutch couple lost most of their belongings, including passports and the French resident permits.

After hearing that, we just sat there humbly, counting our blessings and trying to be patient.

Doris

A little later, we had to face up to another procedure which, in effect, required us to get married all over again. We had acquired an English financial adviser who set up a French bank account for us and helped us compile our annual declaration to the French tax authority. It was he who pointed out, that under French law, property and other assets in France could only be inherited by the nearest relatives. So, on our next trip to England, we were advised to take our existing marriage certificate to the French embassy in London and ask the Consul General there to make a signed declaration that we were legally man and wife. This document must now be taken back to France and presented to a notary in Cannes. He would then draw up a further declaration to be signed by us and listing ourselves and our two daughters as the principal beneficiaries. In due course it would be put on public display, rather like banns of marriage. In the event, because of her mental condition, Louise could not be included, and a separate paper had to be prepared stating the reason for her exclusion. Getting married all over again seemed like a good excuse for a celebratory lunch – and that's exactly what we had on the seafront in Cannes.

With the issue of our resident permits, we now had easy access to the French national health service. It was to serve us well, both on our occasional visits to local doctors and, in my case later on, to a specialist who arranged without any delay admission to a nearby hospital for an internal examination. The hospital had been opened only a few years earlier, and its standards of care and hygiene were quite outstanding. I won't go on about the food – but it was to die for . . .

Gradually we settled into the new pattern of our lives which, once every month, saw us boarding the plane at Nice Airport and heading back to London for a few days. It was a chance to see the family, all of whom we missed a great deal. The very close bond that existed between Sarah and ourselves due to coping with Louise now expanded to embrace the rest of Sarah's family too.

At Eastbourne, we found Louise in good form, though there had been one or two ups and downs, usually linked to changes in medication and her adverse reaction, sometimes, when the staff tried to introduce changes into her social and educational routine. Still, members of staff continued to venture forth on the occasional holiday with her, and she was invariably delighted to see us again on our visits home.

Meanwhile, we had settled gradually into an enjoyable routine at Mougins-le-Haut, where residents had access to their own swimming pool, as well as tennis courts, a gymnasium, jogging trails amid the pine trees, and a place to play boules. We made good use of all of these amenities. Once a week we went to market and we were spoilt for choice. The nearest was close by in Vallauris, a large village closely associated with Picasso, and where some of his major works are on permanent exhibition. Among our favourite markets was that adjoining the old quarter in Nice, which was once part of Italy, and the one in Cannes, where nearly every day was market day. We usually went there on Friday because that's the day when aïoli tops the menu. This is the fish dish featuring the famous garlic mayonnaise of Provence, and it was always available in a little restaurant just across from the market hall.

But I think the market highlight for us was the occasional trip to Ventimiglia, just across the border in Italy. It had a slightly scruffy look compared with the nearby coastal towns in France, but the attractions included a huge market hall just crammed with temptation and, outside, a long row of market stalls stretching along the beach and offering a huge range of goodies. We liked to go there at Christmas time and buy presents, among them cashmere garments at a very friendly price, and plenty of socks, sweaters and scarves for the folks shivering back home.

On one visit to Ventimiglia in the summer, we were sitting on the beach when suddenly there was a commotion as fishermen came running ashore bearing a huge fish, as big as a mature shark. A crowd soon surrounded them as they sliced it up and took half of it away to a fish restaurant nearby. The rest they intended to sell right there on the beach. The slicing process took some while, but when we finally stepped forward one of the fishermen realised we were English and presented us with two huge portions, refusing to take any money. I cooked them in the apartment that evening, and they tasted superb.

Sometimes we went skiing at a small town called Valberg, about an hour's drive up to the mountains north of Nice. We discovered a small hotel where we became friendly with the family who ran it. They advised us to come up during the week to avoid the crowds at the weekend. We managed to cope reasonably well on the lower slopes, though I had an unfortunate habit of turning right when I wanted to go left. One year Sarah, Chris and Lucy joined us, while Joe was taken care of by his other grandmother back in England. We enrolled Lucy in a class for young children and in no time at all she was showing me how to survive on the slopes, while her mum and dad disappeared for a few hours on the more challenging runs. We all have very fond memories of that time.

Ron

On two occasions, we drove the Clio all the way to Surbiton and back, taking the P & O ferry across the Channel. The first time, our return journey took us down the western side of France from St Malo and we stopped overnight at Cahors in south-western France. This was near Montcuq, where Peter Thornton and Lesley Judd were now living. We rang to see if they were at home. They were, and we spent the rest of a happy day at a local restaurant where obviously they were well known and where we seemed to consume every regional delicacy and rather too much local wine. It was good to see Peter in pretty good shape following the two heart operations he had had back in London, and it was obvious he was sticking to a strict exercise regime recommended by the local doctor.

Lesley said we should stop over in their elegant home – or at least have a swim in the pool – but we had an appointment in Nice the following morning, so we decided to set off back to our apartment in Mougins-le-Haut. It was a mistake. The night was wild and windy, and when we reached the motorway going east towards home the rain began to fall with such ferocity that we were forced to stop for some while at a roadside restaurant. The downpour never really let up. Fortunately there was little traffic going in our direction, but progress was very slow.

We finally made it to Mougins, exhausted. The following morning radio and television news bulletins were full of reports of traffic accidents and abandoned vehicles. It's not all sunshine in the south of France. From time to time we also had to contend with the Mistral, the cold north-westerly wind that comes roaring down from the Rhone valley and rattles the shutters. The other seasonal hazard was the outbreak of forest fires in the very dry spells of high summer. None of them came very close to us, but we used to watch from the beach at Golfe Juan when huge Canadian cargo planes specially adapted for the purpose came swooping down to the surface of the ocean and scooped up a huge quantity of water. They then flew off with their cargo and dumped it where the fires were most destructive.

It was in the spring and early summer that we spent a lot of time on our nearest beach, enjoying a swim in the warm water and picnicking under the obligatory sunshade. Come July, the beaches became crowded with holiday visitors and we would head north to Grasse, the perfume capital of France, and set off exploring the small towns in the nearby hills and valleys. Once we boarded a little train from Nice which took us on a bumpy and sometimes precarious track – or so it seemed – all the way up to Digne. There, in the station restaurant of all places, we sat down to a meal as fine as any we tasted in all our time in France.

Down in the valleys there were frequent fêtes and festivals, as well as lakes where you could safely cool off. This was also the time of year when the major jazz festivals took place, notably at Juan-les-Pins, just along the coast, and at Cimiez, up in the hills above Nice. The latter took place in an olive grove surrounding a ruined amphitheatre where the top-of-the-bill bands did their thing. It was a time when many of the great twentieth-century performers were still going strong, and we were lucky enough to see Miles Davis, Dizzy Gillespie, Lionel Hampton's big band, Stan Getz and many others at their peak, not forgetting British trumpeter Humphrey Lyttleton. The amphitheatre was close to a hospital and, in deference to the patients there, by eleven o'clock the big bands, after rocking the amphitheatre at full blast, gave way to a gentle slow blues from a solo pianist. At Juan-les-Pins, under the palm trees and close to the sea, those on the bill included the veteran blues singer B.B. King, and the latter-day trumpet master of jazz ancient and modern, Wynton Marsalis.

One year we flew down to Pisa to have a nervous look at Italy's famous leaning tower, and then drove on to the walled city of Perugia for the annual jazz festival that took place there in July. This opened with a New Orleans marching band parading around the cobbled streets, and we particularly liked the gentler sounds of small groups featuring piano and guitars that played in the restaurants at lunchtime.

Doris

One of the advantages of living so near to Nice Airport was that places like Venice and Barcelona were only an hour or so away. We also flew the short distance across the Mediterranean to Tunisia, where we were the only English visitors in a beach hotel run by a French holiday group. The staff there gave us a warm welcome, in part because they were anxious to improve their command of English in the hope that it would enable them to get jobs in London.

One of the big attractions for us in Tunisia was Carthage, sacked by the Romans in 146 BC. This ancient city had loomed large in our geography lessons at school and now, so many years later, we were there and fascinated to see how carefully the place had been preserved. The other place that captivated us was the souk (the bazaar or market place in Muslim countries). It was full of weird and wonderful things for sale, including a cow's head. Ron wondered how we would get it through French customs at Nice Airport. Was he being serious? I said I had been happy enough on a recent occasion when our son-in-law was visiting the apartment to cook pig's trotters for the pair of them, but the cow's head would stay right where it was.

Ron

During the school holidays we rented a studio apartment facing our nearest beach, at Golfe Juan, and Sarah and Chris came down with the grandchildren to stay there. It meant they had easy access to sea and sand for a fortnight and we joined them most days, sometimes setting off for a trip up to the hills. It was a rare pleasure for us to be all together, and especially so on the day we went by sea to Monte Carlo, followed for much of the journey by a school of dolphins.

The following year, Christopher's mother and father came down too, and this time we rented some extra accommodation for them in Mougins-le-Haut while we went back to the UK for one of our regular visits to Louise.

Yet, much as we enjoyed living in France, as the years went by and the grandchildren grew up, we became more and more aware of the geographical gulf between us and the fact that we were missing out on so much that was happening at home. We began to feel that we were in neither one place nor the other. What triggered this feeling in part was that when we decided to improve our limited ability to speak French by attending weekly evening classes, we would miss out on key lessons every time we went off to see Louise and the rest of the family. The same thing applied to a dancing class that Doris was keen to join.

There was another significant factor, too. In the fifteen years that we had had the apartment in Mougins-le-Haut, the place had changed quite a lot. From our balcony we used to have a clear view of the valley beneath us. Over time, further apartment buildings went up, far more than we recalled seeing on the original master plan. This resulted in swirls of dust and a great deal of noise, driving away much of the birdlife that had been such an attractive feature of the environment. Happily we could still hear the nightingales singing through the night in the early part of summer – but we were dismayed when it was decided to switch off all the elegant fountains around the village and fill in all the small pools where the frogs lived under the water lilies. It seemed that the French had succumbed to the Health and Safety rigmarole that had so affected life back in England. Then there was the decision to widen the pavements by reducing the width of the roads, restricting the opportunity to park outside your front door and unload the stuff you had brought back from the supermarket. It all added up.

So, finally, missing the family as we did, and unsettled by all the changes that had taken place at Mougins over the years, we decided to go back home to the Costa del Surbiton, as we called it, on the south bank of the River Thames.

Doris

I was pleased to be back. By now, our granddaughter, Lucy, was at grammar school in Kingston, and we were delighted to see her appearing in a school play there. She had also learned to play the tenor horn and, indeed, at a family celebration in a restaurant she stood up and performed 'Happy Birthday to You' in my honour.

Later our grandson, Joe, took up the same instrument, but he preferred acting, and we saw him in various performances at both junior and grammar school. He seemed to be following in his father's footsteps: Christopher was a television journalist, but he also appeared on stage and screen as an actor. With the Royal Shakespeare Company, he went on tour in *Hecuba*, starring Vanessa Redgrave, and this took him from London to America and then to Europe. Subsequent tours saw him performing in China. Meanwhile our oldest daughter, Sarah, had become a teacher in media studies and also resumed her earlier role as a radio newsreader.

Lucy went on to study at Manchester University, and I suppose it was inevitable that, during her time there, she should appear on television, putting a question to the panel during David Dimbleby's weekly 'Question Time' on BBC TV. Then Joe, in his first year at Durham University, got himself a walk-on part in an ITV drama filmed in the north-east, starring Martin Shaw.

Sometimes the rest of the family accompanied us on our regular visits to Louise, and together we enjoyed successful trips to the beach or to a restaurant. This was a period of ups and downs for Lulu. She continued her programme of educational and social activities, but reacted adversely to changes in medication. Even so, we were convinced that Park Lane provided her with exactly the right environment and hoped that she would be able to remain there.

Ron

Not long after we came back from France we were saddened to hear of the sudden death of my old comrade-in-arms from LBC days, Peter Thornton. His partner, Lesley Judd, rang me to say he had been taken ill while they were on a short visit to London and died soon afterwards in hospital. Doris and I were among the many LBC employees who attended the cremation ceremony in west London to mourn the passing of a man who was much loved and respected within the world of newspapers and broadcasting.

A few months later, there was worrying news from Lulu's care home in Eastbourne. In the hot, dry summer of 2003, builders and a surveyor had been summoned to Park Lane to check on subsidence at one corner of the building. The roots of nearby trees were exposed above the garden's sandy soil, and in the bathroom cracks had started to appear on the walls. Work began on an attempt to underpin the building, but by late autumn we received a letter saying that the subsidence had increased and alternative accommodation had to be found for all of the residents.

It was especially distressing for us, coming as it did shortly after a review meeting that had revealed that Lulu's behaviour had been declining for some months, with 'increased incidents of screaming, self-injury and violence towards staff'.

At Christmas time, a further letter announced that everyone at Park Lane, including staff, would transfer to Seaford, just a few miles along the coast. There, they moved into Homefield Cottages, that had been a home for old people. It was to prove an unhappy home for Lulu. Some of the staff who knew her well felt that a change in medication shortly before she left Park Lane had had an adverse effect on her. Daily charts on her progress – or lack of it – told a depressing tale of screaming and violence towards staff.

On one visit in high summer, we took her off to Seaford beach, where we planned to have a swim and a picnic. Neither happened because of her constant and noisy distress. Several people approached us expressing concern at what was going on. Somehow we managed to move our protesting daughter off the beach and back into the car. Another noisy scene followed as we got her out of the car, with the help of staff, and back into her temporary home.

On our next visit we decided to have a picnic in the garden behind Homefield Cottages. This got off to a good start as we unpacked a tempting array of goodies from the hamper, but, foolishly, we had overlooked the possible effect of rich and sugary food on someone who was mildly diabetic. On returning home, we rang Homefield Cottages to check, as we normally did, that all was well. All was not well, and we were gently reprimanded by the carer on duty.

As the months went by, most of the Homefield residents were moved elsewhere as and when suitable vacancies occurred in the county's care homes. As for Louise, a written assessment at this time reported that her specific needs made it difficult to find a suitable provider locally. Additionally, there had been a number of 'adult protection incidents' arising from Louise's recent behaviour. It was not until shortly before Christmas that we received a letter from the County Council saying Louise would be moving 'on a temporary basis' to the Greenwood Respite Home in Bexhill. The letter went on: 'Clearly, as this is not seen as a permanent move, the Assessment Team will be continuing to look at alternative options for the future.'

This did not exactly boost our spirits. The letter meant there would be at least two moves for Louise in the near future, with the consequent large amount of stress on each occasion. A subsequent paragraph informed us that it was intended to transfer some of the staff from Homefield to Greenwood, and it was hoped that Louise would continue to maintain 'as far as possible' her links with colleagues and friends in the Eastbourne area. To both our minds, what that seemed to suggest, gloomily, was that she might have to be moved out of the county. Sometime later we heard that the move to Greenwood would not take place after all, because of 'potential conflicts of interest with other residents'. The search went on but, for one reason or another, without success.

Louise was the last to leave Homefield Cottages. Eventually the West Kent and Medway NHS and Social Care Partnership Trust came up with the offer of a place between Hastings and Battle, several miles away. It was in an annexe to an existing care home called 'Pedros' which was being upgraded but which, we were assured, would be available soon. Meanwhile, temporary rented accommodation had to be found. Louise was told she would be going on 'holiday' for a short time and, with two carers, was moved to a converted oasthouse near Sidley, just north of Bexhill.

The 'holiday' was to go on for almost a year. The location was idyllic, deep in the Sussex countryside, on the edge of a small farm, with sheep and cows and a full range of wildlife – not forgetting a goose called Reggie. He was the wildest of them all. He was invariably on guard outside the front door, flapping and snapping at anyone who tried to get past him. You got the same unfriendly treatment every time you tried to leave.

Despite Reggie, the oasthouse seemed at first to be the ideal location for our daughter, but within a few weeks her behaviour had deteriorated and our visits brought back unhappy memories of the screaming and shouting we had faced too often when we went to see her during her time at Laughton Lodge. Still, the carers on duty at the oasthouse seemed to us to have developed magical techniques for restoring calm. One involved getting Louise to join them in a countdown from one hundred to zero, by which time she was all sweetness and light. At first we thought they had given her a shot of something. Not so – but the problems caused by the isolated location of our daughter's 'temporary' home were not so easily resolved. During her time at the two care homes in Eastbourne, she had enjoyed a programme of social and recreational activities which had continued to expand. Trying to recreate that programme from West Oast, which was miles from anywhere, sadly proved impossible.

As the weeks went by, a new social care assessor, Brenda Hughes, took up Lulu's case. She reported that 'the current temporary service is too socially isolating to enable her to have opportunity to interact with a peer group' and that 'the delay in moving to Pedros is likely to affect her acceptance of settling into a smaller home which is in closer proximity to neighbours and noise'.

In July, Mrs Hughes met senior staff of the West Kent and Medway Trust to discuss an action plan. There was talk of Louise attending day centre services and of opportunities to attend college. On a subsequent visit to Louise, Mrs Hughes reported that 'the action plan did not appear to have progressed'. She again expressed her concern about Lulu's isolation and said while it was evident that our daughter was being well supported in domestic and shopping activities, 'the social aspect was limited to her interacting mainly with her carers and occasionally with her parents'.

Doris

To begin with, our visits to Louise at this time had taken place over tea at a restaurant on the seafront at Bexhill, opposite the famous Art Deco building known as the De La Warr pavilion. Two of her carers drove her down from the oasthouse, and the five of us were able to enjoy a happy half-hour over tea and biscuits. Sadly this arrangement came to an abrupt end after an occasion when Lulu, clearly not at her best, began to slide under the table and disappear from view. I reached forward to restrain her, tapping her on the wrist as I did so. She went into a tantrum and the carers had to hustle her out of the restaurant and back into the car.

The sequel to this depressing moment was a meeting with two of the principals of the West Kent NHS and Social Care Trust, Laura Dormer and Angie Simons. It was a tense occasion. Sarah accompanied us and became quite angry over what she regarded as unfair criticism of me. Laura Dormer promised to prepare written guidelines for our future visits to Louise so that she could 'move forward in a positive way'. There was also a discussion about the long delay in moving Lulu from West Oast to Pedros and the consequent strain on all of us. We learned that the Commission for Social Care Inspection (CSCI) still had to approve the changes at Pedros and certify that it was fit for purpose. We had had previous experience of CSCI at Lulu's previous care homes in East Sussex and were impressed by its insistence on the highest possible standards, particularly in matters of safety. Sometimes, we learned, they even turned up unannounced . . .

Laura Dormer sent us a letter summarising our meeting, but unfortunately, in referring to the disastrous café visit, it contained the phrase 'when Mrs Onions had slapped Louise on the hand'. Oh dear, that put us back in attack mode. We wrote back: 'Since we note that this incident is now a matter of record, it is important to emphasise that we have striven over forty years to avoid any form of aggressive physical reaction in responding to Louise, however testing the circumstances. If ever we failed, we are sure that you and your colleagues – far more than anybody else – would have sympathetic understanding.'

Christmas at the oasthouse came and went. Then, to everyone's relief, Louise moved to Pedros at the end of February 2006. Her two-week 'holiday' at the oasthouse had lasted more than ten months. In preparation for the move she had been out shopping with her

carers and chose her own bedroom furniture and curtains. We were
delighted with what we found on our first visit to her new home.
There was a large sitting-cum-dining room and her own garden at
the rear with a rose arch and bird table. If only the kitchen could
have been bigger. She had developed considerable cooking skills at
the Eastbourne College, as she had demonstrated at Christmas in
the large and well-equipped kitchen at the oasthouse. Sadly, though,
the kitchen in the Pedros annexe was far too small for adequate
supervision and the preparation of food, which had to be done at
the dining table.

As she settled into her new home, we were surprised to hear
that she was going on a short holiday to Hayling Island, near
Portsmouth, accompanied by two of her carers. For Louise, the
word 'holiday' had come to mean nearly a year stuck in a remote
oasthouse, with Reggie the goose snapping at you whenever you
went out or returned. So we were not surprised to hear that the
holiday was not quite the success everyone had anticipated.

A subsequent report, though listing all the seaside attractions she
enjoyed, went on to say 'Louise found it difficult adjusting to the
new environment'. Our feeling was that she should have been given
more time to settle in at Pedros.

Soon after they came back, Lulu celebrated her 44th birthday in
great style with a tea party at Pedros, and Sarah and Christopher
joined us on the trip down from London. A month later we went
down again and this time there were six of us, including Lucy and
Joe. We had all been invited to an Easter feast of tea and hot cross
buns. Louise was in great form. She was always delighted to see
her niece and nephew, addressing them excitedly by name and talking
about them – as we learned from her care staff – after we had
gone home.

Lucy (Sarah's daughter)

The various homes where we visited my aunt seemed to get better

217

as the years went by. Less like institutions, basically. I have early memories of white corridors and plastic banisters and endless stairwells. Communal spaces were less like sitting rooms and more like airport lounges or after-school clubs. Louise's room was always a little more cheerful. Clearly the staff recognised the need to add some human touches. I wonder who that was for – Louise, her visitors, the staff? Probably all of us in different ways. As time passed, the places she lived in became smaller, sunnier and more like a normal residence. The staff were more welcoming and there was less plastic and more wood. Sometimes I'm surprised at how well she's looked after, as I just don't expect the State, or anyone really, to do the job sufficiently well. Then she gets moved for the umpteenth time and I realise I'm right to be cynical.

I suppose there's a long tradition in Britain of keeping a disabled relative who lives in a care home away from friends and acquaintances, but I am now quite regretful about how much a misplaced sense of shame affected me as a child. I remember being scared of telling people that I had an aunt who was mentally disabled (or handicapped, as we generally referred to her) and who lived in a special home. I think perhaps I was nervous they'd think I was a freak for having a family somewhat out of the ordinary. I always used to get nervous when we went out with Louise in case she made a scene, threw a loud tantrum or something. Of course, most of our days out were normal days out, sometimes dull, sometimes lovely, often accompanied by coastal winds. Whether at Hill Farm, the Tesco café or Pevensey Beach, nothing terrible ever happened as far as I can remember. I doubt that other people much cared when they witnessed a woman shouting and screaming. So the dread I felt as a child of potential embarrassment was way out of proportion, and the older I got the more rational I became about it.

People talked about the 'tragedy' of a child born mentally disabled. I don't think that all disabilities are tragedies. In Louise's case, my mother, grandmother and granddad didn't go on about tragedy. They shared a principal concern that she was missing out on so much potential. Whenever we visited Louise, you sensed a difference between the way they regarded Louise and the attitude of her carers. The staff showed fond affection, while her parents and sister expressed love, but with it there came an underlying tinge of sadness.

I suppose my dad reacted a little differently, partly because he had never faced the shock of realising that a close relative is going to be permanently brain-damaged. For him, Louise had always been that way. For my brother Joe and me, visiting Louise always induced a childlike uncertainty on the right way to behave.

My mum was always sensitive to ableist jokes, on the 'South Park' television show or wherever else. When my dad started laughing at a magazine piece containing comical descriptions of some of the odder symptoms of Tourette's (written by someone suffering from the syndrome), she showed her displeasure. I remember a moment during my early childhood when I began crying because I perceived that my grandparents preferred my brother to me. My mum assured me this wasn't true, but did point out that the arrival of a healthy grandson at a difficult time in Louise's life had been a particular comfort and source of happiness for them. I never really got my head around this. Maybe it was just because Joe is sporty and cheerful and just plain easier to deal with.

Doris

In the summer we went down to Pedros for the latest of Lulu's regular review meetings. She sat there patiently alongside her care staff as various reports were presented covering medical and social matters and how well she was responding to the new regime. The story so far in her new home was a good one. It was hoped that she would soon be attending college, and meanwhile she was enjoying a busy social life which included swimming, bowling, discos and visits to the pub.

However, we sometimes wondered whether these meetings tended to emphasise the good news while minimising the bad. We usually picked up the latter during our regular telephone calls to

Pedros to see how things were going, or sometimes in individual conversations with her carers during our visits to Louise. That was often the way we would learn that a college course had been abandoned because Lulu had become anxious about it, or that she was not 'well enough' to go to church the previous Sunday or to one of the social activities she so much enjoyed. These occasions reminded us of those times at Laughton Lodge hospital when her obsession with staff rotas and the daily menus sometimes drove her into noisy agitation. It also recalled for us the disastrous visit to that Bexhill café where Louise threw a wobbly, resulting in the compilation of guidelines by her carers governing our future visits. We thought these guidelines were a bit over the top, but they did address the various trigger points in Lulu's life.

One of these resulted from the fact that she had no sense of time and if you told her about some future event, she expected it to happen immediately and would become more and more agitated when it didn't. So now she would be told about our next visit or the other events she enjoyed just one hour before they occurred.

The overall aim of these guidelines was for us to reach the point where, on our visits to Pedros, we could take her out for an hour or so, as we had done in the past at her previous care homes. To begin with we would be accompanied by two of her carers, but the long-term goal would be for us to venture out with Lulu on our own. We were a bit apprehensive about this idea, but we assured each other that such an achievement would be a mark of considerable progress. Would it, could it ever happen?

We continued our regular visits to Pedros, but as the months went by we sensed that all was not well. We felt that Lulu's speech had become slurred, and were concerned to read in the latest report, as she approached the end of her first year in her new home, that 'there had been serious mental health issues which had restricted her presence in the community'. This was hard to take, coming as it did after the previous report had noted her obvious enjoyment during visits to a long list of places throughout East Sussex. The staff had obviously done their best to construct a programme of social and creative activity which concentrated on her fascination with cooking, painting and dancing, and on her love of swimming.

We asked senior staff whether Lulu might benefit from a treatment known as oxygen therapy. The *Daily Telegraph* had run a long feature on its positive effect on patients who had symptoms similar to our daughter's, but her carers, after discussing the idea with doctors, felt it was not an appropriate treatment for Louise. Meanwhile we continued to come across articles about the 'chemical cosh' aspect of some drugs that Louise was taking and wondered if they were doing more harm than good. We continued to worry about the quality of her speech, and also noted that her ability to sign her name on the birthday and other cards she sent us had declined.

So we were left to contemplate the long list of medications she was taking which was a regular feature of her reports. From time to time, some items were discontinued or replaced by something else, but getting the balance right seemed to us then to be mission impossible.

Ron

There is a saying that August is a cruel month. On my birthday, the 27th, I received a letter from the Adult Social Care Department of the county council. It was from someone new to us, a social worker named Cherrill Lawless. She wanted to meet us – as she said, to 'gather your views on Louise's needs'. I rang her and she asked, 'Do you know what this is about?' When I said I did not, she announced that she had been asked to find alternative accommodation for our daughter. I could not believe it.

I told Mrs Lawless that we would do everything we could to resist any attempt to move Lulu from Pedros. We arranged to meet her at her office in St. Leonard's in three days' time. In preparation for that, I did a ring-around to see who else knew about the plan to move Louise. I spoke to Owen Nolan, the manager at

Pedros. He was taken aback. He knew nothing. Neither did the rest of his staff. Next I spoke to senior staff at the West Kent and Medway NHS Trust. We knew them well, as they were responsible for eleven care homes in East Sussex, including Pedros, and we met them from time to time to talk about various matters concerning Lulu's well-being. They, too, were unaware of any intention to move our daughter, but they did reveal that they had been in dispute with representatives of East Sussex County Council over the rising cost of keeping her at Pedros.

So I called County Hall and said I wished to make a formal complaint about what was happening to Lulu. They sent me details of their complaints procedure, which set out three stages we could pursue if need be, and then, if the matter was still unresolved, we could take our case to the ombudsman.

In our first official written complaint, I hammered the point that the unwelcome news about Louise was 'delivered out of the blue by someone with whom we had had no previous dealings and not by one of the principal members of the Pedros staff with whom we enjoy a very good relationship or by one of the two principals of the West Kent and Medway Trust with whom we have met many times and maintain regular contact'.

Our complaint went on to say that Pedros seemed ideal to us, with attractive furnishings and a small enclosed garden at the rear, and that while she had been there, Louise had been able to resume a full programme of outside activities under the care and supervision of a dedicated staff. In due course, there had been some mental health problems, and a period had ensued when our visits were difficult, to say the least, but the observations and recommendations of a visiting psychiatrist had seemed to work wonders, and recent visits had been a pleasure.

It continued:

Louise is now 45 and my wife and I are in our seventies. There could never have been an ideal time to inform us that there was a plan to remove Louise from Pedros, but unfortunately it came after a stressful year during which my wife was diagnosed with cancer and has undergone six months of chemotherapy treatment. She is now in remission but remains under medical supervision.

In trying to find reasons why Louise should leave Pedros, I learned that there had been a dispute between West Kent and County Hall over the amount of money needed to sustain our daughter after her first year there.

As I understood it, the initial amount was £70,000 a year, which I believed to be the budget figure for each of the other residents at Pedros. Amazingly, in Louise's case this figure had risen to £250,000 going into the second year. That is a staggering 350 per cent increase. Surely someone should be held to account for what I can only describe as a budgetary bungle rather than simply require Louise – the innocent party – to pay the price.

I believe that there was eventually some kind of compromise between West Kent and the County Council which will sustain Louise at Pedros until this November. Fortuitously, at the end of November, a new contractor will be announced to succeed West Kent and Medway in the running of Pedros and the other ten homes in the area. This seems to be the proper opportunity to resolve calmly issues like the funding of Louise's accommodation in a purpose-built facility, which has proved so beneficial, both to her and her carers, rather than subjecting her to yet another move which cannot improve – or, indeed match – her present circumstances and will have the deleterious effects that have occurred in the past.

At this point, I would commend to you the minutes of one of the consultation meetings that took place in June about the re-tendering of the West Kent and Medway contract. Projects Manager Martyn Yeats assured parents and carers that there was no agenda to close homes or to move people to other places. This, he said, is not a cost-saving exercise.

In the light of these reassuring remarks, the decision to

find alternative accommodation for Louise seems more than just ill-considered. It is cruel and we will resist it to the last, using whatever assistance and resources we can muster.

Sarah

When I first heard about the threat of yet another move for Louise, I knew we would have to fight hard. The three of us – my father, my mother and myself – sat in my parents' sitting room in Surbiton overlooking the Thames and discussed our tactical approach at the forthcoming meeting with Mrs Lawless.

I had just moved on from a difficult job in education where I had experienced first-hand what I regarded as the negative and aggressive tactics of Her Majesty's Inspectors at Ofsted. However, although bruised, I had learned some lessons in how to fight back. Any action had to be completely focused on looking for the weakness in the opposition's case.

I asked my father to summarise his written complaint to the County Council. Mum quickly became impatient at what she felt was a slow and nit-picking approach, but unusually for me, I told her straight that it was essential if we were to ensure that Lulu remained at Pedros. It was a stressful moment for all of us, and I tried to hug her and tell her how much I loved her. She resisted my embrace but finally accepted the point I was attempting to make, and we continued our fight for Louise in a way that had caused us to be likened to the Three Musketeers over the years.

When we arrived at Cherrill's office in St Leonard's, I was immediately depressed by the scruffy look of the County Council office. It did not exactly lift one's spirits. Mum and Dad had both dressed with care, and it broke my heart to see how this resilient couple were again having to go into bat for their disabled daughter. My father looked handsome in a smart suit with a waistcoat and my mother wore a stylish blue jacket with her trademark red lipstick picking up the tones of her auburn hair.

My father began by saying we had thought about not coming to the meeting with Mrs Lawless, wondering how it could be of any value. We had just delivered to the County Council our views on the 'monstrous' plan to move Louise away from Pedros. In the meeting, my mother described the situation as 'impossible'. To be fair to Mrs Lawless, she remained calm and sympathetic and tried to reassure us about Lulu's future. She said she understood how awful it might be for us if they had to move her, but promised 'it won't be done in a crisis'. My response to that was that moving my sister away from Pedros would undoubtedly constitute a crisis.

Once the meeting got going, Dad showed all of the style and personality that had taken him from a rented terrace house in Enfield to a high-rise BBC apartment in Manhattan. Mum said little, wearing an expression of dignified contempt for whoever might have been responsible for a situation which could adversely affect her child, on whose behalf she had worked so long and hard. I sat and took notes, using my reporter's training to record what was said, only stopping to express my firm support for my parents and sister towards the end of the encounter.

My notes showed that my father used the word 'monstrous' to describe the plan to move Louise and that he told Mrs. Lawless that we would 'bitterly oppose' it. One of his saddest phrases, in referring to Lulu's life, was: 'Louise never goes far without running into problems.' He was scornful of what he described as 'Mickey Mouse economics', referring to the startling jump in the cost of Louise's care from £70,000 to £250,000 a year, and he insisted that both the County Council and Kent and Medway Primary Care Trust must share the blame.

The social worker talked through the money issue with us, trying to show us why the costs had increased so sharply, but we were unable to make sense of the rise. This drove our determination to prevent any attempt to move Louise elsewhere.

Mrs Lawless revealed that she had yet to meet Louise, but she had clearly done her homework on what had brought things to this point. She said she had spoken to colleagues who had been at the

Park Lane care home in Eastbourne, the one that began to fall down when the foundations slipped at the height of a very dry summer. She had been told that Louise had been doing well there until a change of medication affected her adversely, and that it had taken a long while for her to recover, not helped by the frustrations caused by the year-long 'holiday' at the oasthouse.

Ron

About a month after our meeting with Cherrill Lawless, we received a detailed reply from Jim White, commissioning manager in the County Council's department for Adult Social Care. He gave us a painstaking account of how and why the cost of sustaining Louise at Pedros had shot up so dramatically. He dealt first with 'the way in which unwelcome news was communicated to you by someone with whom you had no previous dealings'. He said it would normally be considered good practice to inform the close family, to allow them to represent the interests of their loved one. It should, however, he went on, be recognised that KMPT (Kent and Medway Primary Care Trust) was not indicating its wish to discontinue providing a service to Louise; rather, it was attempting to attain full cost recovery for that service. There remained, he wrote, the possibility that the situation could be resolved by the County Council agreeing to an increased fee, 'without causing undue concern to Louise or yourselves'.

Mr White went on:

> Where the cost of an individual's care and support are subject to significant increase in costs, it is normal practice for the Council to seek clear justification ... and also to consider whether that service continues to represent best value for money. Despite some concerns about Louise's current service package – which provides limited opportunity to mix with her peers – and also concerns about value for money, the Council agreed

to the fee required by KMPT to prevent the need for Louise to move in the short term. It was, however, felt necessary to explore other options for Louise and it was at this point that Cherrill Lawless contacted you seeking to arrange a meeting.

The next paragraph dealt with my phone call to KMPT in which I complained that they had not informed me of Mrs Lawless's mission to find alternative accommodation, and that their response had been that they knew nothing about it.

Mr White's comment on this was that at the point I contacted KMPT, 'they had been informed of the Council's intention to pay an increased fee for Louise and may, therefore, have assumed that Louise's emplacement with them was ongoing. I have found no evidence that the County Council have formally communicated in writing to KMPT their intention to explore alternative service options for Louise. On this point I must, therefore, apologise on behalf of the Council that we had not kept KMPT suitably briefed regarding our intentions and for the resulting confusion.'

Mr White then dealt with my point about a 'budgetary bungle' that upped the cost of sustaining Lulu from around £70,000 to £250,000 a year. He said the expectation of the council had been that she would be partially integrated with the rest of the Pedros service, allowing her the opportunity to mix with her peers, and providing some economies of staffing. Clearly the delay in moving Lulu to Pedros from West Oast had not helped the financial situation. She was to have been there for just one month while work on the new place and the final inspections were completed – but it ended up taking nearly a year.

During this time Lulu was supported by two care workers throughout the day and night 'due to the behaviours being presented . . . and the location of the property'. Mr White went on to say that when she finally moved to Pedros some ten months later these staffing levels continued, due to the work involved in supporting Louise to settle into a new home and her continued behavioural problems.

Jim White reported that a social care review eighteen months later confirmed that Louise continued to be supported on a two-to-one basis. There had been no integration 'due to the high levels of disruption caused by another service user'.

The report then claimed that the level of service received by Louise throughout her stay with KMPT had continually and significantly exceeded the service originally planned and commissioned for her. Mr White went on: 'This may be attributed to an apparent failure by KMPT to correctly assess Louise's care and support needs in the context of the wider service at Pedros and consequently they have provided a service at significant loss to themselves.' He added that 'the impact of this error is that the Council must now consider whether the current service continues to represent value for money in meeting Louise's needs by investigating what alternative options are available to her'.

This bears out what we had been picking up on the grapevine – that there was sometimes a decided lack of sweetness and light in the discussions between the two sides.

The last page of Jim White's report gave us some small comfort. He pointed out that Cherrill Lawless had yet to complete her report, so he could not comment on its outcome, but he went on: 'It should, however, be recognised that there may be scope to improve on the present service ... and provide some opportunity to mix with her peers. If the Council is able to identify such an option, we will, of course, ensure that you are properly consulted.'

While this drama was being played out, we were having to keep track on the other unsettling development that had taken us by surprise earlier in the year. We learned of it in a letter from Kent and Medway NHS and Social Care Partnership Trust, the organisation looking after Louise, who had decided that they would no longer provide a residential service to people with learning difficulties, pointing out that the current national thinking was that this was a job for social care organisations rather than the National Health Service. The letter was endorsed by the County Council, whose responsibility it was to find someone to take over.

A follow-up letter set out the dates of various consultation meetings, some for parents and families, others for care staff worried about their jobs. The changeover would affect 65 people with learning difficulties living in 11 homes, including Pedros, in the Hastings area. The current cost for providing both the residential services and day care activities was getting on for £5 million a year.

Nearly sixty organisations showed some interest in taking over the service, but finally just seven of them were invited to tender for it. In the end, none of them got the contract. All of them wanted too much money. So it was agreed that the existing contractors, the Kent and Medway Trust, would continue to run the service until the spring of the following year. At that point Hastings and Rother Primary Care Trust, which was part of the NHS, would take over, with the County Council working in partnership and providing management of the service. Confusingly, this was not in line with the trend against NHS management, but a letter from the County Council announced that 'it was likely, in due course, that we will look for another provider for the service'.

From our point of view, all of this seemed a bit academic as we awaited the report from Cherrill Lawless on what lay ahead for Louise. The postman delivered her 13-page report just a few days later. Cautiously, we began to read a covering letter which, though still holding on to the possibility of alternative accommodation for Lulu, went on with the good news that Mrs Lawless had been working with KMPT to reconfigure the existing service at Pedros to try and reduce the cost. Together they had set out a plan for Louise's integration with two other residents in the main Pedros building. The idea was that Louise would join with them in activities that they all enjoyed, including cooking and swimming.

The letter went on: 'The long term aim is to integrate Louise with her peers and identify someone with whom she would be compatible to share accommodation. It is not financially sustainable to maintain a single person service for Louise and this is recognised by all the agencies that support her.'

At this point, cautiously, we persuaded ourselves that our protest might have had some effect in challenging the plan to move Louise out of Pedros. Mrs Lawless reported that there had been meetings to consider reducing Louise's medication and to assist 'her integration into the main Pedros house'.

Over the years, we had become all too aware of the long list of pills and potions she was taking each day, but seeing it set out here was a chilling experience. There were more than a dozen different medications, two of them anti-psychotic pills, plus a fortnightly injection of another anti-psychotic, a new drug. Mrs Lawless expressed concern about the considerable risk of toxic and sedative effects caused by large amounts of medication. That problem had been around for several years as successive attempts were made to get the balance right.

The report was unsparing in setting out a decline in Lulu's behaviour during her first year at Pedros. There had been prolonged periods of high-pitched screaming that could last up to ten hours. This brought back sad memories of some of our visits to Laughton Lodge hospital nearly thirty years earlier. The report went on to list various triggers for bursts of bad behaviour. Over the years we had become all too familiar with most of them – such as crowded places, other people crying, screaming or coughing, the menstrual cycle and, finally, constipation, which she had endured since childhood.

It was in June of that first year at Pedros, according to Mrs Lawless, that Louise's various behaviours had started deteriorating to an unacceptable level. The worst period was between September and the following February. During this time, she physically assaulted several members of staff, often resulting in their requiring medical treatment and sick leave. However, the Lawless report acknowledged that there had been several contributing factors, notably staff changes which made it difficult to maintain consistency in Lulu's regular team of carers. There was also mention of the several changes of medication prescribed by a previous learning disability psychiatrist.

We have sad memories of this troubled time in our daughter's life. On one of our weekend visits to Pedros we did not actually come face to face with her. As we arrived we could hear the sound of screaming coming from her room. The staff on duty tried to placate her, but without success, and the noise continued for an hour or more. Finally, we gave up and began the sad journey home, apprehensive about what lay ahead.

On our next visit we learned that there been a discussion about the possibility that Louise might be going into a special hospital for observation and treatment. We feared that this would involve her in the process of being 'sectioned' under the Mental Health Act, and we just hoped that the idea would go away. It did – or at least we heard no more about it until we read the summary at the end of Mrs Lawless's report, where there was a fleeting reference to the possible benefit of Louise spending time in a specialist unit. However, Mrs Lawless felt that a 'single person' service was not in Louise's best interests indefinitely and that she would benefit from integration with other service users. She reported that this view was shared by the 'front line' staff at Pedros because of the opportunity it gave Louise to meet and socialise with others.

We had not expected to, but in fact we derived a great deal of reassurance from the Lawless report. It now seemed that alternative accommodation was no longer the sole option, echoing Jim White's earlier assurance that it was by no means a foregone conclusion that Louise would be required to move.

Even so, we had found Mrs Lawless's report a harrowing read. Inevitably it took us back through the worst aspects of the past four years since Louise had left the Eastbourne area, after the care home there had begun to fall down. Was there ever a time in our daughter's life after we had returned to England from our years in the United States that we could look back on and think that those were good times? Well, yes, there was.

That period had to be the six years that she spent in the two care homes in Eastbourne. Of course there were setbacks at both places, but we now recalled the many happy visits to both of them – especially when Sarah and her family were able to join us – and the pleasure we all had from expeditions into the Sussex country-side for a leisurely picnic, or to Pevensey Bay, where Lulu displayed for all of us her unorthodox skills at swimming and diving.

That was then. Many years had now gone by. So we waited, apprehensively, for the next move in the Pedros saga. Well, nothing happened immediately, and there were no official communications on what might happen to Lulu, but on our regular visits to see her it quickly became clear in conversations with her carers that she was staying put and that the positive aspects of the Lawless report, about our daughter's integration with other residents and the necessity for revision of her medication, were being taken note of.

As Christmas approached, there were further consultation meetings for parents and relatives concerning the takeover by Hastings and Rother Primary Care Trust of the ten learning disability homes in the area, including Pedros. It was the perfect opportunity for Lulu's frazzled parents to ask if she really would be staying at Pedros. The answer was yes. So, on our next visit, we found the door that kept Lulu separate from the other residents had been unlocked and, after eighteen months, her relative isolation had come to an end.

Everyone agreed as the weeks went by that this had been the right decision. There were still problems. Staff told us about a visit to Cooden Beach on a wild and windy day when Lulu wandered out onto the shingle and began screaming at the top of her voice, with accompaniment from a flock of seagulls screeching and swooping above her head. There seemed to be something deeply fundamental about this moment, calling to mind, as it did, 'The Scream', that dramatic painting by Edward Munch. Still, a happier Louise was soon to emerge, and we were now able to enjoy the time we spent with her on our subsequent visits.

Certainly the care staff at Pedros were having to cope with fewer difficult moments. It had also been decided to review the long list of medications that Lulu was taking, and this, too, proved beneficial in bringing about a much less stressful life for our daughter and also for the hard-working carers and doctors who looked after her.

There were four other residents in the care of the Pedros staff – Gary, Colin, Deborah and Patsy. It was Patsy in particular whose calmness seemed to have a soothing effect on Lulu's behaviour, and now she was invariably alongside Lulu on our regular visits to Pedros. Lulu's birthday that year was celebrated in some style at a restaurant in the old quarter of Hastings. Patsy was there, and Sarah and Lucy came down from London. It was a joyous occasion, marred only by the moment when, inadvertently, the waitress placed some broccoli on Lulu's plate. Broccoli was top of the list of her least favourite things.

Sitting alongside her was Di, one of her regular carers, who dealt expertly with the ensuing rumpus, and we all went home feeling we'd achieved some kind of milestone, and that Lulu would resume in full the programme of social and cultural activities that had been devised for her and from which, when she was on top form, she devised so much enjoyment.

Doris

After two more enjoyable visits to Pedros, we decided to go down to our apartment in the south of France for some rest and relaxation. Just a few hours after we arrived, the phone rang shortly after eleven o'clock at night. Ron picked it up. It was Sarah. She had serious news. Lulu was in hospital in a coma. Apparently after supper she had gone into the Pedros kitchen where she picked up the remains of an omelette and started to eat it. The food went down the wrong way. A member of staff encountered her in the passage outside the kitchen. She was in a bad way. Her lips were blue. Particles of the omelette had entered a lung and she fell to the floor, losing consciousness. Her heart stopped but ambulance staff, arriving quickly, managed to get it going again. On arrival at the nearby Conquest Hospital, Lulu was placed on a life-support machine.

Ron and I stared at each other in a mixture of anguish and disbelief, not knowing what to say to each other. Sarah had said she would ring during the night if there was any further news. Otherwise we would talk again first thing in the morning. The two of us, devastated by the news from London, failed fully to comprehend its implication – that tomorrow, somehow, at a busy time of year for Nice Airport, we would have to get ourselves back on a flight to London.

After a restless night, Ron spoke to Sarah and said we would be on our way home as quickly as possible. She said that she and Christopher had no further news, but that they would drive down to the Conquest Hospital and keep in touch with us by mobile phone. Ron then called one of our French friends, Christophe, who had been driving us to and from Nice Airport for many years. He said he would be with us as soon as possible and would stay with us at the airport to help us get the earliest possible flight back to London.

Ron

In the event, Easy Jet thought they would be able to get us on an early-afternoon flight which, in fact, was fully booked, but invariably some passengers would fail to turn up. This was what indeed happened. As the check-in deadline passed, we were waved forward and presented with our tickets. We had been trying without success to reach Sarah on the mobile, but fortunately she got a call through to me just as we were about to enter the aircraft cabin.

Apparently Sarah and Christopher had stopped for fish and chips at lunchtime. Outside the shop she saw a sign promoting Creole Jazz in Bexhill, reminding her of one of her mum and dad's musical passions, and prompting her to call my mobile one more time. She reached me just as we were entering the aircraft cabin to say that they would drive on to Gatwick to meet us. They had come from the Conquest Hospital having visited Lulu a few hours earlier. Our younger daughter was still in a coma.

The plane arrived on time at four o'clock that afternoon, and it was comforting to catch sight of them as we entered the arrivals hall at Gatwick. Christopher said he would drive us cross country to the hospital, where we would be able to talk to the senior doctor in charge of the intensive care unit. At half-past five we signed in at the Conquest Hospital. We were then fitted with protective aprons before being shown into a room where our daughter had been lying for the past forty-eight hours. She was on her back with a tube running into her mouth to sustain her breathing. Her face was puffy as a result of various liquids that had been administered. We kissed her forehead and called her name and sang some of her favourite songs, but there was no response.

The four of us sat down later with the senior doctor on duty. Gently, she took us through the events of the past two days. Three of us had spent much of our working lives in journalism, but we tried not to overwhelm her with questions. Two major points emerged from her patient responses – the first was that the next forty-eight hours would be critical, and the second was that if Louise's heart stopped beating for a second time, there would not be a further attempt at resuscitation.

It was a sombre moment. We left the Conquest with the assurance that they would be in touch with us immediately if there were any significant developments during the night. Little was said as Christopher drove us back to London, where we lived only a couple of miles apart.

The next morning there was bad news. The senior nurse on duty rang us to say that Lulu's condition was deteriorating and we should return to the hospital as quickly as possible. On arrival, our daughter seemed much the same, but we were to learn otherwise when we were briefed by the senior doctor now on duty. He said he had carried out a brain scan that morning and, sadly, this had revealed that Louise was effectively brain dead and that there was no chance of recovery. In those circumstances, he proposed to switch off the life-support machine that evening. By now, Sarah, Christopher and Lucy had arrived, and they shared our grief, as did several of the care workers who had looked after Louise in recent years, at Pedros and elsewhere in East Sussex. Many of them had made several visits to Lulu's bedside over the past two days.

We decided not to be present when Louise's life-support system was switched off. That happened at around seven o'clock, and we were told the following day that Lulu passed away about an hour later. We felt numb.

Then practical considerations took over, like how we were going to cope with the funeral when we lived so far away in London. Fortunately, Angela Simons was ahead of us, in her role as Service Manager of Hastings and Rother Learning Disability Services. She proposed a meeting with us the following day at which she offered – with the help of the care staff at Pedros who were closest to Louise – to look after all the arrangements. It was agreed that there should be a Service of Thanksgiving in the chapel at Hastings Crematorium, and that this should include Lulu's favourite hymn, 'All Things Bright and Beautiful', as well as her favourite popular song, 'Somewhere Over the Rainbow', sung by Eva Cassidy (who had died of skin cancer some years previously).

There would be another essential ingredient – the Lord's Prayer. Louise had learned this during her time at Cobb Memorial School, and over the years had shown – how can we put it? – her displeasure at some of the changes that were introduced by the English churches she attended after we came home. She was happiest at St Mary the Virgin in the ancient town of Battle, where Sunday morning service was conducted by the Dean of Battle, the Very Reverend Dr John Edmondson. It was he who would conduct the Thanksgiving Service which had been set for the second week of June. Before that happened, we received from the East Sussex Coroner's Office an interim certificate listing the causes of Louise's death as respiratory obstruction and aspiration of food particles, subject to confirmation at the formal inquest. Somehow, seeing those words set out so starkly in black and white triggered an emotional reaction that we had been suppressing. All those years, all those fears, all the hopes and aspirations, all the care and dedication shown by so many people who had looked after Louise – and in the end an omelette, a bloody omelette of all things, blows it all away, and this is where it comes to a sudden and brutal conclusion.

Doris

We decided to get away for a few days, and headed back to resume the short holiday in the south of France that had been so shockingly interrupted when Lulu was taken to hospital in the middle of May. It would be an opportunity to rest, catch up on some reading and enjoy some meals out. It didn't work out like that. By day two, Ron was confined to bed, wrestling with a bad stomach. That was very unusual for him. Was it caused by the stress of recent events – or was it, more likely in my view, having consumed some mustard that had been hanging around too long in the fridge? By the fourth day he seemed to have lost all sense of time, complaining at eight o'clock in the evening that it should be getting light. Fortunately we had made friends with a chemist just down the hill from our apartment, and he produced a box of pills from a remote corner of his armoury. It took a while, but eventually they did the trick in time for the journey home.

In the days ahead, as we prepared ourselves for Lulu's Thanksgiving Service, we were sustained by the love and support coming from family and friends, and especially so on the day of the service itself.

Shortly after noon on a perfect summer's day, Lulu left Pedros for the last time as the funeral procession headed for the chapel of Hastings Crematorium. There, the Dean of Battle greeted us and we were surprised to see so many people waiting to follow us inside and take up all the pews behind us. Some we were meeting for the first time, but during the past thirty-five years all of them had played some part in looking after Louise at the various care homes where she had lived in East Sussex.

As a family, we had wanted to make our own contributions to

the service, and Ron had written a tribute to Louise. So had Sarah. In the event, my husband felt the emotion of the occasion might be too much for him to cope with, so we asked Christopher, our son-in-law, if, with his considerable experience as a professional actor, he would take over . . .

It was so sudden, so swift, our daughter's departure from this world. How different from her arrival, forty-seven years ago, after a long and difficult labour.

At six o'clock on a Sunday morning, in a maternity home in Southampton, Doctor Scott said to my wife, in his kindly way: Oh do come along, Mrs. Onions, I shall be wanting to get along to the church!

When, finally, Doris took Lulu into her arms for the first time, her first thought was: "This one's going to need a lot of looking after . . .' And so it proved in a journey that was to take her to far-away places and through so many ups and downs.

One of those places was Cobb Memorial School, a care home run by the Sisters of the Presentation in the mountains of upstate New York.

Recently our first daughter and I were talking on the phone to Sister Mary Thomas, now the principal of the school and the only member of staff remaining there from Louise's five years at Cobb. Sister Thomas said to us: 'You know, if there's one thing I remember above all others about Louise, it's those blue, blue eyes.'

Ah yes, we all remember them . . . and they never shone brighter than when the demons that pursued her had gone away and she was singing, in church or back at Pedros and listening to her record player. Or when she was enjoying herself at one of the imaginative range of social and recreational activities that Pedros staff had arranged for her. Or when she was dancing. And wow! Couldn't she dance! And we have video evidence to prove it! And I'm sure nobody will forget her hair-raising performance on the trampoline.

Lulu had another remarkable skill. She had a photograph from the late sixties showing all the sisters and children who were at Cobb school while she was there and she would astound us by recalling the names of nearly all of them. And, as a bonus, she would add the name of the Reverend Mother's dog, who didn't actually appear in the photograph but Lulu told us anyway that the dog was called Tammy.

Lulu liked dogs, especially barking dogs for some strange reason. Plus goody bags and Nivea Creme. If it wasn't for Louise, Nivea might have gone bust years ago. What she didn't like were crying babies, screaming kids and the sound of someone coughing. And decidedly she did not like broccoli.

Coming home from America was not easy. Decent care homes were few and far between. Visiting her was not always a pleasure. On one occasion, she said suddenly: 'What did you (meaning Louise herself) do to the church window?' First we pretended we hadn't heard and then we hoped this was one of her occasional fantasies.

Another time she came out with the phrase: 'Have you seen a kid with a chicken pie?', conjuring up an image of the staff at Laughton Lodge – where she was then resident – desperately searching for that day's lunch which, mysteriously, had gone missing.

Finally, I pay tribute to everyone who played some part in caring for Lulu, but our family felt that nowhere did it better than Pedros during the three years that she was there.

At this point, Christopher added his own brief tribute to his sister-in-law:

I think that Louise had, despite the terrible handicap that blighted her life, the ability to inspire love. But more than that, she had her own capacity for love. I remember the day I was taken to meet her for the first time before I married her older sister, Sarah. Of course, I was given a careful briefing.

Things might go wrong. Well, I was nervous and she spent an hour or so, as we all talked, carefully scrutinising me. Then, as we were saying our goodbyes, suddenly and unprompted, she gave me a hug and a kiss. I was honoured. It was a moment I have never forgotten.

Our little family, Sarah and me and our children, Lucy and Joseph – who sadly cannot be here because he is sitting his A-Level exams as I speak – have our own memories too, like that blissful day with Louise on Pevensey Beach. Louise was, in her own way, a loving aunt to her niece and nephew.

I think that Louise lived a brave life because she was always, despite her awful misfortune, determinedly and resolutely, her own person: Louise Elizabeth Onions.

Ron

Sarah then followed Christopher with a gracious reminiscence, thanking everyone who over forty years had helped to look after Louise, both in America and England. Many of them were there in the chapel as she revealed that we had been at work on a book telling the story of Lulu's life and the people who had played some part in it, not least New York's Doctor Giannini, who made the key diagnosis of our daughter's brain damage, and was to become an adviser to the American president, George Bush, on children with special needs.

Afterwards, we went back to Pedros, where a buffet reception had been arranged. The crowded dining room had been decorated with some of the outstanding photographs that had been taken as a record of Lulu's various activities, and with some impressive paintings she had done in art class. We met for the first time various people who had played some part in helping Lulu through life. One was the aromatherapist she visited regularly – an indication of just how meticulously she was looked after within the Pedros family. From others present, we sensed a deep undercurrent of shock and sadness over what had happened to Louise. Carers who had looked after her on a day-to-day basis had been much affected, especially those who were on duty on the day she was rushed to hospital. We learned that a counselling service had been set up for everyone on staff, and that the Primary Care Trust responsible for Pedros was about to launch a full investigation.

One of the senior members of staff gave us great comfort with a few words he had prepared on behalf of his colleagues indicating how deeply they had been affected by Louise's sudden death. It was an overwhelming moment for him and for all of us, and I struggled to make a coherent response.

Now it was time to go home, though there would be reasons to return to East Sussex. The coroner had issued an interim certificate on the cause of death, but because of the particular circumstances there would have to be further inquiries before a formal inquest could take place. Nine months passed before that happened. Christopher, Sarah, Lucy and Joe accompanied us then to the coroner's court in Hastings. Most of the people who gave evidence were well known to us. It was especially difficult for those who were on duty at Pedros on the evening of Lulu's sudden collapse. The coroner told us that we were were free to question any of the witnesses. Christopher and I did so. The whole painstaking process took two hours before the coroner recorded a verdict of accidental death.

Finally, in the autumn of that year, Lulu's ashes were scattered in a special place outside her church, St. Mary the Virgin in the town of Battle.

From the *Daily Telegraph*, Friday, 8 August 2008

A family who planned a new life in Canada say they were refused entry because their daughter has learning difficulties.

Paul and Barbara-Anne Chapman sold their home in Wokingham, Berks, and bought a farmhouse in Nova Scotia. But after a six-hour flight the family claim they were told by a border guard that because Lucy, seven, is disabled she would not be allowed into the country.

Canadian immigration officials have suggested that the Chapmans might have been turned back because they lacked the necessary work permit. The family say they believed they had all the paperwork down to the clearance for their Labrador.

Mr Chapman, a former Metropolitan police officer, claimed that when the border guard looked at their passports at Halifax airport, she asked him: 'Why have you brought your daughter to this country?' He said: 'I asked why I shouldn't bring her and was told that because she was disabled she had a lifetime ban. We couldn't believe what they were saying.'

Lucy suffers from a rare genetic condition called Angelman syndrome, which means she has a reduced mental age and cannot speak. She does not require additional medical care or drugs.

Mrs Chapman, 45, also a former police officer, said: 'My dog was allowed to stay. My dog has a higher status than my daughter in Canada.'

The Canadian Supreme Court lifted a blanket ban on disabled immigrants in 2005.

A spokesman for Citizenship and Immigration Canada could not comment specifically, but said: 'People with disabilities can come to Canada. It is not that we do not want them (the Chapmans) here, they just have to follow the proper process, which includes ensuring the residency permit is in place.'